S0-AKA-056

Done Deal?

The Politics of the 1997 Budget Agreement

Done Deal?
The Politics of the 1997 Budget Agreement

Daniel J. Palazzolo
University of Richmond

CHATHAM HOUSE PUBLISHERS
SEVEN BRIDGES PRESS, LLC
NEW YORK • LONDON

Done Deal?
The Politics of the 1997 Budget Agreement

SEVEN BRIDGES PRESS, LLC
P.O. Box 958, Chappaqua, New York 10514-0958

Copyright © 1999 by Chatham House Publishers of Seven Bridges Press, LLC

All rights reserved. No part of this publication may be reproduced, stored in a retrieval system, or transmitted in any form or by any means, electronic, mechanical, photocopying, recording, or otherwise, without the prior permission of the publisher.

Publisher: Robert J. Gormley
Managing Editor: Katharine Miller

Project Editor: Melissa A. Martin
Production Services: Robert Kern, *TIPS* Technical Publishing
Composition: Scriptorium Publishing Services, Inc.
Cover Design: Inari Information Services, Inc.
Printing and binding: Versa Press, Inc.

Library of Congress Cataloging-in-Publication Data

Palazzolo, Daniel J., 1961–
    Done Deal? : the politics of the 1997 budget agreement / by
    Daniel J. Palazzolo
    p. cm.
    Includes bibliographical references and index.
    ISBN 1-889119-20-2
    1. Budget–United States. 2. Budget–Political aspects–United States
    3. Separation of powers–United States. I. Title
    HJ2051 .P34 1999
    352.4'8'0973–dc21   99-6031
                                                                 CIP

Manufactured in the United States of America
10 9 8 7 6 5 4 3 2 1

For Jennifer, Sarah, and Elena

Contents

Acknowledgments

From January to August 1997, I served as a Congressional Fellow for Congressman Robert L. Ehrlich Jr. (R-Md.). Mr. Ehrlich had just been appointed to the House Budget Committee, and I was seeking a position as a legislative assistant for budget policy. I hoped to use the opportunity to learn more about the budget process and develop my research on entitlement reform. I thought the budget would dominate the 1st Session of the 105th Congress, and in January it appeared that President Clinton and congressional Republicans might attempt to negotiate a bipartisan budget deal. Of course, no one could reliably predict whether they would be successful, and I never dreamed the process would be completed during my short stay in Washington. As history and fortune would have it, I was precisely in the right place at the right time. So when the budget agreement was announced on 2 May 1997, I set aside my research on entitlement reform and focused on writing a book about the budget agreement that would be instructive to students and engaging to scholars.

Done Deal? is a story about the politics of the 1997 budget agreement from a political scientist's perspective. The story is couched in general terms about how the separation of powers system works under a divided government, and it is based on document analysis and participant observation. My appointment with Congressman Ehrlich placed me in an ideal position to see the process unfold as I was performing my duties as a legislative assistant. I attended Republican Budget Committee caucuses and weekly Republican Party whip meetings; I worked with Budget Committee staff; I watched the process and analyzed policy for Mr. Ehrlich; I talked with Mr. Ehrlich after he returned from Republican Conference meetings; and I received a slew of faxes and memoranda from the party conference, Dear Colleague letters, and communications from interest groups. In addition to keeping a daily journal, I collected information from various sources and interviewed key members of Congress and staff personnel. I could hardly imagine a better situation.

Thus, I am greatly indebted to Congressman Ehrlich. He not only granted me access to the process but also shared his observations, insights, and analysis of budget politics throughout. We should all be so lucky to know such a talented representative and skilled practitioner of politics. I also wish to acknowledge the congressman's Washington, D.C., staff, including Diane Baker, Richard Cross, Lisa Ellis, Steve Kreseski, Marjorie Kwah, Greg Muth, and J.P. Scholtes. Each contributed in some way to the development of this study, and each made the fellowship educational, exciting, and enjoyable. They also put up with my ceaseless enthusiasm for "the book."

If Congressman Ehrlich and his staff made my experience special, the American Political Science Association (APSA) made it possible. I am grateful to the Selection Committee for offering me the fellowship, and I thank Christopher Deering, Lisa Foust, and Mark Hyman for advising me on the appointment with Congressman Ehrlich. I also learned a great deal from talking regularly with Pat Sellers and Rich Forgette, two congressional scholars in the APSA program. Pat and Rich added valuable perspectives to the research project in its formative stages, and our conversations helped to sharpen my focus and broaden my perspective. Roger Davidson and Bill Connelly also commented on the initial book prospectus.

Most of the book was written after I left Washington, though I continued to be well-served by outstanding colleagues. Most political scientists know about Charles O. Jones's contributions to our understanding of Congress, the presidency, the policy process, and the separation of powers system from his many books. I have had the opportunity to benefit directly from Chuck's scholarly advice since the late 1980s when I was a graduate student at the University of Virginia. Anyone familiar with Chuck's work will readily discern his influence on this book. I cannot thank him enough for sharing his time, wisdom, advice, and personal warmth. I also relied on the insightful comments of Randall Strahan, a good friend and another student of Chuck Jones, who has taught me a lot about congressional leadership and tax politics. Randy reviewed a first draft of the entire manuscript and discussed it with me extensively on several occasions. His observations and editorial suggestions greatly improved the book. Bill Swinford and John Whelan, my colleagues at the University of Richmond, made helpful suggestions on selected chapters. Several former or current students, including Andy Rich, Sean McMenamin, and Michael Thames, reviewed parts of the book as well. I appreciate the editorial assistance of Irene Glynn and the professional guidance of the resourceful people at Chatham House, especially Bob Gormley, Katharine Miller, and Melissa Martin. Finally, hats off to Bob Kern of *TIPS* Technical Publishing, Karen Brown and Sarah O'Keefe of Scriptorium Publishing Services, Inc., and Paulette Miley for facilitating final production of the book. All of the above individuals did nothing but strengthen and improve this book, leaving me responsible for any remaining shortcomings.

Anything worth doing is a product of the mind and of the heart. So I dedicate this book to my wife, Jennifer, and two daughters, Sarah and Elena. They stayed in Richmond while I spent weeknights in Washington during the fellowship year, only to endure the long hours I needed to research and write the book when I returned to teaching at the University of Richmond. They are more patient, supportive, and loving than a father or a husband could ever expect. Some guys have all the luck.

1

The Puzzle of Budget Politics

The scene in the rotunda of the U.S. Capitol on Friday, 2 May 1997, was joyful and triumphant. Speaker of the House Newt Gingrich (R-Ga.) and Senate Majority Leader Trent Lott (R-Miss.) gathered behind a cluster of microphones to make a historic announcement beneath a backdrop of a life-size portrait depicting the signing of the Declaration of Independence. Congressional Republicans rejoiced in telling the press and the American public that after months of negotiations, a Democratic president and Republican congressional leaders agreed to a five-year plan to balance the budget. Senator Pete Domenici (N.Mex.) and Representative John Kasich (Ohio), the leading Republican participants in negotiations with the White House, clasped their hands together and raised them to express their excitement over fulfilling a goal that had defined their respective careers in Congress.

At the other end of Pennsylvania Avenue, President Bill Clinton and Vice-President Al Gore celebrated with broad smiles and high fives in the Oval Office. Clinton then departed to join happy Senate Democrats on retreat in Baltimore to announce his support for the bipartisan budget agreement. Clinton stated confidently, "We have reached an agreement in broad but fairly specific terms . . . with Republican leaders today that would balance the budget by 2002." Clinton went on to praise Republican leaders: "I want to thank them [Senator Lott and Speaker Gingrich] personally for negotiating with me openly, candidly, and, I'm convinced, in good faith."[1] By 1 August, three months later, bipartisan majorities in Congress passed and President Clinton signed into law two major budget bills codifying the general terms of the budget agreement. One bill contained budget savings that enabled the federal government to reach a balanced budget for the first time since 1969; the other cut taxes for the first time in sixteen years.

Just eighteen months prior to the historic announcement of 2 May, the situation in Washington could not have been more different. In fall 1995, grave looks and sober frowns on the faces of leaders representing both parties were almost daily occurrences in the White House press gallery and at media briefings with reporters on Capitol Hill. The news featured a steady diet of partisan stalemate, press leaks that generated distrust and anger among party leaders, accusations of betrayal on the part of negotiators, and even a sulking Speaker of the House, who claimed he was snubbed by the president on a trip back from Jerusalem aboard Air Force One.

By November 1995 the public had scorned both parties, but especially congressional Republicans, for playing politics as government services came to a halt and 800,000 federal workers were sent home. After the parties agreed to a short-term solution, the government was shut down a second time, and the parties remained gridlocked until Republicans withdrew from further negotiations. The rancorous partisan politics and high-stakes political standoff spilled over into the 1996 election campaigns. Democrats exploited the budget issue, blaming Republicans for shutting down the government, portraying Republican incumbents as extremist clones of Newt Gingrich, and chastising them for wanting to "slash," even "destroy," Medicare. Republicans returned the favor by attacking Clinton's personal character and calling Democrats liberal puppets of labor union bosses.

The stark contrast between the joyful display of bipartisanship that culminated in the 1997 budget agreement and the partisan strife that defined the budget debacle of 1995–96 is an intriguing puzzle. How did it happen? How did a Democratic president and a Republican Congress reach agreement at a time of intense partisanship, mutual distrust, and suspicion? How was it possible that leaders of opposing parties, who appeared to be so far apart in terms of their priorities, were able to negotiate a good-faith agreement to balance the budget, reduce spending for Medicare, and cut taxes? How were leaders able to garner support for the agreement from skeptical members of Congress? Does the agreement truly deserve the praise given by its supporters or the criticism dealt by its opponents?

Those questions cannot be answered by applying conventional views of Washington politics that portray an antiquated separation-of-powers system hopelessly ridden with partisan politics and political gamesmanship or distorted by the perverse and self-serving demands of "special interest groups." This perspective, which I call the *inevitable gridlock* model, fails to account for the complex workings of the policymaking process and the flexibility of the separation-of-powers system. The only way to explain the turnabout from the partisan stalemate that produced government shutdowns in 1995 and 1996 to the bipartisan budget agreement of 1997 is to apply what I refer to as a *realist expectations* perspective to the possibilities and limitations of the American political system. The realist expectations view identifies the inherent constraints on policy reform but recognizes the system's capacity to adapt to changing circumstances and produce important changes in policy, specifically as it relates to the federal budget. Partisanship and interest-group politics are parts of a more elaborate system of policymaking, and their capacity to create gridlock depends on a variety of other factors. This chapter elaborates on the distinction between the realist expectations perspective and the inevitable gridlock model, specifies how the realist expectations view solves the puzzle described above, and outlines the contents of the remaining chapters.

Inevitable Gridlock

For years, scholars and journalists have tried to convince Americans that the deficit was an intractable problem that could never be solved. Various studies claimed, for one reason or another—petty political games, party politics, the intractability of interest groups, a lack of political courage and leadership, a lack of public understanding—that the political system failed to face up to the "tough choices" that go with balancing the budget. Variations on the inevitable gridlock model go back to the late nineteenth century, with Woodrow Wilson's critique of the American system of separation of powers.[2] Wilson argued that by dividing the powers of government between the legislative and executive branches, the Constitution rendered the system inefficient, unresponsive to the public's will, and incapable of enacting major policy changes to address national problems. To cure those ills, Wilson advocated a parliamentary form of government.

Though Wilson's vision of a new parliamentary system of government never evolved, the basic premises of Wilson's theory eventually led to the responsible party school of thought. Responsible party advocates argued that the only way the system can avoid gridlock is for the voters to elect a president and congressional majorities of the same party.[3] In the view of responsible party theorists, when voters elect unified party government they send to Washington representatives and senators who are predisposed to cooperate with a president of their own party. Policymakers with the same party affiliation can presumably overcome the constitutional barriers embedded in a system of separation of powers and checks and balances. Moreover, voters can hold the majority party accountable for government policy. Conversely, according to this view, when voters elect a divided government, they essentially vote for gridlock. Divided government leads to inefficiency and ineffectiveness, and it undermines accountability because the voters do not know which party to punish if they think government policy fails, or which party to reward if they think government policy succeeds.[4] Under this arrangement, gridlock is inevitable; some scholars even argue that divided government results in larger budget deficits.[5]

In their account of the budget battles of the 1980s and 1990s, George Hager and Eric Pianin apply an inevitable gridlock perspective to explain why neither major political party can solve the deficit problem. Ironically, their book *Mirage* was published in spring 1997, in the midst of the bipartisan budget negotiations that led to the budget agreement. Hager and Pianan's study led them to conclude that "the politics of deficit reduction have always been more partisan than deficit reduction, a game of advantage seeking whose goal is to win back control of Congress or the White House." Hager and Pianin draw a simple lesson from their review of recent budget battles: "It is all but irresistible for policy-makers to score political points rather than work toward a bipartisan plan to balance the budget."[6] Thus the two major parties are caught inevitably in a "revenge cycle" wherein the political rewards go to those who obstruct and the losses go to those who cooperate and compromise. History, Hager and Pianin contend, shows that budget politics is a "mirage," as politicians promise to reduce the deficit, talk about bipartisanship, and appear to struggle for the public good. Fearful of being attacked by their opponents, and worried that they risk major losses at the ballot box, each party waits for the other to make the first move. Meanwhile, a balanced budget looms in the hazy distance, a horizon politicians can never reach. As Hager and Pianin put it: "The deficit has so badly polarized the two political parties that the problem seems, at times, beyond the power of democratic government to fix."[7] Unless confronted with a crisis, policymakers never succeed in making unpopular choices.

Party politics is not the only obstacle to solving the deficit problem, and partisanship is not the only cause of inevitable gridlock. Some scholars argue that members of Congress, regardless of party ties, are unwilling to make the tough choices needed to reduce the deficit because they might offend some important constituency and risk losing the next election.[8] Others attribute the problem of gridlock mainly to a lack of public understanding about the fundamental causes of the deficit and the public's unwillingness to tolerate cutbacks in popular entitlement programs.[9] Public opinion surveys invariably show that Americans do not understand that Medicare and Social Security are the most costly government programs, and they strongly oppose reducing spending in those programs for the sake of a balanced budget.[10] Since politicians naturally respond to public opinion, so the argument goes, they will avoid reforming entitlement programs unless the public becomes more willing to accept efforts to change them.

Many scholars place at least part of the blame on interest groups.[11] As Peter Peterson points out, the "entitlement revolution" of the 1960s and 1970s facilitated an increase in the number of interest groups. Behind every government program are hosts of organized groups that exist primarily, if not exclusively, to defend those programs. Some of these groups serve narrow political or economic interests, while others represent a fairly significant population of program beneficiaries.[12] But all groups share a common goal: ensuring that their particular programs remain intact. As the theory goes, existing commitments to programs and beneficiaries of entitlements make it virtually impossible for politicians to reduce the deficit. The advent of new programs and the explosion of groups in the 1960s and 1970s within a fragmented political system make the job of cutting spending mighty difficult.[13]

Electoral vulnerability, party politics, public opinion, and interest groups provide an oversupply of reasons for perpetual gridlock. Each of those factors has undoubtedly played an important part in budget politics over the past twenty years. Taken together, they pose serious obstacles to policymakers seeking to reduce budget deficits. But does the system inevitably grind to a halt? Have those obstacles prohibited politicians from developing policy designed to reduce the deficit? Does divided party control of the White House and Congress incapacitate the separation-of-powers system?

Realist Expectations

The realist expectations perspective contends that despite the obstacles, the political system is not destined to result in gridlock. Instead, the separation-of-powers system can produce various governing arrangements, and leaders play critical roles in identifying opportunities for and constraints on policy change. The prospect for policy change depends on a variety of political, institutional, and policy conditions, and on the manner in which leaders interpret and adapt to those conditions. Thus, divided party control of the White House and Congress alters the expectations of party leaders, but it does not inevitably result in partisan stalemate. Members of Congress are worried about reelection and seek to represent their particular constituencies, but they are also concerned about solving such national problems as the deficit. Interest groups will lobby hard to change policy in their favor or prohibit policy change if doing so harms their clients, but they do not always succeed.

The realist expectations model is rooted in the Framers' concept of governing in a separation-of-powers system. As political scientist Jessica Korn argues, Wilson based his critique of the separation of powers on a false notion of the Framers' intentions. The separation of powers was designed not just to encourage institutions to check power, "but also to produce a division of labor so that members of the different branches would develop specialized skills in pursuing the responsibilities of legislating, executing, and judging."[14] This division of labor may obstruct the president's party from developing a national electoral mandate and translating it into public policy, but it does not create a less effective system of governing. Instead, the separation of powers creates a situation in which policymaking is shared by the executive and legislative branches, and policy outcomes result from bargains struck by elected representatives. Those representatives will most likely be responsive to public opinion, but they are likely to represent more than one "public." As political scientist Charles O. Jones contends, since the president, senators, and members of the House of Representatives are all elected for different terms and serve different constituencies, representation is likely to be "mixed," rather than given to one party. Consequently, responsibility for government policy is more likely to be "diffused," that is, given to more than one party.

The prospects for successful legislating are not doomed by divided government. To the contrary, Jones argues that "diffusion of responsibility may permit policy reform that would have been much less likely if one party had to absorb all of the criticism for past performance or blame should the reforms fail when implemented."[15] Jones urges us to look beyond a single model of how the American political system should work (with one party in charge), and adjust our expectations of Congress and the president by accepting the political realities they must face. Political scientist David Mayhew, who conducted a thorough analysis of legislative productivity in times of divided government since World War II, found that a president and Congress of opposite parties are just as likely to achieve significant legislation as a president and Congress of the same party. According to Mayhew, the key factor in determining the success or failure of policy change is whether the country is in the "mood" for change.[16]

As to the budget deficit, the realist expectations model views it as a serious policy problem (rather than a political football) that policymakers address in various ways and with varying degrees of success. The political system normally will take uneven steps toward solving a big problem, and the realist does not assume that a major overhaul in spending or taxes is necessary to make progress toward reducing the deficit. In the next chapter I review the major attempts to reduce the deficit during the 1980s and 1990s using a realist expectations perspective of budget politics. I argue that previous budget battles were more than mere political games that undermined efforts to reduce the deficit. I do not quarrel with the point that partisan posturing is part of the budget process; it always has been and always will be. Moreover, the practice of political gamesmanship can be distasteful and potentially destructive. When power is divided between the parties, the screaming gets louder, the feelings grow more intense, and the differences are exaggerated for political effect. But we should not be so surprised by, or fed up with, the political games and party differences that we overstate their effects on the budget process. We should not assume that the quest for political advantage must end in bad policy, partisan revenge, or stalemate. The realist understands that politics does not equal gridlock.

In addition to politics, budget battles have been about trying to find ways to reduce the deficit and address other national priorities: a strong national defense, adequate retirement security and health-care benefits for senior citizens, and the like. Since the 1980s, policymakers have been obsessed with the deficit as a public policy problem, not just a political wedge issue. Parties and leaders fight during the budget process because the stakes are high and the policy consequences are real. One of the main tasks of leaders is to build a consensus in an uncertain process crowded with hundreds of interest groups and representatives pursuing various political goals and policy priorities.[17] The record of budget policy during the 1980s and 1990s shows that Congress and the president made progress toward increasing revenues, controlling spending, and reducing the deficit.

From the realist perspective, concerns about reelection, partisan differences, and interest-group demands are obstacles to consensus and not conspiratorial forces that inevitably undermine efforts to reduce the deficit. Since the main problem is trying to find a consensus, it is a mistake to assume that all politicians are unwilling to make tough choices, that *no* politicians will take the risks that go with leadership, that the parties are *always* seeking political advantage, or that interest groups *always* undermine efforts to reduce the deficit. In fact, budget policy decisions are often the result of a complex mixture of governing principles, political calculations, rational policy analysis, and responsiveness to public opinion.

History shows that elected officials from the president down to first-term members of Congress have initiated proposals to reduce the deficit; some succeeded, some failed miserably, and some fell just short of winning enough support.[18] Some attempts were undermined by conflicts between parties, others failed because of breakdowns within a party. Sometimes, interest groups limited the capacity of policymakers to make major reforms; other times, groups bore the brunt of policy changes that cut back spending or increased taxes in ways that directly affected their clients, the elderly included. Though members of Congress are always concerned about reelection, many of them remarkably cast votes to raise taxes, reduce spending, or forego spending increases in popular programs in order to reduce the deficit. Some budget deals were made right after a president was elected, others were approved during midterm election years, and most passed in divided government situations. There is no simple standard explanation for success or failure.

The only way to explain the variations in budget politics is to begin from a more complex and less deterministic perspective of governing. The realist expectations model explains why the system is neither destined to produce gridlock in times of divided party government nor sure to succeed when one party controls both the executive and legislative branches of government. Although party politics, interest groups, public opinion, and concerns about reelection place constraints on major policy change, they have not prohibited Congress and the president from addressing the deficit. Those who see a system destined to be in gridlock have been so busy trying to explain the failure of grand plans to balance the budget that they missed the gradual progress toward restoring revenues and reducing the rate of growth in government spending from 1982 to 1996. While searching for a primary culprit for the "crime," too many investigators failed to notice that some of the main suspects were addressing the deficit problem in the messy, inconsistent, uncoordinated, and incremental way that a realist expects of a separation-of-powers system with widespread opportunities for representation.

Realist Expectations and the 1997 Budget Agreement

The realist expectations perspective helps explain why the political system went from partisan gridlock to a bipartisan agreement in just over one year. Since the Constitution permits a variety of governing arrangements, a bipartisan pattern of presidential-congressional interaction is one possibility under divided government.[19] In 1997, after the two parties had battled for two years over budget priorities and voters returned both parties to control their respective institutions, key leaders from both parties believed that the best way to advance their political interests and policy goals was to negotiate a bipartisan agreement. Party leaders adjusted their policy goals to political realities; they interpreted the 1996 elections as an indication the public wanted the parties to work together; and they believed they could concede points to the other side while maintaining their core principles and advancing their political aims. The process of putting together the components of a bipartisan agreement—a balanced budget by the year 2002, caps on total government spending, targeted tax cuts, large reductions in the rate of spending growth for Medicare, an extension of health coverage to more children, and several targeted initiatives for welfare recipients—was also facilitated by a strong economy.

Identifying the key conditions that explain the formation of the 1997 budget agreement is a good beginning, but it is only a beginning. The realist expectations view has important implications for understanding how the budget process works in divided government. Those implications represent the central themes developed in the book and deserve special mention at the outset.

First, the 1997 budget agreement should be considered part of a long-term project to balance the budget that has spanned many years and has included episodes of stalemate, incremental policy changes, and major deficit-reduction efforts. Each year offers a new opportunity and a connection to the past, and policymakers apply lessons from previous experiences to the prevailing circumstances. President Clinton and Republican leaders had spent the previous two years debating priorities, trying to figure out each other's commitments, and narrowing their differences over taxes and spending. So when they began the process in 1997, they had already laid the groundwork for a deal, and they could essentially pick up from there. Moreover, Republicans learned the hard lesson of partisan stalemate in a divided government: if one side loses, both sides lose. Thus, after a failed attempt at dramatic reforms in 1995 and 1996, they were willing to accept incremental policy changes in 1997. Indeed, the 1997 bipartisan budget agreement could not have come together without the partisan battles that preceded it. It would be no exaggeration to say that the glow of bipartisanship emerged from the ashes of partisan stalemate.

Second, even though leaders engaged in a bipartisan process in 1997 to achieve certain common goals (a balanced budget and Medicare savings), they did not abandon their partisan interests. Bipartisanship implies that both parties want to pursue common goals, but partisan priorities do not disappear at the bargaining table. Bipartisan policymaking is not simply a noble and voluntary effort to set aside partisan differences. Instead, the realist expectations view assumes that parties enter bipartisan negotiations because they see them as a feasible way to advance particular priorities under the circumstances. As they seek partisan advantage in a bipartisan process, leaders constantly wrestle with the difficult tradeoffs between party principles and feasible compromises. They engage in a sort of tug-of-war, with each side yanking hard at times and then yielding ground. In 1997 the two parties continued to pursue different priorities but realized that in a divided government they needed to settle for less than the ideal.

Third, a bipartisan process is likely to produce tensions within the parties over which priorities are most important and what is the best strategy for achieving them. Liberal Democrats and conservative Republicans who opposed the budget agreement believe it prohibited them from advancing their policy aims and political interests. Leaders try to accommodate as many partisan colleagues as they can, but the reality is that some members are going to oppose a bipartisan compromise, because it either violates their principles or weakens their political standing. As leaders attempt to build a coalition of members to support their budget, they must disappoint certain members on the left and right who are unwilling to accept a bipartisan compromise.

Fourth, a bipartisan budget agreement depends on the capacity of leaders to achieve their parties' goals and address national problems. Leaders are essential to recognizing opportunities to govern, understanding the possibilities and limits of policy change, staying focused on realistic goals, persuading their colleagues to accept their judgments, and organizing the institutions effectively to close a deal. As leaders attempt to develop and maintain a broad consensus on budget decisions, they need to consider the reactions of hundreds of colleagues representing different constituencies. They must be able to manage the obstacles that stem from internal party divisions, interest-group pressures, and concerns about reelection. They also must be willing and able to accept the compromises and tradeoffs that go with bargaining in a representative system of government.

Finally, we must take into account the variety of political, institutional, and policy conditions that affect budget decisions as the budget agreement makes its way through Congress. The budget process involves multiple decisions (informal agreements, budget resolutions, and spending and tax bills plus amendments to those bills) made at various stages of policymaking (behind closed doors, in congressional committees, and on the House and Senate floors.) These decisions are motivated by a complex mix of principles, political calculations, rational policy analysis, and responsiveness to public opinion. Opponents of the budget agreement, consisting mainly of interest groups and factions within the parties, are always lurking in the shadows, waiting for an opportunity to scuttle the deal. Thus the budget must undergo a series of adjustments in which individuals and factions in both parties constantly push the boundaries and alter the terms of the original agreement in order to achieve their policy objectives and political goals. As the budget process develops from presidential-congressional negotiations to congressional committees and to the House and Senate floors, the strategic situation is constantly changing. For example, while some decisions made in Congress were passed by majorities of both parties, others broke along party lines. Leaders play crucial roles in negotiating differences between the parties, combating opponents, convincing colleagues of the benefits of compromising with the opposing party, and overcoming the various obstacles in the budget process.

Only through a close analysis can we understand how complex the process is and why the budget deal never seemed to be "done." At each stage along the way, right up until the end, just as policymakers wiped the sweat from their brows and proudly smiled at their handwork, an unpredictable and sometimes treacherous legislative process placed the terms of the deal in jeopardy. One reason this book's title, *Done Deal?*, includes a question mark is to highlight the endless efforts to adjust, alter, and shape particular tax and spending decisions.

Another reason for the question mark is that the 1997 budget agreement was historic but at the same time limited, calling into question what it achieved and what remains to be done. Ultimately, a process that demands each party to compromise in order to succeed places limits on the extent of policy change and leaves skeptics unhappy with the final product. The 1997 budget agreement reflects the political system's bias toward incrementalism, a gradual change in policy that accomplishes limited aims and not a major overhaul of federal budget priorities. Even the most ardent proponents of the agreement admitted that over the long term more difficult decisions would have to be made if the budget was to stay balanced after the year 2002.

Despite the budget agreement's limitations, those who contend the budget deal was a minor achievement or "a political contraption designed to let different kinds of politicians brag" fail to understand or appreciate its importance.[20] The 1997 budget agreement is the linchpin connecting serious efforts of the past twenty years to reduce the deficit and address other fiscal priorities with the bigger challenges facing policymakers in the future. It also represents a shift in priorities from Democrat-leaning deficit-reduction plans emphasizing mainly tax increases and defense spending cuts to Republican-leaning policies emphasizing reductions in entitlement spending and domestic spending restraint to balance the budget and cut taxes. The 1997 budget agreement is not the deal to end all deals; no such deal exists because the long-term process never ends and problems will never be "solved" to the satisfaction of everyone. It is, however, a major development in budget policy born out of a political system and a process that is designed to yield much less and that rarely produces more.

Plan of the Book

Chapter 2 begins with a primer on key budget concepts, trends in spending and revenues, and the deficit problem. It then reviews major attempts to reduce the deficit in the 1980s and 1990s. Despite numerous obstacles, policymakers made progress toward reducing the deficit and, as the realist expectations view suggests, no single formula explains why some attempts succeeded and others failed.

Chapter 3 describes the governing and policy conditions at the outset of the 105th Congress and the key leaders in the budget process. One tenet of the realist perspective is that policy can be formed from a variety of conditions and that leaders play key roles in the process. At the outset of the 105th Congress, some elected officials and political analysts were optimistic, others were pessimistic, and still others had no clear expectations about the prospects for a bipartisan agreement. Moreover, a significant number of congresspersons from both parties believed their leaders should not engage in a bipartisan process to develop a budget agreement. Thus, conditions offered an opportunity, though not a certainty, for successful bipartisan negotiations.

Chapters 4 and 5 cover the bipartisan negotiations between the White House and congressional Republican leaders and the major policy decisions that culminated in the budget agreement. While the potential for an agreement was evident, the process had its usual false starts and included the partisan gamesmanship that had become common practice over the years. There was a complex interplay of political conditions and leadership skills as each side tried to advance its objectives, and negotiators attempted to balance each party's principles with the practical need to compromise. Ultimately, both sides compromised in order to achieve feasible policy changes.

Chapter 6 traces the budget agreement's course through the House and Senate. The tentative agreement reached by bipartisan negotiations had to be translated into a congressional budget resolution, win the endorsement of the House and Senate budget committees, and pass both chambers. The chapter underscores the principles and politics that affect budget decisions and shows the importance of leadership.

Chapter 7 shows how the politics of budget reconciliation played out as the congressional committees worked through the details of the spending bill. Varying degrees of partisan and bipartisan decision making took place as members sought to advance their policy goals. Party leaders attempted to strike a delicate balance between preserving the terms of the bipartisan agreement and satisfying the interests of committee chairs.

Chapter 8 explains the contrast in committee politics between the House and the Senate on tax policy. Whereas the House Ways and Means Committee featured a bill that divided the parties, it also exposed the tensions within the Republican Party over taxes. The Senate Finance Committee, on the other hand, produced a bipartisan tax bill.

Chapter 9 analyzes the conference stage of the reconciliation process, where the final decisions were made. Instead of splitting the difference between the two houses, the conferees traded one issue for another, expanded on the work of both chambers, and revamped parts of the tax bill with active participation from the White House. The conference also served as a weeding-out mechanism, discarding contentious and politically risky components of the bills and restoring bipartisan comity after it had broken down in the House. The deal was nearly blown apart at the last minute and then passed just before Congress adjourned.

The concluding chapter reflects on the lessons that can be drawn from the politics of the 1997 budget agreement and explores the policy achievements and limits of the deal. The chapter argues that while the budget agreement marks a significant step in the long process toward balancing the budget and addressing other national priorities, it leaves plenty of work to be done.

2

Budget Choices and Deficit Politics: 1980–96

At the outset of his presidential campaign in 1992, independent presidential candidate H. Ross Perot claimed that balancing the budget was simple. Perot proposed an off-the-cuff plan to cut spending by $480 billion by reducing Social Security benefits to wealthy senior citizens, eliminating "waste, fraud, and abuse," requiring U.S. allies to fund joint security operations overseas, and modernizing the Internal Revenue Service. Simple as that, Perot exclaimed, "and you haven't even broken a sweat." Yet, at the time, Mr. Perot had no idea how difficult it was to balance the budget mathematically, much less politically. After critics pressed Perot for more details, he hired John White, a former Office of Management and Budget (OMB) official under President Carter. Using White's analysis, Perot presented the boldest deficit-reduction proposal ever contemplated in a presidential campaign. The five-year, $744 billion deficit-reduction plan contained several politically risky proposals: $300 billion in new taxes, huge cuts in defense spending, and major reforms in entitlement programs, including higher taxes on Social Security recipients and higher premiums for Medicare beneficiaries. This time, Perot admitted the choices would not be easy. He likened the process to walking across a desert with limited water, and he warned the voters that "if you want Lawrence Welk music, I'm not your man."[1]

Perot learned a lesson that all elected officials ultimately learn in an era of deficit politics: balancing the budget is difficult. To begin with, budgeting involves more than figuring out the "best" way to balance the budget. Though most elected officeholders want a balanced budget in good economic times, some see it as a higher priority than others. A balanced budget must compete with numerous other priorities: a strong national defense, more health-care coverage, lower taxes, and the list goes on. The process is never easy, and "solutions" are never simple. Politicians quarrel about whether programs are worth maintaining, cutting, or expanding, and their disagreements can be based on their philosophy of government, their constituents' needs, a friendly interest group's support, their analysis of a program's benefits, and several other reasons.

This chapter defines key budget concepts, charts major fiscal trends, and describes the ongoing deficit problem. Though one could argue that policymakers should have done more to reduce deficits, they have not been unwilling, afraid, or unable to address the problem. As political scientist Aaron Wildavsky has pointed out, "it is fair to argue that, facing tough choices, Congress and the president have bargained responsibly, balancing the costs and benefits of both lower deficits and the policy choices to get there."[2] Despite numerous obstacles, policymakers made progress toward reducing the deficit during the 1980s and 1990s.[3] The ultimate challenge of budget politics is for leaders to build a consensus among competing political interests, values, and priorities. Yet such obstacles are not insurmountable. Though most of the successful efforts to reduce the deficit contained incremental amounts of budget savings, on two occasions (in 1990 and 1993) Congress and the president enacted five-year budget plans with over $490 billion in savings. A brief historical review indicates there is no standard explanation why some budget proposals succeed and others fail. Variations in governing, policy, and leadership produce a wide range of strategies and policy outcomes, and numerous cases defy conventional assumptions about why, as some critics argue, the political system is destined to gridlock.

Budget Basics: Many Purposes, Many Goals, and Many Budgets

On one level, the federal budget is a complex and massive document that only experts can ever hope to understand. It is filled with spreadsheets and cost estimates of how much money the federal government needs to raise and how much each federal agency plans to spend. Yet behind the numbers, a budget contains basic choices about taxes and spending. Thus, without oversimplifying the budget, we can identify the key budget concepts and trends in taxes, spending, and deficits that one needs to know to understand the problems confronting policymakers.[4]

- In *economic* terms, the budget defines the nation's fiscal policy by stating how tax and spending decisions are expected to affect the nation's economy.

- In *technical* terms, the budget contains mathematical models including projections about how the economy is going to perform in the future.

- In *political* terms, the budget specifies how the nation's priorities match up with the preferences of the general public, the principles of the two major parties, and specific policy goals of interest groups.

- In *public policy* terms, the budget distributes financial resources to achieve certain outcomes: a better educated citizenry, cleaner air, a capable military force, and the like.

- In *legal* terms, the budget is a contract of mutual obligations between the federal government and the people.

- In *moral* terms, the budget reveals how the country distributes resources and the debt it passes on from one generation to another.

Once we shed the technical terminology, though, we are left with fundamental questions of governing: who gets what, when, and how from the federal government. Behind the numbers lie the values and priorities of the individuals who make the budget. Some priorities reflect national issues that concern all Americans, others serve narrow interests or constituent needs. How much should Americans pay in taxes, and in which kinds of taxes? How much should be spent on national defense, and for what purposes? How much should be spent on domestic programs to help the elderly? How much should be devoted to education, crime, transportation? If the budget is to be balanced, which programs should be reduced and which taxes should be raised? These questions, and thousands more, lie behind a vast array of numbers that can overwhelm anyone.

The president is required to submit to Congress the Federal Budget of the Executive Office on the first Monday in February for the upcoming fiscal year, beginning 1 October. The president's budget appears to be *the* federal budget because it contains the most precise accounting of the financial transactions entered into by executive agencies. The president normally introduces his budget at about the time he gives a State of the Union address, and the proximity of these two events leaves the impression that the president is responsible for establishing national priorities and deciding the government's fiscal policy.[5]

Yet while the president performs the first official political act in the annual budget drama, he does not have the only budget in town. The Constitution grants Congress the power to make laws regarding taxes and appropriations, and so members of Congress have the power to accept, reject, or change the president's budget requests. Congress's role expanded with passage of the Budget Act of 1974, which enabled Congress to create budget committees in the House and Senate, formulate a congressional budget resolution separate from the president's budget, and establish an independent Congressional Budget Office (CBO) to crunch all the numbers. The Budget Act also established a timetable for formulating and approving a congressional budget resolution and procedures for coordinating the budget resolution with specific spending and tax legislation. Before the Budget Act, Congress could change specific tax laws and spending bills; after 1974 Congress could propose a general budget plan similar to the president's.[6]

Once Congress could formulate a budget resolution, trying to identify a single federal budget became very complex. Members of Congress used the budget process to express their values and advance their priorities. In its annual ritual to pass a congressional budget resolution, Congress always considers budget resolutions drafted by the House and Senate budget committees, but it also entertains alternatives devised by various members. Liberal Democrats, conservative Democrats, conservative Republicans, the black caucus, and moderate factions of both parties frequently attempt to pass budget resolutions through Congress. Many of these groups try to balance the budget, but they disagree about how it should be done. George Hager and Eric Pianin point out that in 1995 "more than 80 percent of the House—360 of its 435 members—had backed some plan to balance the budget."[7] The variety of budgets helps explain why it is so difficult for politicians to reach a consensus on a single deficit-reduction plan.

Slicing the Budget Pies and Charting Trends in Revenues and Outlays

Most presidents and most members of Congress are not budget-policy wonks. Fortunately, for them and for most Americans, a detailed understanding of the budget is not necessary to engage in an informed conversation about national priorities, fiscal policy, and the role of government in society. In order to simplify the array of complex decisions in the budget, let's consider a few key concepts.[8] (Readers less familiar with budget terminology may wish to refer to the Glossary of Terms at the back of the book.)

The federal budget has two sides: one for *outlays*, the total amount of money the government spends in a year; and one for *revenues*, the total amount of money the government receives in taxes and user fees.[9] The difference between revenues and outlays equals the annual deficit or surplus. As figure 2.1 illustrates, the federal government ran annual deficits since 1969. The deficits grew dramatically in the early 1980s and, after declining for a few years, increased again in the late 1980s and early 1990s, reaching $290 billion in 1992. Since that time, the budget deficit has declined, reaching its lowest level in 1997. For the fiscal year ending 30 September 1997, the federal government took in $1.579 trillion and spent $1.601 trillion, leaving an annual deficit of $22 billion. By January 1998 the CBO and the OMB were projecting budget surpluses in the future.

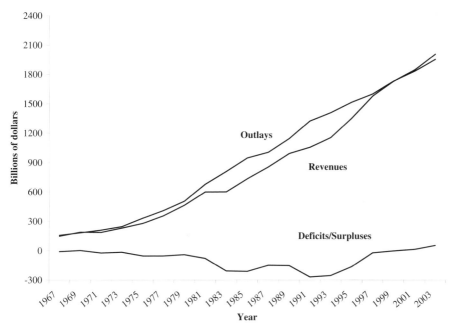

Figure 2.1
Outlays, Revenues, and Deficits/Surpluses, 1967–2003

Source: The Economic and Budget Outlook for Fiscal Years 1999–2008
(Washington, D.C.: Government Printing Office, 1998).

Despite the impending surpluses, years of annual deficits have piled up a mountain of debt. Like any individual who borrows money from a bank, the federal government has to borrow money when outlays exceed revenues. In order to finance its operations when revenues fall short of outlays, the government sells debt in the form of U.S. Treasury securities. The national debt is the accumulation of all the money borrowed by the federal government to finance annual deficits plus the interest that has compounded over the years.[10]

Figure 2.2 (p. 18) divides revenues into tax receipts from various sources: individual incomes, corporate profits, social insurance (payroll) taxes earmarked for Social Security and Medicare, and various "other" revenue raisers, such as excise taxes from sales, estate and gift taxes, customs duties, and user fees. Comparing the revenue columns of 1997 with 1967, we see a shift in the share of revenues from various sources. While taxes from corporate profits decreased as a share of all revenues, social insurance taxes earmarked for Social Security and Medicare increased.

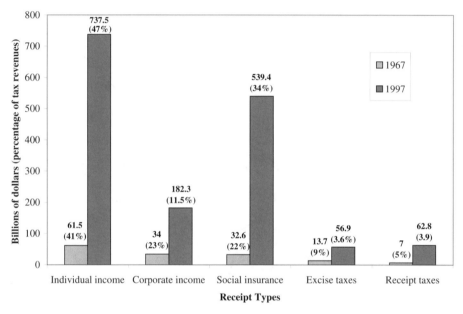

Figure 2.2
Composition of Tax Receipts, 1967 and 1997

Source: *The Economic and Budget Outlook for Fiscal Years 1999–2008*
(Washington, D.C.: Government Printing Office, 1998).

Figure 2.3 (p. 19) slices a spending pie into seven pieces, illustrating spending levels for large mandatory programs and two areas of discretionary spending (defense and nondefense). Mandatory spending includes entitlement programs, which are commitments by the government to transfer payments directly to individuals who meet eligibility requirements specified by law.[11] The largest entitlement program is Social Security, a government pension plan for senior citizens, which accounted for $362 billion, or about 22 percent of all government spending in FY 1997. The main eligibility criterion for Social Security is that an individual be at least sixty-five years of age, though the actual amount of money paid to individuals is based on a complex formula. Senior citizens are also eligible for

Medicare, a government health-care program, which consumed 12 percent of total spending.

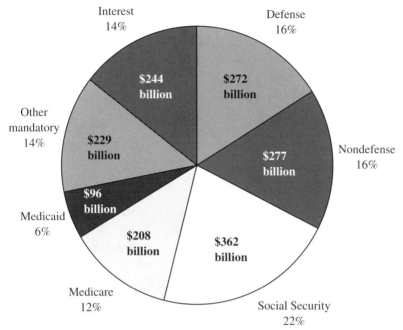

Figure 2.3
Federal Spending in Major Program Areas, FY 1997

Source: The Economic and Budget Outlook for Fiscal Years 1999–2008
(Washington, D.C.: Government Printing Office, 1998).

Unlike mandatory programs, which must be funded and do not require annual appropriation approved by Congress and the president, spending for discretionary programs must be enacted into law on an annual basis. Thus, each year Congress has *discretion* to change spending for those programs. Discretionary spending is normally divided into defense and nondefense spending. Defense discretionary includes all the government expenditures for weapons systems, operations, personnel, and the like. Nondefense discretionary includes everything from transportation programs to education grants to salaries for members of Congress and executive branch officials. As figure 2.3 illustrates, the federal government spends roughly the same amount on defense and nondefense discretionary programs. Also note that the government spends more on Social Security, a single mandatory program, than on all defense or nondefense discretionary programs. We can also see the toll taken by years of accumulating deficits: net interest on the national debt nearly equals the amount spent on defense or nondefense discretionary programs.

The growth in mandatory spending and interest on the debt creates a major challenge for policymakers. As figure 2.4 illustrates, entitlements and interest on the national debt dominate the budget. Trends in spending and revenues begin to explain how the deficit emerged and why it is so difficult to deal with. A General Accounting Office (GAO) study found that "a few large entitlement programs—Social Security, Medicare, and Medicaid—and interest payments have accounted for over three-quarters of total outlay growth since 1971. Overall, spending for entitlement and other mandatory programs arising outside of the annual appropriations process grew more than four times faster in real terms than appropriated (i.e. discretionary) spending."[12] With entitlements leading the way, federal spending increased steadily over the past twenty-five years, whereas federal revenues grew at a slower rate before rising sharply beginning in 1994.

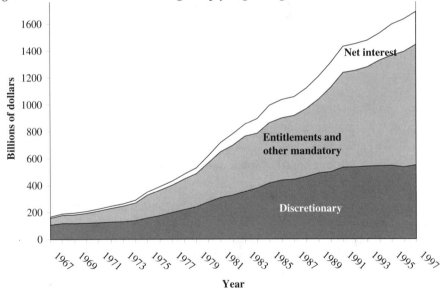

Figure 2.4
Spending in Major Budget Categories: 1967–97

Source: The Economic and Budget Outlook for Fiscal Years 1999–2008 (Washington, D.C.: GPO), 1998Government Printing Office, 1998).

The Deficit Problem

The federal government ran deficits for sixty-eight of ninety-seven years from 1901 to 1997. Until the 1970s, though, most deficits occurred during recessions or wars, and these short-term deficits were easily erased in good economic times by budget surpluses. As political scientist James Savage argues, balancing the budget was a moral imperative and an entrenched symbol of American politics until the 1960s.[13] Since the 1970s, deficits grew larger and became more persistent, continuing even in good economic times. These "structural" annual deficits produced unprecedented levels of borrowing and drove up the national debt.

The partisan debate in Washington over the causes of the large structural deficits is all too familiar and unfortunately misleading. Republicans blame the deficit on excessive domestic spending that began with President Roosevelt's New Deal during the 1930s and expanded with President Johnson's Great Society programs of the 1960s. Democrats blame President Reagan's "borrow and spend" and supply-side economic policies during the 1980s, including tax cuts and increases in defense spending. Most nonpartisan analyses contend that both parties share the blame. Both agreed to substantial increases in entitlement programs without collecting sufficient tax revenues to pay for them, and neither anticipated the effects of recession and inflation on government spending. Persistent annual deficits resulted from an assortment of economic troubles and policy decisions beginning in the 1960s. As Wildavsky points out: "A reasonable conclusion would be that all who govern now and in the past half century share some of the blame for the deficit, some more than others, but few are guiltless."[14]

Analysts debate the extent to which various economic forces, policy choices, and political developments explain why the deficit grew during the 1970s and persisted into the 1990s. But most agree that deficits stem from a combination of an expansion of entitlement spending, slow economic growth combined with inflation through the 1970s and early 1980s, and tax cuts and defense spending increases in the early 1980s.[15] Some analysts say the origins of deficits can be traced to Keynesian economics during the Great Depression of the 1930s. The British economist Lord John Maynard Keynes challenged the traditional view by arguing that instead of worrying about balancing the budget, the principal objective of government economic policy should be to balance the economy. In good economic times, governments should run surpluses and pursue policies of fiscal restraint to lessen consumer demand. During recessions, surpluses are counterproductive, and the government should engage in deficit spending to spur economic growth by stimulating consumer demand.

After a post–World War II economic boom, economists and policymakers gradually reached a consensus in support of Keynesian economics, and by the 1960s they thought they had figured out how to manage economic cycles. Policymakers agreed that deficit spending was fine during recessions when the economy needed the stimulus from additional government spending or tax cuts. Yet politicians lacked the discipline required to make Keynesian theory work in practice. In the world of economic theory, spending and tax policies are timed so that the economy is balanced in the short term, perhaps with budget deficits, and the budget is balanced in the long term. In the world of politics, there are taxes to cut and programs to finance, with less regard for the patience and precision that go with disciplined fiscal management.

Optimism about economic growth spurred politicians to make unprecedented commitments to entitlement programs in the 1960s and early 1970s. Congress and the president passed major health-care entitlements, Medicare for the elderly and Medicaid for the poor; food stamps; guaranteed student loans; supplemental security income (SSI); and expansions in welfare and Social Security benefits.[16] From 1967 to 1972, when Congress and the president passed several increases in Social Security, average annual benefits increased by 14.5 percent above the rate of inflation.[17] To cap off a five-year binge in benefit increases, in 1972 a Republican president and Democratic Congress raised Social Security benefits by 20 percent and indexed Social Security benefits to the rate of inflation in the future. Indexation ensured that senior citizens would enjoy automatic cost-of-living-adjustments (COLAs) to shield them from the adverse effects of rising prices, but it also meant that federal spending on Social Security would automatically rise with inflation.

The expansion in social programs was not merely a matter of spending a lot of money, but of how the money was being spent. The shift from a budget based primarily on discretionary programs to a budget driven by entitlements has profound implications for spending control. Spending for discretionary programs can be adjusted annually in the appropriations process, but spending for entitlements depends mainly on the number of eligible beneficiaries, costs of the benefits, and such uncontrollable forces as the state of the economy, demographic changes in the population, and the price of health care. Of course, Congress and the president can change the level of spending for entitlements by passing legislation that alters benefit formulas and eligibility criteria for entitlement programs. Yet it is more difficult to change laws in mandatory programs than it is to change the level of spending for discretionary programs.

Medicare, one of the most expensive and fastest-growing entitlements, provides a good example of the difficulties of controlling entitlement spending. The president and Congress cannot simply look at projected costs in the Medicare program and say, "It is obvious Medicare is getting expensive, why don't we spend less this year?" Under existing law, doctors and hospitals expect to be reimbursed, and beneficiaries expect medical services and treatment. Total annual spending on Medicare depends on the costs of those services and the number of eligible Medicare beneficiaries who use the health-care system. In order to reduce Medicare spending, the laws specifying eligibility must be changed first, which means reducing the benefits or increasing the costs to senior citizens, or cutting reimbursements to doctors and hospitals.

The economy also affects revenue and spending trends. If inflation increases, the government is going to spend more on entitlement programs, such as Social Security and veterans' pensions, and all other programs indexed for inflation.[18] Conversely, if inflation is low, government will spend less on these programs. If economic growth is strong and unemployment is low, revenues will increase with large corporate profits, high wages, increased investment income, and total national income, and the government will pay less in unemployment and income-support programs.

Just after the major thrust of policy innovations in entitlements and a successful twenty-five-year run of reasonably stable economic cycles, the early 1970s brought an unexpected economic slowdown. A combination of high unemployment and inflation fueled spending for nearly all entitlements, though Social Security led the way as inflation soared well beyond expectations. Timothy J. Penny and Steven E. Schier summarize the effects of the economy on Social Security expenditures:

> The 1972 increase would spell disaster for Social Security within five years. . . . The Social Security Administration (SSA) erred in believing high economic growth and fiscal slack would continue. SSA, in supporting the 1972 benefit hike, estimated 15 percent inflation and 12 percent real wage growth from 1973 to 1977. In reality, inflation zoomed 41 percent, whereas real wages rose 1 percent. Higher benefit checks had to be paid, but revenue from the payroll tax stagnated.[19]

In addition to economic stagnation combined with inflation, unexpected demographic changes placed further burdens on entitlement spending. Life expectancy increased faster than anticipated, birthrates declined, divorce rates doubled, and out-of-wedlock births tripled, placing additional pressure on means-tested entitlement programs, such as unemployment compensation, food stamps, and Aid to Families with Dependent Children (AFDC). In the early 1980s, when recession hit again, unemployment increased, and more individuals received government support from means-tested entitlement programs. Then, large increases in health-care costs above the rate of inflation accounted for the dramatic increase in Medicare and Medicaid in the 1980s. Between 1975 and 1995, Medicare grew an average of 15 percent, or 6 percent above of the rate of inflation.[20]

The rise in deficits cannot be attributed solely to poor economic conditions and increases in entitlement spending. In 1981, tax cuts further reduced overall revenues, and large increases in defense spending added to deficits in the early 1980s. The Economic Recovery Tax Act of 1981 (ERTA) cut tax rates by 25 percent over three years. Contrary to President Reagan's expectations that tax cuts would spur revenue growth, total federal revenues as a percentage of gross domestic product (GDP) declined from 19.7 percent in 1981 to 17.4 percent in 1983 and did not return to 19 percent until 1996. Meanwhile, defense spending more than doubled during the first six years of the Reagan administration, rising from $134.6 billion (or 5 percent of GDP) in 1980 to $274 billion (or 6.3 percent of GDP) in 1986.

Deficit Reduction: Economics, Policy, and Politics

Ever since the budget deficit became a major policy problem, critics have said that politicians were too busy playing partisan games, placating special interests, and worrying about getting reelected to "do the right thing" to balance the budget. Now that the budget is balanced, many critics say the economy is responsible. Yet a review of economic trends and budget policy in the 1980s and 1990s reveals a more complex picture. If recession coupled with inflation on the heels of large increases in entitlement spending in the 1960s and early 1970s, followed by defense spending increases and tax cuts in the early 1980s, propelled the deficit, then arresting or reversing those trends would be necessary to balance the budget. Certainly, strong economic growth with low inflation during the 1990s produced large increases in expected revenues and decreases in spending growth, which ultimately brought the budget into balance. But reducing the deficit has been a long-term project, and the budget would not be balanced today without the policy changes in the 1980s and 1990s that reduced spending and increased taxes.

President Clinton's FY 1999 budget underscores the powerful effects of economic growth on deficit reduction. The OMB predicted that the legislative changes (tax increases and spending cuts) in Clinton's budget package of 1993, the Omnibus Budget Reconciliation Act (OBRA), would reduce deficits by $505 billion. In fact, since the passage of OBRA, deficits are $811 billion lower, a reduction by over $300 billion more than expected. Why the difference? According to the Clinton budget, "the answer lies in a continuing surge of receipts, and in spending that came in below expectations. That surge is rooted in an especially strong economy."[21] Table 2.1 shows the difference between the projected and actual levels of outlays, receipts, and deficits from FY 1994 through FY 1997. Each year, actual receipts were higher and actual outlays lower than projected after the passage of OBRA. In 1997 alone, the government received $74 billion more and spent $90 billion less than projected in 1994; consequently, the deficit for FY 1997 was a whopping $164 billion less than projected just four years earlier.

Table 2.1
Projected versus Actual Receipts, Outlays, and Deficits/Surpluses,
FY 1994 to FY 1997 (in billions of dollars)

	1994	1995	1996	1997
Receipts				
Projected	$1,249	$1,354	$1,427	$1,505
Actual	1,259	1,352	1,453	1,579
Difference	10	2	26	74
Outlays				
Projected	1,483	1,519	1,597	1,691
Actual	1,461	1,516	1,561	1,601
Difference	-22	-3	-36	-90
Deficits				
Projected	-235	-165	-170	-186
Actual	-203	-164	-108	-22
Difference	-32	-1	-62	-164

Source: Budget of the United States Government, Historical Tables, Fiscal Years 1995 and 1999.

Important policy decisions that preceded the economic boom of the 1990s, including the 1993 OBRA, also contributed to balancing the budget. Table 2.2 (p. 27) outlines the legislative changes Congress and the president have made over the years to reduce deficits and identifies the partisan control of the presidency, the House, and the Senate. The progress toward deficit reduction has been uneven and diverse, touching on nearly every major part of the budget. Some savings have been small, and occasionally they were based on gimmicks rather than real policy changes. Sometimes spending cuts in one part of the budget were offset by spending increases in another part of the budget. Moreover, the deficit wreaked havoc on the budget process, and partisan posturing often took the place of hard bargaining.[22] One can certainly argue that policymakers *should* have done more to reduce the deficit sooner, but such expectations may be unrealistic. Moreover, contrary to conventional wisdom, in many cases, interest groups did not get their way, tough political decisions were made, and budget savings were genuine. It would be a mistake not to recognize the gradual progress toward deficit reduction. Over time, through a series of legislative acts, both large and small, policymakers racked up an estimated $1.5 trillion in budget savings since 1980.[23] Table 2.2 gives a chronological sketch of legislative changes, with subcategories for each part of the budget. For the sake of brevity, the following discussion is organized by major budget categories: entitlements, revenues, discretionary spending, and enforcement procedures.

First, while entitlement programs have driven overall spending, incremental steps have been taken to slow entitlement spending. After the rapid program expansion in the 1960s and 1970s, policymakers generally stopped adding more entitlement *benefits* by the mid-1970s. The growth in overall entitlement spending after 1974 resulted from demographic, economic, and social trends and from health-care inflation. Thus, even though in the 1980s and 1990s entitlement programs grew more than discretionary programs, except for Medicare and Medicaid, they grew at a slower pace.[24] Moreover, in the 1980s policymakers managed to nick nearly every major entitlement program, from food stamps to civil service reform, and even Medicare and Social Security. Regarding Medicare, Marylin Moon and Jannemarie Mulvey point out that in nearly every year since 1981, the program was changed by "either reducing payments to providers of the services Medicare covers or raising beneficiaries' required contributions."[25] The CBO estimated that program changes in Medicare during the 1980s reduced overall program spending by 20 percent.[26] Social Security was reformed in 1982 in a crisis atmosphere, despite public misgivings and opposition from well-organized interest groups.[27] Wildavsky points out: "In 1982 . . . despite strong opposition of civil service unions, members were required to contribute to social security, which was subtracted from their pensions. The unions did everything right politically; they launched a major campaign against inclusion. The trouble was their little juggernaut was overwhelmed by a much bigger one, the gripping concern that social security retirement might become insolvent."[28]

Second, the lure of tax cuts ended in 1981, and through several reconciliation bills passed during the 1980s, Congress and the president gradually raised

Table 2.2

Highlights of Budget Savings and Policy Changes from Legislative Acts under Varying Political Conditions, 1981 to 1996

Period I, 1981–86: Republican president, Democratic majority in the House, and Republican majority in the Senate

Legislation (savings)	Percentage of majority party voting in favor	
	House	*Senate*
1982 Omnibus Reconciliation Act ($13.3 billion over 3 years) *Mandatory.* Reduced spending for government pensions, farm programs, food stamps, and veterans' benefits.	Democrat 39%	Republican 89%
1982 Tax Equity and Fiscal Responsibility Act (TEFRA) ($115.8 billion over 3 years). *Mandatory* ($17.5 billion). Reductions in Medicare, Medicaid, and welfare programs. *Revenues* ($98.3 billion). Closing tax loopholes.	Democrat 51%	Republican 79%
1983 Social Security Reform ($165 billion over 7 years) *Mandatory.* Raised the retirement age, delayed CO-LAs by six months, increased payroll tax, expanded pool of eligible Social Security beneficiaries to include federal employees.	Democrat 75%	Republican 80%
1983 Reconciliation Act ($8.2 billion over 3 years). *Mandatory.* Delayed COLA for federal and military retirees, and delayed pension increases for civilian retirees. (This bill passed the House in October 1983 and the Senate in April 1984.)	Democrat 53%	Republican 96%

Table 2.2 (Continued)

Period I, 1981–86: Republican president, Democratic majority in the House, and Republican majority in the Senate

Legislation (savings)	Percentage of majority party voting in favor	
	House	*Senate*
1984 Deficit Reduction Act ($149.2 billion over 3 years). *Mandatory* ($35.2 billion). Includes Medicare: increased out-of-pocket cost to beneficiaries and imposed 15-month freeze on physician reimbursements. *Revenues* ($50.8 billion). Includes loophole closings, taxes on liquor, telephone services, and restructured tax breaks on real estate. *Defense Discretionary* ($58.3 billion). *Nondefense Discretionary* ($3.9 billion).	Democrat 73%	Republican 83%
1985 Omnibus Budget Reconciliation Act ($18 billion over 3 years). *Mandatory* ($12.1 billion). Includes student loans, veterans' benefits, and Medicare reimbursements to doctors and hospitals. *Revenues* ($6.1 billion). Includes cigarette taxes, custom fees, pension insurance premiums. (This bill passed the Senate in December 1985 and the House in March 1986.)	Democrat 39%	Republican 97%
1986 Budget Reduction Act ($11.7 billion over 3 years). Medicare and Medicaid, asset sales, and various accounting gimmicks.	Democrat 91%	Republican 76%

Table 2.2 (Continued)

Period II, 1987–92: Republican president, Democratic majority in the House, and Democratic majority in the Senate

Legislation (savings)	Percentage of majority party voting in favor	
	House	Senate
1987 Budget Summit Agreement ($76 billion over 2 years) *Mandatory* ($30 billion). Includes Medicare and other programs. *Revenues* ($26.6 billion). *Defense Discretionary* ($13.7 billion). *Nondefense Discretionary* ($5.9 billion).	Democrat 79%	Democrat 89%
1990 Budget Enforcement Act (BEA) and Omnibus Budget Reconciliation Act ($496.2 billion over 5 years).[a] *Mandatory* ($99.1 billion). Includes $2.9 billion in Medicaid savings and $44.2 billion in Medicare, including additional beneficiary deductibles and premiums, and increasing the wage base for Medicare payroll taxes. *Discretionary* ($182.4 billion). *Revenues* ($146.3 billion). Includes increase in the top marginal rate of taxation from 28% to 31%. Half of the new revenues came from new excise taxes (gas, transportation, beer, wine, distilled spirits, tobacco, and luxury tax). *Interest* ($68.4 billion). *Budget Procedures*. The BEA placed caps on discretionary spending in defense, domestic, and international programs for 3 years and then just in defense and nondefense. A pay-as-you-go (PAYGO) provision stipulated that all tax cuts and entitlement increases had to be "deficit neutral," i.e., offset by tax increases or entitlement cuts. *Additional Spending* ($22.5 billion, including expanding the Earned Income Tax Credit. Expanded children's health coverage $1.1 billion).	Democrat 71%	Democrat 64%

Table 2.2 (Continued)

Period III, 1993–94: Democratic president, Democratic majority in the House, and Democratic majority in the Senate

Legislation (savings)	Percentage of majority party voting in favor	
	House	*Senate*
1993 Omnibus Budget Reconciliation Act ($490 billion over 5 years)[a] *Mandatory* ($89.3 billion). Includes $55.8 billion in Medicare and $7.1 billion in Medicaid savings. *Discretionary* ($68.5 billion). *Revenues* ($240.6 billion). Raised the top rate on income taxes from 31% to 36% for taxable income of $140,000 (married couples) and $115,000 (individuals) and added a 10% surtax on income of more than $250,000. (About 90 cents of every dollar of revenues came from families earning more than $100,000 per year.) Increased the percentage of Social Security benefits subjected to taxes from 50% to 85% for individuals with income above $34,000 and for married couples with incomes above $44,000. Also increased corporate taxes, and a host of smaller provisions, including a gasoline tax increase. *Interest* ($46.8 billion). *Budget Procedures.* Extended BEA rules until FY 1998.	Democrat 84%	Democrat 89%

Table 2.2 (Continued)

Period IV, 1995–96: Democratic president, Republican majority in the House, and Republican majority in the Senate

Legislation (savings)	Percentage of majority party voting in favor	
	House	*Senate*
1996 The Personal Responsibility and Work Opportunity Act ($54 billion over five years). *Mandatory.* Repealed Aid to Families with Dependent Children and replaced it with block grants to the states. Most of the savings came from reducing benefits for food stamps and legal immigrants (some of which was restored in 1997).	Republican 99%	Republican 100%

Source: Various CBO publications and annual editions of *Congressional Quarterly Almanac.*

a. CBO later reestimated the 1990 and 1993 budget packages and found the 1990 BEA saved $482.1 billion and the 1993 OBRA saved $432.9 billion.

revenues by closing tax loopholes.[29] Then, in 1990 and especially 1993, policymakers dramatically increased taxes, mainly on upper-income earners. Raising taxes is always politically risky. The tax-loophole closings that made up much of the revenue gains in the 1980s were passed despite opposition from traditionally powerful interest groups.[30] The 1990 and 1993 tax increases came with a huge political price, first for President Bush, who subsequently lost his reelection bid to Bill Clinton in 1992, and then to congressional Democrats who voted for the 1993 budget bill.[31]

Third, while budget savings from entitlement programs and taxes were achieved through policy changes contained in budget reconciliation bills, savings in discretionary spending were achieved through the appropriations process. Discretionary spending since the 1960s has varied depending on the program, with periods of expansion normally followed by periods of decreased spending. Spending for nondefense discretionary programs has gone up and down since the 1960s, with most of the growth occurring before 1980. In fact, after growing at a real average rate of 4.9 percent per year from the early 1960s to 1980, nondefense discretionary spending declined by 2.9 percent per year from 1980 to 1987.[32] From 1987 to 1995, spending increased at an average annual rate of about 3.3 percent, only to decline again by 2.2 percent during 1995 and 1996. While nondefense spending declined during the Reagan years, as noted earlier, defense spending doubled from 1980 to 1985, reflecting both the political climate and legitimate concerns about beefing up national defense. But since 1986, real defense spending has declined at a rate of about 3.8 percent per year, dropping from 6.3 percent of GDP in 1986 to about 3.4 percent of GDP by 1997.

Finally, in addition to policy changes, lawmakers enacted several procedural enforcement mechanisms to try to control spending. In 1985 Congress passed and the president signed into law the Balanced Budget and Emergency Deficit Control Act, also known as Gramm-Rudman-Hollings (GRH). GRH created a five-year sliding scale of deficits from $172 billion in FY 1986 to $0 by FY 1991 and a sequestration process that automatically cut spending across the board if Congress and the president failed to pass spending and tax legislation to achieve annual deficit targets. Annual deficits declined for two years under GRH, and the law helped control spending and focus attention on deficit reduction. But GRH failed to balance the budget, mainly because entitlements were exempted from automatic spending cuts, and because politicians relied on optimistic economic assumptions and accounting gimmicks rather than real policy changes to avoid automatic spending cuts.[33] In 1987, when small adjustments were no longer enough to meet the deficit target, Congress and the president raised the targets and extended the schedule for balancing the budget by two more years.

In March 1990, when Bush administration officials realized the deficit would exceed the GRH target for the upcoming fiscal year by over $200 billion, they entered into negotiations with a Democratic-controlled Congress and agreed on a plan that replaced GRH with the Budget Enforcement Act (BEA). The BEA did away with the deficit targets and automatic spending cuts in GRH and replaced them with discretionary spending caps and a pay-as-you-go (PAYGO) requirement for tax cuts and entitlement benefit increases. The spending caps set specific spending levels for defense, nondefense, and international affairs from 1991 to 1993, and overall discretionary spending caps for the following two years. Across-the-board cuts would be imposed if spending exceeded the caps. Under the PAYGO rules, any tax cut or entitlement increase had to be revenue neutral, or sequestration would apply to mandatory programs. Though GRH failed to achieve its ultimate goal of balancing the budget, Congress and the president have complied with the spending caps and PAYGO rules since 1990.

The Politics of Deficit Reduction

If Congress and the president succeeded on numerous occasions in passing legislation that reduced the deficit, how did it happen? Conversely, how do we explain gridlock when the system fails? In keeping with realist expectations of governing, the answers to those questions are far from simple. As table 2.2 illustrates, successful budget deals were cobbled together under different governing circumstances and were supported by various partisan alignments within the legislature. For example, President Reagan signed two large reconciliation bills including tax increases (1982 and 1984) and a few smaller ones, which Republican Majority Leader Bob Dole (R-Kans.) led through the Senate. At the time, Democrats controlled the House, though a majority of Democrats voted for one bill (1982) but not the other (1984). In 1987 another reconciliation bill passed a Democratic-controlled Congress, and again Reagan signed it. The only common denominator in previous budget deals was that a majority of both houses of Congress and a president ultimately agreed on the mixture of spending and tax decisions. When the system failed to produce a consensus, the reasons for failure varied from case to case. Let us review a few prominent cases that explain successful and failed attempts to reduce the deficit.

Deficit Reduction and Divided Government: 1990

The two largest deficit-reduction packages in history—the 1990 and 1993 budget deals—were passed under entirely different political circumstances. In 1990, under pressure from the GRH deficit ceiling and a dismal economic situation, President Bush reneged on an explicit campaign promise not to raise taxes. Determined to solidify the support of Republican conservatives at the 1988 Republican National Convention, Bush dramatically emphasized his opposition to tax increases with his famous phrase "Read my lips, no new taxes!" On 26 June, the GRH target backed Bush into a corner—he could either revoke the campaign pledge or face a near-certain disaster if automatic spending cuts in defense and domestic spending ensued just prior to the 1990 midterm elections.[34] Bush capitulated and agreed to include "tax revenue increases" in a budget agreement to be negotiated between the White House and congressional Democratic leaders. Bush hoped for a quick agreement, but a bitter and confrontational process ensued, and negotiations dragged on for four months. When the budget agreement finally reached Congress in September, it was torn apart by the liberal and conservative wings of the two parties. Liberal Democrats objected to taxes that fell disproportionately on lower- and middle-income Americans and complained about higher premiums, deductibles, and copayments for Medicare beneficiaries. Conservatives, led by Minority Whip Newt Gingrich (R-Ga.), opposed any tax increases. Shortly after the summit agreement was announced, Gingrich formally rejected the deal and rallied most of the Republican Party whips to work to defeat the bill in the House. With liberal Democrats and conservative Republicans splintering off, the budget bill was rejected by a vote of 179–254.

When negotiators went back to the drawing board, with congressional Republicans on the sidelines, the White House was forced to meet the objections of liberal Democrats. The next round of negotiations produced a decidedly Democratic budget, including a tax increase on the wealthiest taxpayers and scaled-back taxes on alcohol, tobacco, and gasoline (see table 2.2 for a breakdown of budget savings). This budget passed the House by a vote of 228–200; only 27 percent of House Republicans voted for the bill compared with 71 percent of House Democrats. With the combination of budget savings and budget enforcement provisions, the OMB predicted the budget would be close to balance by 1995. But an economic recession and unexpected increases in Medicaid spending drove the deficit to unprecedented levels. As Bush faced the voters in 1992, the deficit climbed to $290 billion, the largest in history. Campaign consultants for his Democratic opponent, Bill Clinton, persistently reminded Bush and the voters: "It's the economy, stupid."

Deficit Reduction and Unified Party Control: 1993

Clinton's electoral victory in 1992 meant that one party would control both chambers of Congress and the presidency for the first time in twelve years. But Clinton won only 43 percent of the popular vote in a three-candidate field, and Democrats lost ten House seats and broke even in Senate contests. Even before he took office, Clinton faced the cold, hard realities of deficit politics. During the campaign Clinton promised a middle-class tax cut and more spending for a lengthy list of domestic programs: Americorps, Head Start, welfare reform, health care, and "investments" in job training, education, technology, and the like. Two weeks before his inauguration, Clinton received the first bit of bad news; the OMB estimated that the budget would be $327 billion in the upcoming fiscal year. His budget priorities also had to fit within the spending disciplines put into place by the 1990 BEA. Clinton grudgingly accepted the advice of congressional Democratic leaders and several top advisers to propose a serious deficit-reduction package.[35] A lower deficit, Clinton reasoned, would reduce interest rates, spur investments, produce economic growth, and, he hoped, enable him to spend more on his new domestic initiatives. Yet reducing the deficit meant that Clinton had to forego his tax cuts and pare back his domestic "investments."

Once Clinton sought to reduce the deficit, he had to balance his own priorities with those of liberal Democrats in Congress. In January 1993, Senate Majority Leader George Mitchell strongly opposed ideas floated by OMB Director Leon Panetta to cap the COLA for Social Security benefits and increase beneficiary premiums on Medicare.[36] That left defense spending and tax increases as the only viable means for significant deficit reduction, two issues that reduced Clinton's chances of garnering Republican support in Congress from slim to none. Thus, Clinton had to build a majority coalition in the House and Senate from the factions within the Democratic Party. Though Democrats quickly adopted most of the president's five-year economic plan in the budget resolution, they struggled to pass the budget reconciliation bill containing legislation to attain Clinton's budget goals. Moderate and conservative Democrats were not pleased with the amount of savings from defense and the heavy reliance on tax increases to reduce the deficit. After several adjustments in the taxes and entitlement savings in the original budget, Democrats barely passed the reconciliation bill; not a single Republican in either chamber voted for the bill, and Vice-President Al Gore had to break a tie vote in the Senate in order to pass it.[37]

Failed Attempts to Make the "Tough Choices"

Deficit hawks commonly blame politicians for either ignoring the entitlement problem or failing to support legislation that reduces benefits for senior citizens. But the record is actually mixed. As illustrated, numerous changes in entitlement policy have been enacted into law. Several other major proposals were put before Congress; some were defeated, others passed one chamber but fell short of winning a majority in the other, and others passed both the House and Senate but were vetoed by the president. For example, in May 1985, Senate Republicans succeeded in passing a highly controversial budget resolution crafted by Senate Budget Committee Chairman Pete Domenici (R-N.Mex.) that reduced the deficit by $300 billion over three years, including a freeze in the COLA applied to Social Security and government pensions. But with Democratic Speaker of the House "Tip" O'Neill leading the opposition, and with the consent of House Republicans, the COLA freeze was soundly defeated in the House by a vote of 56–372. O'Neill and President Reagan conspired to kill the idea during bipartisan negotiations over the budget.[38]

In August 1993, under different circumstances, Democrat Congressman Tim Penny (D-Minn.) teamed up with Republican John Kasich (R-Ohio) and led a bipartisan task force to develop a five-year package with $90.4 billion in spending cuts—$52.2 billion in discretionary spending and $37.9 billion in entitlements.[39] Congress had just approved the 1993 budget reconciliation bill, but Penny and Kasich wanted to do more to control spending. The Penny-Kasich bill faced broad opposition from President Clinton, House Democratic leaders, Republican appropriators, and numerous liberal interest groups. The bill was narrowly defeated by a vote of 213–219, with 90 percent of Republicans voting for and 78 percent of Democrats voting against.

The two previous examples of failed attempts to reduce the deficit occurred under different circumstances. In 1985 Republicans controlled the White House and the Senate, while Democrats held a majority in the House. In 1993 Democrats controlled the White House and both chambers in Congress. A third example, the 1995 Republican congressional budget, fits the description of a partisan conflict scenario that ended in stalemate. Since the 1995 budget debate serves as an important comparison with the 1997 budget agreement, we should describe the case in more detail.[40]

Republican Revolution and Partisan Stalemate

In the 1994 congressional elections, Republicans won a majority in the House for the first time in forty years. Speaker Newt Gingrich commissioned House Budget Committee Chair Kasich to draft a budget resolution that balanced the budget by 2002 and at the same time cut taxes, increased defense spending, and left Social Security untouched. Senate Republicans followed suit, and after the two bodies resolved their differences over tax and spending levels, they agreed to a seven-year plan that would reduce spending by $983 billion, cut taxes by $245 billion, increase defense spending by $33.7 billion, and balance the budget in the year 2002. The budget contained unprecedented spending reductions in entitlement programs: $270 billion in Medicare, $180 billion in Medicaid, and $170 billion in other mandatory programs (e.g., federal retirement, food stamps, farm subsidies, AFDC, EITC, SSI, student loans, and unemployment benefits). In June 1995 the House and Senate passed the budget resolution along party lines.

After sitting on the sidelines throughout most of the spring, on 13 June President Clinton offered an alternative ten-year plan to balance the budget. Clinton relied on more optimistic economic assumptions, and his budget contained smaller reductions in Medicare ($128 billion) and Medicaid ($54 billion). Though Clinton's offer fell far short of the GOP budget, it provided an opportunity for bipartisan negotiations. But when Clinton introduced his plan in June, congressional Republicans were not interested in compromising. Though the president could veto legislation passed by Congress, Republican leaders operated on the assumption that Clinton would do anything to avoid a confrontation and a government shutdown. House Republican Conference Chairman John Boehner (R-Ohio) expressed the GOP perspective: "We just assumed that given enough pressure, Clinton would do what he always had done—cave and cut a deal." The strategy was to force the president either to sign their spending and tax bills or face a government shutdown in the fall. Gingrich explained: "You had to find a trump to match his trump, and the right to pass money bills is the only trump that is equally strong."[41]

Yet by the fall of 1995, political conditions had changed substantially. The luster of the Republicans' dramatic electoral victory had worn off, public support for the Republican budget had declined, and President Clinton benefited from the public's disapproval of the GOP plan and its backlash against the party's chief protagonist, Newt Gingrich. As the 1 October deadline approached to complete the spending bills for the upcoming fiscal year, Clinton and Congress agreed to a continuing resolution that would fund government operations until 14 November. When Republican leaders went to the White House to negotiate an agreement with the president to avoid a government shutdown, Clinton shocked them with his steadfast opposition to major cuts in education, job training, and Medicare. At one point, Clinton turned to Gingrich and said, "Look, you guys don't get it. If you want a president to sign your budget, you're going to have to elect someone else to do it." Pointing to the chair behind his desk in the Oval Office, he said, "You may not believe this, but I'm willing to lose this seat rather than take a budget like this. . . . I'll let Bob Dole do that if he's in that chair."[42]

When the Republican Congress sent Clinton another continuing resolution containing major cuts in several of Clinton's domestic priorities and an effective increase in cost of future Medicare premiums, the president vetoed the bill. The next day, all but the most essential government personnel, about 800,000 government employees, were sent home. Six days later, the two sides agreed to a temporary continuing resolution and held more negotiations on a budget deal. Bitterness and confrontation soon replaced a passing moment of hope that the two parties would come together. By then, Clinton had developed a clear tactical advantage, as the public blamed Republicans by a margin of 2 to 1 for the government shutdown. Freshman Republicans who had been unwilling to compromise all along looked suspiciously on a budget summit involving White House officials and Republican leaders that Gingrich had promised would never take place. The process was bogged down in a partisan stalemate over major policy differences. Information from the proceedings was leaked to the press, and misunderstandings about budget assumptions or deceptive tactics left Republican negotiators frustrated, confused, and angry.[43] A process ridden with partisanship, confrontation, and political gamesmanship ended in stalemate. After one more government shutdown, the Republicans finally gave up.

Budget Politics and Realist Expectations

This chapter provides evidence to support three points about budget politics in a deficit era: (1) elected officials are not cowards who always shy away from the tough choices; (2) Congress and the president have made progress toward reducing deficits since 1981, and without such efforts deficits would have been much larger; and (3) no single explanation accounts for why Congress and the president succeed in some cases and fail in others. The chapter applies a realist expectations view that treats the deficit as a public policy problem and assumes that the main challenge in addressing that problem is building a consensus among representatives with various political and policy goals and divergent values and priorities. It may be reasonable to conclude that I have focused only on the "bright side" of budget politics, though that is not the intention of the chapter. The main point is to illustrate the complexity of the decision-making process, identify the myriad spending and tax policies that have produced budget savings, and show the variable conditions that affect budget politics and policy outcomes. It is certainly relevant to cite examples of partisan gamesmanship, excessive political fighting, and an unwillingness on the part of some politicians to make responsible choices. Indeed, these examples only underscore the complexity of the process.

The dark side of deficit politics still lives, and others have told that side of the story. Several political scientists have argued convincingly that deficits heightened partisanship, created delays and contorted the budget process, produced various forms of gimmickry, and brought out the worst in elected officials.[45] The GRH law typified and hastened those aspects of the process. In the absence of consensus, GRH tried to force politicians to do something they were unwilling to do individually or unable to do collectively: make the tough choices required to balance the budget. If politicians could not do it, an automatic procedure would do it for them. The policy effects of persistent deficits are debatable, but most agree that deficits weaken the economy by sapping savings and placing upward pressure on interest rates, constrain government's ability to set priorities and respond to other vital public needs, and leave a pile of debt for the next generation. The critical analysis brought to bear by scholars and policymakers uncovers the serious economic, political, and moral dangers of large deficits. Few would dispute the claim that the country would have been better off if elected officials had found a way to balance the budget sooner.

Yet finding a way brings us back to the realist expectations view. Politicians have trouble reaching agreement. The problem of building consensus makes it extremely difficult to explain precisely why individual politicians behave as they do and why the system produces certain policy outcomes but not others. We cannot say that liberal Democrats like Speaker "Tip" O'Neill, who strongly opposed Senator Domenici's freeze on COLAs for Social Security recipients, were "ducking a tough choice" or not "doing the right thing." It is more plausible to assume that they were fighting for a public policy in which they strongly believed. That O'Neill resorted to political tactics to win that fight does not erase the basic principle behind his actions. There is no question that the deficit would have been lower if Congress and the president enacted Domenci's COLA freeze, or Penny-Kasich's Medicare reforms, or the Republican budget of 1995. Yet those are not the only ways to reduce the deficit. Like Mr. Perot, every elected official thinks he or she knows the best way to balance the budget, but each one has a different idea about how to do it.

Policymakers, analysts, political scientists, and the public all agree that during good economic times, the best budget is a balanced budget, but we will probably never agree on the ideal level of spending and revenues at which it should be balanced, much less which policies should be employed to reach those levels. Moreover, we will disagree about how much progress has been made over the years in terms of reducing deficits. Yet we should recognize the complexity of reconciling competing political goals, policy priorities, and basic principles. Consequently, the budget battles of the past contained a rich variety of decision making processes and policy outcomes. Sometimes policymakers attempted a partisan strategy, other times they tried a bipartisan approach. Sometimes major entitlement reforms died early in the process, sometimes they passed one or both chambers of Congress, and other times they were enacted into law. Most of the time, even under Republican presidents, tax increases have been part of the mix of budget savings. There is little certainty in a system where Republican presidents sign huge tax bills; where one major deal was passed in a divided government situation, the other when the same party controlled both the presidency and Congress; where one major deal was passed in an election year, the other during the president's first year in office; and where some interest groups win and others lose. In the light of previous budget battles, it would have been wise to ask after the 1996 election, "What's next?"

3

Aligning the Stars . . . Governing, Policy, and Leadership

After the 1996 elections, which returned President Clinton to the White House and Republican majorities to the House and Senate, political analysts engaged in ritual speculation over how Congress and the president would relate to each other in the upcoming 105th Congress. Optimists believed a bipartisan plan to balance the budget by 2002 was "doable." Stanley E. Collender, chief budget analyst for Burson-Marsteller, noted: "Politically, it's still tough because you've got to take on the seniors and all that. But you've got the possibility of all the stars, the moon and sun aligning just right. . . . You've got a better shot at this than you've probably had in a decade."[1] Yet, as noted earlier, the budget process is filled with uncertainties. It is never clear which of the many forces interacting in the budget process will be responsible ultimately for pushing negotiators together or pulling them apart. Therefore, at the beginning of the budget process, it is nearly impossible to predict whether Congress and the president will succeed in reaching a budget agreement, much less what the agreement will look like.

The governing circumstances at the beginning of the 105th Congress offered the opportunity for cooperation and bipartisan compromise, but they hardly guaranteed a positive outcome. After the intense partisan battles of the 104th Congress (1995–96) and a bloody election campaign, each party distrusted the other. Since the 1996 elections did not change the partisan makeup of Congress and the presidency, the inevitable gridlock model would predict another year of stalemate. As it turned out, the budget battles of the 104th Congress (1995–96) and the 1996 election campaigns served useful purposes: they clarified the limitations and possibilities for the budget process in 1997. After two years of debate, President Clinton and Republican leaders had a much better idea of their differences. Once it became clear both sides were serious about negotiating a bipartisan agreement, President Clinton, Republican congressional leaders, and budget negotiators from the White House and Congress played pivotal roles in keeping negotiations on track despite obstructionist forces on both sides. In spite of the split-party results of the 1996 elections, leaders from both parties agreed that the voters wanted Republicans and Democrats to work together in 1997.

Potential Barriers to Cooperation

Several analyses of the 1996 elections concluded the voters wanted bipartisan cooperation. Republicans barely held on to a majority in the House, and only after they agreed with President Clinton to pass legislation that increased the minimum wage, protected health insurance coverage for workers who lost or changed jobs, and increased domestic spending for education, child-care grants, public works projects, and environmental clean-up.[2] After cutting discretionary spending from $508 billion to $488 billion in 1995, Republicans succumbed to White House pressure to increase spending to $503 billion in 1996.[3] Presumably, Republicans gave way to Clinton's priorities to avoid the political fallout from another government shutdown.

Yet the apparent incentives to cooperate masked underlying divisions between Democratic and Republican electoral constituencies. Though the electorate as a whole voted for divided government, individual voters were not necessarily calling for moderation or "centrist" policies. A postelection analysis conducted by Thomas B. Edsall and Mario A. Broussard found that voters did not split their tickets in favor of a new "vital center," as President Clinton called it. Only one in seven voters actually voted for divided government; the vast majority voted for a president and a member of Congress from the same party. Edsall and Broussard concluded: "The country will be governed for the next two years by a White House and a congressional majority that owe their elections to two separate and bitterly opposed voting coalitions." Exit polls revealed that President Clinton was elected by a coalition of voters who were "more apt to be female, Catholic, single, ideologically moderate to liberal, satisfied with the financial situation and less concerned about character than those who made up the congressional electorate." In contrast, "the Republicans' coalition is richer, whiter, more male-dominated, more pessimistic, more Protestant, more conservative and more likely to own a gun, and places a much higher priority on the deficit, taxes and honesty than those who backed the president."[4] Thus the election results reflected the preferences of two distinct publics—one Democrat, the other Republican—and each could claim responsibility for electing one branch of government. To the extent politicians seek to represent the people who vote them into office, the situation favored partisan politics.

Prospects for bipartisanship seemed just as dim inside Congress, where the two parties harbored deep ideological differences. In recent years, the House had become a virtual hotbed of partisanship and unprecedented party voting.[5] The House was pulled to ideological extremes: Republicans had become more conservative and Democrats more liberal. In the Senate, where Republicans gained two seats from the previous Congress, party membership became even more conservative. In the 1996 Senate elections, retiring Republican moderates Hank Brown (Colo.) and Nancy Kassebaum (Kans.) were replaced by conservatives Wayne Allard (Colo.) and Sam Brownback (Kans.). Conservative Republicans Jeff Sessions (Ala.), Tim Hutchinson (Ark.), and Chuck Hagel (Neb.) won seats occupied by Democrats.

Republicans in Congress might also have found it difficult to trust President Clinton after a hard-fought election campaign featuring attacks on Republicans for their vote to reduce Medicare spending in the 104th Congress. The AFL-CIO and the Democratic National Committee spent millions of dollars to unseat incumbents from marginal districts. In Arizona's Sixth District, where Republican freshman incumbent J.D. Hayworth was struggling to win reelection against Democrat challenger Steve Owens, the AFL-CIO ran a thirty-second television spot that read: "Where do the candidates stand? J.D. Hayworth voted to cut Medicare funding by $270 billion." Steve Owens "opposes those Medicare cuts. When it comes to Medicare, there is a difference." The National Republican Congressional Committee (NRCC) countered with their own advertising campaign. One ad said that the "big labor bosses" are "spending big bucks on Steve Owens. . . . Call the union bosses. Tell them Arizona is not for sale."[6]

Though most Republicans survived the onslaught, twenty did not, and numerous returning incumbents were reelected by narrow margins. As political scientists Lawrence C. Dodd and Bruce I. Oppenheimer point out: "Although Republicans can take comfort in retaining their House majority, they did not do so without a scare. The class elected in 1994 barely dodged a bullet. Of the fifty-seven who were reelected, twenty-two won with 53 percent or less of the vote." [7]

It was not clear that the wounds of the campaign would heal sufficiently for Republicans to carry on genuine bipartisan negotiations with President Clinton. Under the circumstances, George Hager, coauthor of *Mirage*, predicted that without a crisis to force the parties to act together, there would be no bipartisan budget deal in 1997.[8] At the least, electoral divisions, distrust of the other side, and partisan politics would lead to another turn of the "revenge cycle."

Aligning the Stars

From another perspective, the political and policy conditions provided the basis for compromise. The campaign and the budget battles of the 104th Congress offered lessons that might have encouraged bipartisan cooperation. After two government shutdowns, a failure to achieve the revolutionary goals of the 104th Congress, and a bruising election campaign in 1996, many Republicans were ready to compromise. The heyday of the Contract with America was over, and the campaign was a sobering experience for Republican incumbents. Reality had set in. Members who hoped to build successful political careers had been through the fight of their political lives, had lost their revolutionary zeal, and were tired. Moreover, they were wary of confronting President Clinton, believing he eventually would win the battle of public opinion. As one Republican staff person on the House Budget Committee put it: "This left us with an 'If you can't beat 'em, join 'em' attitude."[9]

Moreover, though the budget process of 1995–96 failed to produce successful legislation, it forced the parties to narrow their differences. Senate Budget Committee Staff Director William Hoagland, a participant in the 104th Congress negotiations, observed: "When one goes back and looks at where the negotiations left off in 1996 and compares the numbers, there were a lot of similarities. The 1995–96 negotiations clearly gave us some understanding on the fundamental differences, particularly on taxes and Medicare. All of this built the framework for putting together an agreement for 1997."[10]

Table 3.1 illustrates the savings in major budget categories sought by Clinton and congressional Republicans in 1995–96. These data show that initial budget offers were far apart, especially on Medicare, discretionary spending, and tax cuts. But in January 1996, after the second government shutdown and before talks broke up, negotiators had come much closer together. The gap between the two parties in terms of total net savings went from $350 billion in November 1995 to $66 billion in January 1996.[11] Of course, Democrats and Republicans disagreed on the changes in Medicare and Medicaid to produce the estimated savings, they had different priorities in terms of discretionary spending, and they remained far apart on tax cuts. But when White House negotiators sat down with Republican budget makers in 1997, both sides had already laid most of the groundwork for an agreement. Moreover, Republicans learned an important lesson from the previous Congress: do not overshoot the president's mark on spending reductions for popular entitlement programs. This became evident during the first few months of 1997 as Republican members of the House Budget Committee deliberated on the budget resolution they would propose if the bipartisan negotiators failed.[12] In the absence of a bipartisan agreement, Republicans planned to use the same budget savings in Medicare and Medicaid that the president proposed in his budget.

Table 3.1

Differences in Budget Savings and Tax Cuts
between President Clinton and Congressional Republicans,
January/June 1995 versus January 1996 (in billions of dollars)

	January/June 1995			January 1996		
	Republicans	*Clinton*	*Difference*	*Republicans*	*Clinton*	*Difference*
Medicare	$226	$97	$119	$154	$124	$30
Medicaid	133	38	95	85	59	26
Discretionary	409	138	271	349	295	54
Welfare	64	38	26	60	43	17
Other mandatory[a]	49	-6	55	69	60	9
Tax cuts[b]	-245	-105	135	203	-87	116

Sources: Alissa J. Rubin and George Hager, "Chances of a Budget Deal Now Anyone's Guess," *Congressional Quarterly Weekly Report*, 13 January 1996, 90; and George Hager and Andrew Taylor, "GOP Looks for New Strategies as Talks Stall Yet Again," *Congressional Quarterly Weekly Report*, 20 January 1996, 150.

a. Other "mandatory" includes spending on agricultural subsidies, student loans, and sale of broadcast spectrum rights.

b. Gross figures, before subtracting various tax increases.

A strong economy also improved prospects for a bipartisan agreement. As noted earlier, economic growth increases revenues, decreases government spending, and reduces the deficit. As negotiations between White House officials and congressional policymakers progressed in spring 1997, economic conditions continued to improve, and the amount of budget savings required to balance the budget in five years declined substantially. The economy made the job of balancing the budget much easier.[13]

Politically, election results and campaigns can produce ambiguous messages. After a dramatic victory in 1994, in which Republicans won fifty-three House seats and a majority in both chambers for the first time in forty years, they pursued a strategy of partisan confrontation, and it failed. A "near miss" at losing the majority in 1996 sent a warning signal and made Republicans realize that toning down the partisanship, moderating policy goals, and seeking the gradual changes that go with compromise made more sense.[14] Moreover, Republicans were operating with a smaller majority in 1997; the party ratio in the House declined from 235 Republicans and 197 Democrats in 1996 to 227 Republicans and

207 Democrats in 1997. The small majority placed moderate Republicans in a pivotal position. Representative Michael N. Castle (R-Del.) observed: "Any 10 people, if they band together, can prevent something from happening."[15] Despite Edsall and Broussard's analysis of national survey data, many Republicans were from liberal or moderate districts. House Budget Committee Republican Robert L. Ehrlich (Md.) noted: "Sure we want to do more in terms of tax cuts and spending cuts, but the reality is Bill Clinton is in the White House, and we do not have a conservative majority in the House of Representatives."[16]

In terms of the implications for governing, election results are often less important than the way elected officials interpret them. After the 1996 election, leaders of both parties appeared willing to compromise. President Clinton remarked: "America has told every one of us—Democrats, Republicans, and independents—loud and clear, it is time to put politics aside, join together and get the job done for America's future."[17] In response to questions about relations with the White House, Speaker Gingrich said he saw "no reason we can't find common ground." And "I don't start this new process automatically expecting us to get into a confrontation."[18] Senate Majority Leader Trent Lott said the divided results "gave us all another chance to work together and do what needs to be done for our country."[19]

Those comments suggested a very different attitude from 1994. Despite clear partisan differences in the electorate, party leaders perceived the 1996 elections as a call for cooperation. Faced with at least two more years of divided government, leaders of both parties could see advantages in cooperation over confrontation. Rather than wish for unified party control, leaders on both sides appeared ready to see if they could work together. Of course, until the hard negotiating began, it was not clear whether the public statements of a Democratic president and a Republican Speaker were genuine expressions of goodwill or merely political posturing.

Party Leaders and Policy Leaders

If political circumstances present the opportunity, but not the certainty, of a bipartisan budget agreement, then leaders are crucial to the process. When conditions prohibit cooperation and compromise in the first place, no amount of individual motivation or political skill will bring about a budget agreement. So when the opportunity presents itself, leaders must take advantage of the situation.

The two kinds of leaders involved in the negotiations can be classified as party leaders and policy leaders. Elected party leaders, sometimes referred to as "principals," establish the general framework for the negotiations by stating their parties' basic goals, communicating points that are nonnegotiable, and settling any issues between the parties that the policy leaders cannot resolve through negotiations. The key party leaders in 1997 were Democrats President Bill Clinton and Vice-President Al Gore and Republicans Speaker of the House Newt Gingrich and Senate Majority Leader Trent Lott. Policy leaders, who negotiate over specific parts of the budget and try to reconcile their differences, for the White House included Special Assistant to the President John Hilley, White House Chief of Staff Erskine Bowles, and OMB Director Franklin Raines. Major policy leaders negotiating for congressional Republicans included Senate Budget Committee Chair Pete Domenici (N.Mex.) and House Budget Committee Chair John Kasich (Ohio).

The division of labor between principals and policy leaders is not always clear cut, and it can affect the outcome of the negotiation process. The complexities of the budget require negotiators with experience and expertise to represent the interests of their parties. According to several Republicans, one difference between the budget battles of the 104th Congress and the negotiations in 1997 was that Republicans were better served by policy leaders in 1997.

> In 1995, Kasich and Domenici were negotiators for most of the time. But when it didn't go anywhere, we moved it up to the higher levels. And there were literally meetings in which they kicked Kasich and Domenici out and they brought [House Majority Leader] Armey in there. It was all over in the Oval Office. So, it was the President, the Vice President and Leon [Panetta] and Gingrich and Dole and Armey, and they tried to work out the budget agreement. I mean they were just ill-equipped to do it. They're leaders, they're not experts in budget policy, they can't be expected to know that stuff. . . . That group isn't able to make decisions. It is a recipe for failure.[20]

Comparing the difference between 1995 and 1997 in terms of his relationship with Speaker Gingrich, House Budget Committee Chair Kasich said:

> I think the biggest single difference was Newt let me do my thing and let me get it to the point where he needed me to be in the room to resolve some of the issues we were not capable of resolving—the level of taxes, that sort of thing. But really I carried the thing all the way to where the train was leaving the station. He just let me do what I needed to do.[21]

Chairman Kasich's description of his relationship with Speaker Gingrich offers a window into the complicated range of opportunities and constraints under which policy leaders operate. Kasich suggests that while policy leaders must represent the general intentions of the principals and the broad interests of the party, they have discretion to push certain items during the negotiations. (In the next two chapters we see that despite regular communication between principals and policy leaders, at times Kasich and Domenici diverged from the specific preferences of the principals.) At the same time, policy leaders are constrained by two factors: (1) the principals can veto decisions made by policy leaders in the negotiations process; and (2) once negotiations are finished, policy leaders must convince their colleagues in Congress to vote for the budget agreement.[22] Ultimately, the principals have the final word.

The Principals: "Where There's a Will, There's a Way"

Though the principals are not always directly involved in negotiations, they must support the process and be willing to reach an agreement. They must decide whether to compromise in order to achieve some policy goals or forego that progress in favor of the political gains that might be made by attacking the other party's budget priorities.[23] As one Republican put it: "Where there is a will, there is a way, but there must be a will, and that will must come from the leaders."[24]

Republicans believed that President Clinton's main objective in 1995 and 1996 was to win reelection and that attacking the Republican budget was the best way for him to achieve it. Once Clinton was reelected and the Republicans retained their majorities in the House and Senate, the president seemed willing to compromise. As one high-level Republican Budget Committee staff person put it:

> Now I think the biggest contrast between '95–'96 and today is that in 1995–96 Congress wanted a budget deal, but the White House didn't. It didn't matter how much we moved in their direction. At the time, we tried to show after the negotiations finished in January 1996, we moved over half way toward them on every issue, and they still didn't accept the deal. . . . They had every incentive to try to create the crisis. They were winning the PR battle. The Republicans were blamed for shutting down the government. The media claimed the plan was giving tax cuts to the rich. . . .
>
> In 1997, however, the White House took a different approach. They pushed. They were the ones who wanted to meet. They were the ones who initiated discussions. They said, "We could fulfill a balanced budget plan."[25]

Congressman David Hobson (R-Ohio), a close confidante of Chairman Kasich and Speaker Gingrich's liaison to the Budget Committee, agreed: "A major difference was that the President had the will to get it done this time."[26]

Though we can only speculate about how an individual politician's motives affect behavior, we can establish whether there is reason to cooperate. For Clinton, compromising with Republicans offered the chance of leaving a historical legacy: the president who balanced the budget, the defining political issue of the last quarter of the twentieth century, and achieved several additional policy goals. Immediately after the 1996 elections, Clinton told ABC News broadcaster David Brinkley that if he were "able to accomplish only one thing . . . I would pass a balanced budget that would . . . open the doors to college to all Americans and continue the incremental progress we've made in health care reform."[27] Those objectives simply could not be achieved without attempting a bipartisan compromise. Gene Sperling, national economic adviser to the president, said after the budget agreement was announced: "Our marching orders since December were very clear: We were supposed to try to create a bipartisan atmosphere that would produce a bipartisan agreement."[28]

Congressional Democrats were fully aware of the president's intentions, but many distrusted the Republicans. Congressman Ben Cardin (D-Md.), a member of the House Budget and Ways and Means Committees, explained: "The strategy early on between the House Democrats and the White House was very different. The White House wanted an agreement. They wanted to negotiate. We wanted a separate budget all along. So, we were far more skeptical of the specifics in the agreement."[29] Other Democrats wanted to highlight the differences between the parties. From the standpoint of pursuing the political goals and policy interests, many House Democrats preferred a confrontational approach.[30] One liberal Democrat on the House Budget Committee lamented:

> Sure [Clinton] wanted a deal. He thinks this is going to preserve his place in history; that he balanced the budget in 1997. You know, the president could be running over these guys if he would use [the minority party] as a backstop. But they chose not to go the confrontational route. They were going to capitulate to whatever they had to do. The whole strategy was wrong. You don't start negotiations by putting out your final offer. Clinton doesn't care about us.[31]

Vice-President Gore was also a principal in the process. Gore, looking ahead to the 2000 presidential campaign, wanted a positive record to carry into the Democratic primaries. A failed Clinton presidency did not bode well for Gore's prospects, and the window of opportunity for reaching a budget agreement would not last long. Of course, by compromising with Republicans, Gore risked a backlash from key Democratic voting blocs; labor unions generally opposed the negotiations, and elderly groups opposed proposals to reform entitlements. As we see in chapter 5, Gore spoke on behalf of seniors when it came time for negotiators to make the final decision over whether to adjust the CPI and reduce the COLAs for entitlement benefits. Still, throughout the budget process, Gore's presence set up an intriguing intraparty clash between the White House and House Democratic Minority Leader Richard Gephardt (Mo.). The White House chose to negotiate directly with congressional Republicans and leave Gephardt out of the process. Gephardt regularly complained that the White House was conceding too much to Republicans, and ultimately he voted against the budget resolution, the tax cuts, and the reconciliation spending bill. In so doing, Gephardt was representing the liberal wing of the Democratic Party and positioning himself in case he decided to run for the Democratic presidential nomination in 2000.[32]

On the Republican side, Speaker Newt Gingrich and Majority Leader Trent Lott had incentives to cooperate with the White House. For Gingrich, who was reeling from an ethics investigation that nearly cost him his Speakership, a bipartisan budget agreement would be a signal achievement, evidence that House Republicans could govern and he could be an effective leader. Perhaps the past—the government shutdowns, the confrontational image, and the "extremist" label—would be forgiven and forgotten if a Republican Congress passed historic legislation to cut taxes and balance the budget. After losing the battle of the budget in 1995 and 1996, Gingrich had begun to shift toward a more pragmatic, conciliatory approach.[33] In 1995 he clung to the Contract with America and used a vanguard of freshman lawmakers to push for "dramatic" change. Gingrich believed the 1994 election was a revolutionary experience that carried a clear mandate: balance the budget, save Medicare, transform welfare, and reduce taxes. He was not willing to compromise on those basic points.[34] By autumn 1996, Gingrich's views had changed significantly. Reflecting on the previous Congress, Gingrich said, "One of the lessons I've learned in the last two years is you go slower, you prepare the ground, you make sure people understand." And "in retrospect, if I were doing it again, we would consciously avoid the government shutdown. It was clearly wrong."[35]

For Lott, the budget process offered the chance to make good on his reputation as a pragmatic conservative. As a Senate Republican staffer noted: "Trent was a new leader in the U.S. Senate that had established his bona fides as one who wanted to get things done and who wanted to show that progress could be made."[36] Lott knew he had to work with a Democratic president for at least four years, maybe eight if a Democrat won in 2000. How long should he wait to try to accomplish some Republican legislative goals? After the agreement was announced, Lott described his relationship with Clinton: "We don't agree politically. We're of different parties. But he's where he is and I'm where I am. The president of the United States and the majority leader of the United States Senate need to communicate and deal with each other in good faith."[37] Lott's comments reflect a realist perspective of the prospects for governing in a divided government.

Gingrich and Lott, of course, would not make a deal simply for the sake of it. They faced constant pressure from the right wing of the Republican Party to avoid negotiations with the White House unless they could get substantial tax cuts and major spending cuts. At the least, the agreement had to move in a Republican direction—a balanced budget, tax cuts (capital gains, child tax credit, and estate tax reform), and savings from entitlement programs. Once Republican leaders believed Clinton was willing to come their way, conceding to Clinton a few domestic programs and tax cuts for higher education seemed a small price to pay.

The Policy Leaders

Policy leaders must be in sync with the strategic goals of the principals and negotiate an agreement that members of their party can support, but they have important roles to play in their own right. One Republican staff involved in negotiations during the 104th and 105th Congresses explained the task of White House negotiators: "In 1995, Leon [Panetta] had a job to do. His job was to protect the president's interests. Whereas Bowles, Hilley and Raines believed it was in the president's interest to cut a deal. In other words, whatever goals they wanted to achieve . . . they went out and tried to do it."[38]

President Clinton assembled a new team of negotiators in 1997. The three main policymakers were White House Chief of Staff Erskine Bowles, John Hilley, and Office of Management and Budget Director Franklin Raines. Bowles, a coolheaded former investment banker and long-time friend of President Clinton, agreed to serve as Clinton's chief of staff with the understanding that the president was committed to pursuing a balanced budget. A self-described "deal maker" and "creature of the private sector," Bowles was just as concerned with the process as he was with the policy. In characterizing his view of the budget negotiations, Bowles admitted, he is "not the most ardent politician. I believe there's good and bad on both sides."[39] Whereas Panetta conducted negotiations himself, Bowles rarely met alone with Republican negotiators and normally left policy details up to Raines and Hilley.

Bowles was critical in developing strategy for administration talks with congressional leaders. He took a very businesslike approach to the process. After assembling a team "with a common buy-in to the goal," the idea was to develop a "framework to get to yes both from a policy and process standpoint." In reference to meeting with Lott and Bowles, Speaker Gingrich pointed out, "We're all three southerners. . . . There was a chemistry there. It was totally businesslike—no posturing, no ego." House Democrat Minority Whip David Bonior said of Bowles: "He represents the center—his views, his allegiances, his way of carrying himself. That's where he is and that is where the [budget] deal is." After White House and Republican leaders reached an agreement, Bowles reflected on the comity and cooperation that had become part of the budget negotiations: "There was extraordinary good faith on the other side of this deal and on our side also."[40]

John Hilley, President Clinton's chief congressional liaison on the budget, is given credit for restoring trust between congressional budget leaders and the White House. After a long and bruising battle in the previous Congress, Republican budget makers were naturally skittish about entering into earnest negotiations with the White House. Hilley was mainly responsible for convincing Republican policy leaders Domenici and Kasich that the president wanted a budget deal. He also played an instrumental role in keeping negotiations on track when they were about to fall apart. As Congressman Hobson put it:

> Hilley was the fixer; the driver in the sense that he knew how far people could go. He seemed to be the key element to keep things moving along. . . . He was very helpful because when things would breakdown, John and Pete Domenici could go to Hilley and say, "Hey, you know, this is what we can do, this is what we can't do. Find us a way we can get this done." And that trust enabled them to work together.[41]

As Budget Committee Chairman Kasich explained it: "Hilley was the guy who really made up his mind that he wanted to get this done. We made a pact with each other that we would trust one another, and he and I were constantly talking about how to get through the roadblocks."[42]

In contrast, Republicans believed the lead negotiator for the White House in 1995, Leon Panetta, a former Democrat chair of the House Budget Committee, had made it more difficult for the two sides to negotiate an agreement in 1995. As one Republican on the House Budget Committee put it:

> One of the big disappointments with the last time is that John [Kasich] thought he could work with Panetta, but it didn't happen. . . . I think this is really key, the team the President had this

> time didn't have the warts from the legislative side. The team be-
> fore had this old legislative House attitude that Democrats have
> to win. . . . This time, Erskine Bowles comes from a different
> background of business, not the Congress. He knows how to ne-
> gotiate a deal in the real world. You had Raines, who had been
> around, but didn't have the warts that other people had. And
> you had John Hilley who had an insider's perspective but didn't
> have a House background.[43]

Speaker Gingrich made a similar observation about the difference between Bowles and Panetta: "Erskine brought a commonsense, southern moderate approach and he didn't have the personal investment in the programs. Whereas Leon Panetta was a liberal Democrat who had created the very programs we were trying to change."[44] William Hoagland, Republican staff director for the Senate Budget Committee, took a similar view:

> The personalities shifted slightly [from 1995 to 1996]. And there
> was some change in the philosophies of some underlings in the
> White House, and I am thinking specifically of Chief of Staff Mr.
> Bowles as well as the Special Assistant to the President John Hil-
> ley. While I have a lot of respect for Mr. Panetta, he had a certain
> luggage he carried with him from his time in Congress and some
> of the battles he had with Chairman Kasich.[45]

The White House negotiating team in 1997 also had less in common and weaker ties with Democratic lawmakers in the House of Representatives. Panetta knew Gephardt very well and communicated regularly with the minority leader in 1995 and 1996. Hilley, Raines, and Bowles were not nearly as close to House Democratic leaders. Though White House officials occasionally consulted House Democrats, Gephardt and Senate Minority Leader Tom Daschle (S.D.) regularly complained about not being informed of developments in negotiations.[46]

John Kasich, the young, energetic chair of the House Budget Committee, brought experience, charisma, and a conservative perspective to the bipartisan negotiations. Some White House officials regarded him as brash, hyperactive, sarcastic, moody, and unpredictable, "sort of a wild card" among budget negotiators.[47] The budget battles of the previous two years had left Kasich disappointed and distrustful of President Clinton. When the 1997 session began, Kasich was less optimistic than Domenici about the prospects for reaching a budget agreement with the White House. Kasich assumed that major reductions in taxes and entitlement spending were not possible under the circumstances, and he realized that any agreement would take only a small step toward advancing the Republican agenda of less government, lower taxes, and returning power to the states and to individuals. Moreover, Kasich had presidential ambitions of his own, and it was unclear whether a bipartisan compromise was the best way to serve his political goals. He would be content if the negotiators could make a deal that moved the budget in a Republican direction, but if the GOP had to compromise too much, he was more than willing to walk away.

In many ways Kasich's blend of fiscal conservatism, skepticism, and pragmatism made him a perfect negotiator for House Republicans. A true believer in balancing the budget, reducing entitlement spending, and cutting taxes, he had the trust of conservative Republicans in the House. At the same time, his zeal for smaller government sometimes led Kasich to work with Democrats who supported cuts in defense spending and corporate welfare programs. Kasich was also motivated by the fact that this would be his last term as House Budget Committee chair, possibly his last chance as a member of the House of Representatives to affect the future of government spending and tax policy. As long as the White House was willing to deal on Republican terms, Kasich was willing to work out an agreement. Kasich's public position was this: "first of all . . . I want to get this budget done." Still, he noted: "I feel passionately about the fact that the Republican Party has stood for less government and for more power to the people—which includes tax cuts for people."[48]

Pete Domenici, a pragmatic fiscal conservative, spent most of his twenty-five years in the Senate trying to balance the budget. Political scientist Richard Fenno described Domenici as knowledgeable, hardworking, truthful, and policy-oriented. According to Fenno: "Pete Domenici is an educator; and he operates from a wealth of knowledge about his subject. As chairman, it was his style to design the best public policy he could, explain to whomever would listen, wait patiently for the right time to push it and, only then, reach out to make accommodations to build a majority."[49] And "his preference was to lead by economic argument and then to bargain incrementally, at the margins, over the budget numbers needed to attract majority support."[50]

As a symbol of his ongoing efforts to balance the budget, Domenici kept in his office a framed drawing of the Greek mythological character Sisyphus, who was condemned to Hades and the fate of rolling a huge stone up a hill, only to have it roll down again. Domenici liked to compare his trials with those of Sisyphus: "He's struggling mightily to get this load off his back."[51] For Domenici, the stone was the federal budget. His pursuit of a balanced budget meant he was less committed to tax cuts than Kasich. After guiding President Reagan's tax cuts through the Senate in 1981 only to watch deficits balloon, Domenici became skeptical about cutting taxes.[52] On several occasions during the Reagan administration, Domenici assisted Bob Dole (R-Kans.) in efforts to raise taxes as a means to balance the budget, and he was willing to pursue bipartisan approaches to reduce the deficit. At times, Domenici's cautious approach to tax cuts placed him at odds with supply-siders, who believed tax cuts should be the first priority of the Republican Party.

A Matter of Realist Expectations

The governing, policy, and leadership conditions described in this chapter make up the general framework for explaining how the budget agreement came together. The underlying uncertainty about the prospects for a bipartisan agreement at the outset of the 105th Congress fits the realist perspective. The 1996 campaigns and election results created the potential, though not the certainty, of a bipartisan governing process. Key leaders ignored the inevitable gridlock interpretation of the elections that highlighted party differences and mixed messages and focused on the public's rationale for electing a divided government. Rather than wait four more years for the electorate to deliver a single-party victory, the leaders accepted the voters' judgment and set their sights on making the system work.

The White House's strategy to engage Republican leaders in negotiations, despite objections from congressional Democrats, also conforms with the realist perspective. Since the Republicans controlled Congress, it made sense for President Clinton to negotiate with Republican leaders and ignore congressional Democrats, who believed they benefited more from partisan stalemate than bipartisan cooperation. While bipartisan cooperation was the only way Clinton could hope to attain certain policy goals in his second term, partisan conflict was the best way for congressional Democrats to prevent Republicans from building a successful legislative record. The contrasting motives of the White House and congressional Democratic leaders even affected their conceptions of trust: Republican negotiators trusted White House negotiators more than did liberal Democrats in Congress. The internal party divisions correspond with realist expectations of governing in a system where parties consist of factions that hold different views.

By identifying the key governing and policy conditions and characterizing the key principals and policy leaders, this chapter sets the stage for a complex drama. In the chapters that follow, we see how policymakers formulate and build support for a bipartisan budget agreement under divided-party control. We shall see how leaders adapt to opportunities and constraints as they move the budget through a complex process requiring multiple decisions and demanding the input of hundreds of legislators with a wide variety of motives and policy preferences.

4

Tug-of-War

On 4 February 1997, President Clinton identified his budget priorities in his State of the Union address to Congress: "In two days I will propose a detailed plan to balance the budget by 2002. This plan will balance the budget and invest in our people while protecting Medicare, Medicaid, education, and the environment. . . . It will balance the budget and provide middle-class tax relief to pay for education and health care, to help raise a child, to buy and sell a home." He called upon Republican members of Congress to work with him to make the tough choices in the budget process: "The people of this nation elected us all. They want us to be partners, not partisans. They put us all right here in the same boat, they gave us all the oars, and they told us to row."[1]

The president's appeal to bipartisan cooperation left Republican lawmakers with two choices. They could declare the president's budget dead on arrival, ignore Clinton's plea for cooperation, and draft a separate budget resolution containing their priorities. Or they could try to negotiate a bipartisan agreement with the White House. But they could not change the fact that Clinton was president, which meant eventually he would be positioned to either sign or veto the spending and tax bills approved by Congress. When Republicans on the House Budget Committee met in February 1997 to consider their approach to President Clinton's budget, Committee Chair John Kasich reminded his colleagues of the political realities. Like it or not, Kasich contended, Clinton's reelection disrupted the policy revolution Republicans pursued after the 1994 congressional elections. Whether Republicans agreed to work with the White House or draft a separate plan, a major overhaul of federal spending and tax law was not politically feasible. Republicans, Kasich said, are in a "tug-of-war" with the White House, and the objective was not to win a giant Republican victory, but to "pull them over to our side."[2] Kasich was setting realistic expectations and asking his colleagues to do the same.

Still, as Kasich and his colleagues recovered from the partisan hangover of the 104th Congress, bipartisan cooperation was far from certain. From January to about the middle of March, the budget process experienced a series of jump starts and false starts. The principals established contact, Republican policy leaders and White House negotiators tried to establish trust, and President Clinton's budget became the initial starting point. Bicameral differences emerged, as the White House favored negotiating with Senate leaders at first, and Senate Republican leaders looked more optimistically on the prospects for a bipartisan agreement. Throughout the process, negotiators on both sides tried to perform a delicate balancing act of negotiating secretly in good faith with representatives of the opposite party and responding to the concerns of rank-and-file members of Congress within their parties. Negotiators gradually developed mutual trust as they discussed various issues. But it was easier for policy leaders meeting face-to-face to trust each other than it was for them to convince their colleagues to trust their partisan rivals. Thus, while Republican leaders agreed to use President Clinton's budget as the basis for negotiations, it was also fair game for public criticism and partisan banter. Meanwhile, Democrats in Congress believed the arrangement gave the Republicans a free ride and an unfair political advantage because Republicans were allowed to negotiate modifications in the president's budget without having to introduce one of their own. The challenge for the negotiators was to work deliberately to find common ground before suspicious rank-and-file members of Congress from both parties withdrew support for the process. By the middle of March, the process appeared to be going off track.

Jump Starts and False Starts

Suspicion and distrust do not vanish with the glow of a new Congress, the anticipation of a president's second term, and a few upbeat speeches and press conferences. Many Republicans in Congress were still smarting from the last round of budgeting with the Clinton administration and licking their wounds from a brutal election campaign. Congressional Democrats were melancholy about vanished dreams of returning to the majority and bad memories of what they viewed as President Clinton's surrender to Republicans on welfare reform in 1996. Many Democrats thought Clinton would relinquish traditional party principles and cut a conservative budget deal with Republicans. So before anything major happened in the budget process of 1997, the major participants had to get used to each other.

Before the president introduced his budget to Congress, early signs of a bipartisan process were under way. On 12 November, less than a week after the elections, the president met with Republican leaders at the White House to discuss arrangements for negotiating a budget agreement. On 27 December, Clinton met privately with Ways and Means Committee Chair Bill Archer (R-Tex.) to discuss

Medicare and tax cuts. Archer, a staunch fiscal conservative with a reputation for doggedly pursuing tax cuts, expressed his willingness to compromise with the president. Both men were operating with a sense of urgency in terms of meeting their policy goals. A rule passed by the House in 1994 placed a term limit of six years on committee chairs, and Archer had already served two years. A top Ways and Means aide reported that Archer started the meeting saying to the president, "I have four years, and you have four years."[3] On 26 January, Archer published an editorial in the *Washington Post* entitled "Let's Make a Deal, Mr. President." Archer urged the president to present a budget in February that contained permanent tax cuts, broad capital gains tax relief, no new taxes, a plan to address the immediate deficit in the Medicare Trust Fund without accounting gimmicks, no additional welfare spending, and realistic economic assumptions.[4]

President Clinton sent early signals that he was willing to compromise with Republicans on Medicare and taxes. An early draft of Clinton's budget contained $100 billion savings in Medicare over five years (mainly through reductions in payments to doctors and hospitals), a cap on federal Medicaid payments to the states, a $500 per child tax credit, education tax breaks, and a targeted cut in capital gains taxes. At a news conference in January, Republican Senate Budget Committee Chair Pete Domenici, Democrat Senate Minority Leader Tom Daschle, and Clinton expressed optimism that White House and congressional Republicans could reach a budget agreement. Kasich was less enthusiastic. The president vowed to "make a clear effort to reach out to [Republicans] and meet them halfway to get this job done."[5] (See table 4.1 for major developments in the budget process.)

Table 4.1
Key Developments in the Budget Process, February–March 1997

President Clinton's State of the Union address	4 February
President Clinton presents his FY 1998 budget to Congress	6 February
Senate Budget Committee hearing with OMB Director Franklin Raines	7 February
House Budget Committee hearing with OMB Director Franklin Raines	11 February
House Budget Committee hearing with CBO Director June O'Neill	13 February
House votes on H.Res. 89	13 March
Chairman Kasich presents budget to House Budget Committee Republicans	14 March
Speaker Gingrich delivers speech speculating about delaying tax cuts	17 March
House Republican Conference on tax cuts and the CPI	19 March
President Clinton convenes meeting of Republican and Democratic leaders	19 March

Bicameral Differences

In the earliest stages of the budget process (January and February) the White House gave more attention to the Senate than the House. A few days after inauguration in January, and three weeks before the budget was submitted to Congress, Senator Domenici held his first private meeting with John Hilley. Beginning with that meeting, Domenici and Senate Budget Committee Staff Director Bill Hoagland operated on the presumption that there would be an agreement between the White House and congressional Republicans and that agreement would form the basis of the Senate budget resolution. As Hoagland described the situation in the Senate:

> Literally, Senator Domenici and myself began discussions with Hilley and Bowles even before the inauguration. And we knew from the outset that Mr. Bowles and Mr. Hilley, representing the President—they spoke for the President—we knew we all had the same objective in mind. As we went through this negotiation we knew there would be issues, but it was agreed to at the outset we were going to get an agreement.[6]

House Republicans were much less confident of reaching an agreement. On 8 January, Republican members of the House Budget Committee gathered for an "orientation" meeting, which turned into a ninety-minute strategy session in which members expressed the pessimism and distrust left over from the previous Congress.[7] Members emphasized the need to communicate a Republican vision to counteract the president's public relations efforts, the importance of a coherent political strategy for dealing with the White House, and efforts to manage intraparty differences over tax and spending priorities.

Kasich voiced three major concerns. First, he expected that the president's budget would include optimistic economic projections, accounting gimmicks in Medicare, and "phony" tax cuts that would terminate after a couple of years if the deficit grew unexpectedly. Second, Kasich worried that House Republicans, stinging from the last budget round, would not have the stomach to support a "real" budget with conservative economic assumptions and "real" cuts in entitlement spending. Third, he was not sure how much leeway he would be given in the negotiations. Kasich reminded colleagues that in 1995 he and Domenici were left out of key meetings involving the president, the Speaker, and the Senate majority leader.

Reflecting later on the prospects for a bipartisan agreement when negotiations started in February, Kasich said: "I was neither pessimistic nor optimistic. I was just completely neutral on what would happen. I thought it was very important not to have any expectations, because when you have expectations you build energy." Even when negotiations got under way, establishing trust across party lines did not come easily, as party leaders tried to balance their hopes for a successful agreement with their responsibility to meet the policy goals and political interests of elected officials from their respective parties. Kasich noted: "The White House came to see me and the fact is they were very positive and we started to have discussions that were very positive, but I just never tried to anticipate one way or the other how it was going to go."[8]

Rank-and-file House Republicans were even more skeptical about negotiating a deal with President Clinton. House Budget Committee Staff Director Rick May described the mood among House Republicans at the outset of the budget process:

> Republicans were gun shy at first. They said, "Wait a minute, what are they up to? Is this a trap? Are they gonna suck us into negotiations and pull the rug out at the last minute?" All the battle scars from the last time made us suspicious from the beginning. I don't know how many people came to me and said, "I can't believe you guys are doing this with these people. These guys are gonna kill us. They're gonna beat us at the PR game. They're just doing this to make themselves look good."[9]

Leaders from both parties reflected a mixture of caution and optimism after the president sent his budget to Congress. President Clinton said, "There are still differences between the parties about how we should do this, but I am convinced these differences can be bridged. . . . We've got the best chance in a generation."[10] Speaker Gingrich and Senate Majority Leader Lott maintained their view that congressional Republicans would not deem Clinton's budget "dead on arrival." Though both Domenici and Kasich criticized the budget's economic projections, limited tax cuts, rising deficits until after Clinton left office, and limited spending cuts, Domenici described the president's budget as "a very good starting point." Kasich called it a "rickety agreement."[11] The House Budget Committee issued a press release acknowledging the president's willingness to recognize Republican principles: a balanced budget, tax relief for American families, and the need to address the fact that Medicare was going bankrupt. Yet the main body of the press release indicated how Clinton failed to address six key questions Republicans used to evaluate the president's budget:

1.	Balance the budget by 2002 and *keep it in balance*?	No
2.	Provide *permanent* family tax relief?	No
3.	Seriously try to bring deficits down steadily each year?	No
4.	Refrain from on-again off-again budget plans?	No

5. Save Medicare without a shell game?   No

6. Shift power, influence, and control
    back to people in their communities?   No

After the president submits a budget to Congress, the budget committees hold hearings at which key administrative officials testify. Here again, the Senate took more kindly to OMB Director Franklin Raines. Hoagland noted:

> OMB Director Raines testified before the Senate Budget Committee the day after the president submitted his budget. The day after that we had a personal private meeting out at his residence in Northwest Washington. We knew even as he was testifying on this committee on that Friday, that that was just a starting point. Maybe other people were chastising the president's budget as not real and out of line, but Senator Domenici and I knew from our private meetings that this was an opening bid and that there was going to be an agreement on a bipartisan basis and we were going to work it out. So we never got terribly upset with some of the things in the president's first budget, because we knew it was a positioning budget.[12]

In contrast with the Senate strategy of cooperation with the president, House Republican leaders planned a two-track strategy for the budget process. The first track was to negotiate with the White House and try to reach an agreement consisting of a balanced budget over five years using conservative economic assumptions, reductions in entitlement spending, and tax cuts. If that failed, the Republicans on the House Budget Committee would draft a separate "politically safe" budget resolution and send the president separate bills containing the spending cuts Clinton proposed for Medicare and Medicaid. When Raines testified before the House Budget Committee on 11 February, Republicans mounted a partisan, frontal attack on the president's budget. Committee staff prepared a memorandum for the hearing titled "Abracadabra: How President Clinton's Balanced Budget Appears and Disappears." The "major themes" of Raines's visit would be: (1) "the President accepts our policy goals rhetorically, but doesn't deliver"; (2) "he fails our six-point credibility test"; (3) "the era of big government is back"; and (4) "no hard choices—not a bold budget."

Kasich began the Raines hearing by pointing out that the economy was not doing well when we looked at the impact on families; the national debt continued to climb; and the administration budget pushed too many cuts into the last two years. He also complained about the economic assumptions in the president's budget. John Spratt (D-S.C.), the ranking Democrat on the House Budget Committee, responded by touting the Clinton administration record on economics and noting that the administration's economic assumptions were similar to those of the Congressional Budget Office (CBO) and perhaps even more accurate. Raines proved to be a savvy, composed, and persuasive witness. He rebutted Kasich's criticisms and defended the president's policies without insulting the chairman or closing the door to bipartisan negotiations. One of the main Republican concerns of Clinton's budget was that 73 percent of the savings would come in the last two years of the five-year plan, after the president was out of office. All budgets tend to be "backloaded," a term used to describe the cumulative effect of large savings in the last years of a budget plan, because the savings from spending reductions made in the first two years compound over the length of the plan. But in Clinton's budget, most of the actual spending cuts were delayed until much later compared with previous budgets. Raines urged the Budget Committee to view the proposed budget as part of a ten-year project of deficit reduction that began when President Clinton was elected to office in 1992. From that perspective, Raines concluded, only about 10 percent of the savings would come in 2001 and 2002. Several dumbfounded Republicans shook their heads and snickered, and Chairman Kasich did all he could to sit back as he twisted and chewed on his glasses and smiled occasionally at the budget director's clever rejoinders. He told Raines House Republicans were willing to work with the administration, but he expected they would have to do "Washington tango" for a while, implying the two parties would dance around the core issues before getting to serious negotiations.

Politics and Economics

On the morning of 13 February, prior to a hearing featuring CBO Director June O'Neill, committee Republicans caucused in a small room behind the Budget Committee hearing room in the Cannon House Office Building.[13] Kasich reminded his colleagues of the two-track strategy he explained at a retreat for House Republicans in Williamsburg the previous weekend. By this time, Kasich had met with Hilley, and he was willing to negotiate in good faith. Meanwhile, the House Budget Committee began working on a separate budget resolution. Several members voiced their concerns about negotiating with the White House. One member argued flat out, "We should forget negotiating with Clinton; he can't be trusted. Why not just draw the lines between us and the Democrats and take it to them in 1998?" Kasich objected: "No. We're not trying to fix the problem this year, but we should take what we can now. This is a tug-of-war, and the idea is to pull them over to our side, and gradually move the budget in our direction." Most members seemed to accept the approach because, as Kasich later indicated: "Nobody thought an agreement was possible anyway."[14]

One of the first major sticking points in the process was over the arcane but crucial issue of economic projections in Clinton's five-year budget plan. Because the economy plays such an important role in determining spending, revenues, and deficits, projections about economic growth, unemployment, inflation, and interest rates are critical elements to a deficit-reduction plan. Projections of high economic growth, low unemployment, low inflation, and low interest rates increase revenues, reduce spending, and lower the deficit without any spending cuts or tax increases. Kasich took no comfort in the political cover afforded by optimistic economic assumptions. He preferred using the most conservative economic projections so that budget negotiations would focus on achieving real spending cuts, not just making the numbers work out to a balanced budget. Thus, Kasich's main strategic purpose during the February hearing with CBO Director June O'Neill was to get a qualified budget analyst to say the president's budget was not grounded in conservative economic assumptions. Kasich also used the occasion to remind Republicans on the Budget Committee that he insisted on using conservative economic projections. Kasich worried that Republican Party leaders would try to cut a quick deal with the Clinton administration by agreeing to optimistic economic assumptions in exchange for larger tax cuts.

Despite Kasich's efforts to get O'Neill to accentuate the problem of economic assumptions in Clinton's budget, the CBO director lived up to her reputation as a cautious economist. Though the CBO made only a "preliminary analysis" of Clinton's budget, O'Neill said the plan could result in a $50 billion deficit in 2002, instead of the administration's projected $17 billion surplus. Still, she concluded, the administration's budget was an "honest effort." Helped along by the ranking Democrat John Spratt, O'Neill conceded the apparently large difference in the deficit/surplus estimates for 2002 between the president's OMB and the CBO resulted from relatively minor differences in economic projections. Yet the political spin coming out of the Budget Committee focused only on the bottom line. The committee faxed a News Alert before O'Neill's hearing had even finished announcing: "CBO Says Clinton Budget Doesn't Balance." It was too early in the process to give the Clinton administration an advantage on the economic assumptions that would define the range of choices and possibilities in the budget agreement. The negotiations had just begun and Kasich wanted to stake out a clear position: any balanced-budget agreement would be based on conservative economic projections.

The political jockeying over economic assumptions obscured two basic economic facts.[15] First, recent OMB and the CBO forecasts were too pessimistic in projecting the size of the deficit in 1996. For example, in May 1996, about four months before the end of FY 1996 (30 September), CBO projected a deficit of $144 billion, which was off by 34 percent of the actual $107 billion deficit for the year. Second, because so much government spending is determined by the performance of the economy, very small differences in future economic projections can lead to large differences in the amount of savings needed to balance the budget over a five-year period. This was true in 1997. As table 4.2 illustrates, the main difference in the two agencies' projections occurred over slightly more optimistic assumptions by OMB in three areas: income shares, inflation, and interest rates.[16] In fact, neither CBO nor OMB could be certain about the actual inflation rate, interest rates, or income shares a year from the time they made their projections, let alone five years into the future. Former CBO Director Rudolph G. Penner pointed out: "Given the range of uncertainty when you're talking about the deficit of 2002, the two forecasts are essentially identical."[17] Yet those slight differences enabled the president to estimate a balanced budget by 2002 with $236 billion in net savings over five years, whereas congressional Republicans using CBO projections needed $387 billion in net savings, a difference of 60 percent.

Table 4.2
Comparison of CBO and OMB
Selected Economic Assumptions in 2002 (in percentages)

	CBO	OMB	Difference
Income shares[a]	47.3	47.7	.4
Inflation	3.0	2.7	.3
Interest rates	5.1	5.5	.4

Source: George Hager, "War Over Predictions Goes on Despite History of Bad Calls," *Congressional Quarterly Weekly Report,* 29 March 1997, 735–36.

a. Wages and salaries as a percentage of the nation's total economic output (GDP).

Seeking an equal playing field, Republicans used a 3 March CBO analysis to charge that the president's budget was not real. CBO reported Clinton's budget would increase the deficit in the next year by $33 billion and would result in a $69 billion deficit in 2002. The CBO analysis gave Republicans the ammunition needed to spark an episode of partisan posturing and confrontational politics. Kasich told reporters he was "astounded" by the CBO's conclusion that 98 percent of deficit reduction would occur in the last two years of Clinton's five-year plan. "The president doesn't do anything, frankly, to balance the budget until he and

Al Gore leave office in this term." Kasich went on to say: "We would be better off if we didn't have this budget. . . . I think the president and his team ought to send us another budget."[18]

Yet the White House argued the CBO's economic assumptions were not superior to or more accurate than the administration's. OMB Director Raines called on Republicans to offer an alternative budget and publicly urged further negotiations: "We'd like to hear what the alternatives are. The president has the only plan that is on the table that is a complete budget plan. . . . I'm prepared to go back into a room with [Republicans] to negotiate. We're ready." [19] Meanwhile, congressional Democratic leaders joined the fray. Senate Minority Leader Tom Daschle quipped: "My question to Pete Domenici and John Kasich is: 'Where's yours?' I am increasingly frustrated with our Republican colleagues who would rather play political games than roll up their sleeves and get to work." Daschle sounded a pessimistic warning: "There appears to be the same sort of political approach now to budget consideration that we saw two years ago. And, I believe that, unless something changes, that political approach is going to lead to the same political result, which is a shutdown of Government and complete chaos again."[20]

On 13 March, House Republicans brought the conflict over economic projections to a head. House Republican leaders scheduled a vote on H.Res. 89, a resolution requesting that the president introduce a budget using CBO economic assumptions. The debate over the resolution was the clearest sign yet that partisan battle lines were about to be drawn, jeopardizing hopes of a bipartisan agreement. Republicans railed against the President's "rosy" economic scenario, the "backloaded" savings, and the "phony gimmicks," such as "disappearing tax cuts" and spending cut "triggers" that would never materialize. Democrats repeatedly took the floor to ask Republicans, "Where is your budget?" Spratt argued: "What we are trying to do is distract attention from the fact that the majority would prefer not to have to put up its own [budget] resolution. This resolution [H.Res. 89] is a waste of time."[21] The House voted 231–197 along party lines to request that President Clinton submit a new budget to Congress.

Kasich was well aware of the minor differences in the assumptions, but he believed that any budget agreement should rest on the most conservative economic projections: the more conservative the assumptions, the better the chance of extracting a higher level of budget savings from an agreement with the White House. If the budget was balanced earlier as a result of a better economy, so be it; besides, Republicans could always compromise on the economic assumptions later in the negotiation process.

Politics and the Consumer Price Index: Is There a Leader in the House?

On 14 March, the day after the House passed H.Res. 89, Republicans on the House Budget Committee met for three hours to take a "first cut" at a budget resolution and "jump start" the process, as Kasich put it.[22] Budget Committee staff had been working on various budget scenarios for several weeks, but the committee was in limbo while Kasich negotiated with the White House. Kasich said he was in no hurry to draft a budget resolution, but he called the meeting because some members expressed concerns that the Budget Committee was not moving quickly enough. Despite the partisan rancor evidenced by Republican criticisms of the economic assumptions in Clinton's budget and Democratic complaints that Republicans had still not presented a budget proposal, Kasich was learning to trust White House negotiators. Kasich later pointed out: "I felt that what we really needed to do is to just plod along."[23] As long as the Republicans did not present a budget resolution, the Democrats in Congress would have nothing to criticize, no targets to hone in on. Republican negotiators benefited from the diffusion of responsibility that goes with a divided government. But as part of the balancing act leaders must perform, Kasich agreed to put together a budget resolution.

To start the meeting, Kasich introduced a four-year plan to balance the budget. Kasich's proposal called for a freeze in domestic discretionary spending, a slight increase in defense, savings in Medicare and Medicaid comparable to Clinton's plan, savings from the Earned Income Tax Credit, and half the president's projected savings from sales of the Electromagnetic Spectrum. Reflecting on the past year's experience, Kasich said there would be no premium increases in Medicare and no block grant for Medicaid, two policy ideas in the 1995 budget that became the source of campaign attacks by Democratic candidates. The proposal included $100 billion in tax cuts, but in exchange for the tax cuts the budget assumed $70 billion in savings from a .5 percent reduction in the Consumer Price Index (CPI).

Adjusting the CPI was not a new idea, but it had gained momentum after a report released in December 1996 by the Advisory Commission to Study the Consumer Price Index, headed by a former chairman of the Council of Economic Advisers, Dr. Michael J. Boskin. The Boskin commission found that the CPI overstated the actual annual rate of inflation by somewhere between .8 and 1.6 percent.[24] During a House Budget Committee hearing on 4 March, Federal Reserve Chairman Alan Greenspan strongly endorsed an adjustment to the CPI. Since such major government entitlements as Social Security are indexed for the rate of inflation, an overstatement of the rate meant the government was spending more money than it needed in order to keep its promise of annual COLAs for Social Security benefits. Even small changes in the CPI could produce large budget savings. The CBO estimated that shaving .5 percent off the annual increase in benefits and tax brackets would reduce the deficit by $70 billion over five years.

While Kasich's proposal reflected the constraints of prior budget battles with the White House, it also indicated his willingness to push his colleagues to consider major entitlement reform. He knew Republicans were just recovering from the Democrats' "Mediscare" campaign of 1996, and they would oppose another round of large Medicare cuts. It made sense politically to adopt the president's number for Medicare savings. Yet budget priorities are not based solely on political considerations, and Kasich's proposal to adjust the CPI reflected his hope of achieving as much entitlement savings as possible and paying for the tax cuts. Kasich viewed the CPI adjustment as a feasible source of savings. He was doing what budget leaders had done for years—pushing the envelope, trying to reduce the deficit with substantive changes in entitlement benefits.

In his effort to persuade his colleagues to support a .5 percent reduction in the CPI, Kasich pointed out that moderate Democrats favored an even larger reduction (.8 percent). Though Kasich knew Republicans were skittish about taking on a potentially explosive political issue, he urged Budget Committee Republicans to show leadership. Kasich told a story that conveyed his concept of political leadership and his concern about the lack of political will on the part of Republican members. He said a Republican member expressed concerns about the political consequences of voting to reduce the CPI and urged Kasich to leave it out of the budget resolution. "We're in the majority now," the member told Kasich, "let's keep it that way." Kasich said he looked at the member, astounded by his suggestion, and said, "We're in the majority? To do what? What good is it to be in the majority if we can't change anything?" Kasich pleaded with his colleagues: "Somebody needs to provide leadership here, and we're the committee to do it." Moreover, Kasich was not going to rely on optimistic economic assumptions to finance a tax cut. He said pointedly, "No CPI change, no tax cuts."

Kasich also revealed that President Clinton was willing to adjust the CPI but worried about liberal Democrats in Congress. Kasich said he would be talking with White House negotiators later that day and asked the members to give him the leeway to negotiate a reduction in the CPI. The responses were mixed, but most members expressed their distrust of the president and were opposed to letting Kasich raise the issue with White House negotiators. Kasich responded by asking: "Why are we here?"

The members turned to other possibilities. After a long discussion of strategies and ideas, the group was left with three general scenarios for a balanced budget by 2002:

1. No tax cuts, but no change in CPI.

2. Adjust the CPI and include tax cuts.

3. Tax cuts, no adjustment in the CPI, and dramatic cuts in discretionary spending.

Kasich ended the meeting by notifying members that the following week the Republicans would meet again and put together a budget resolution. He told the members, despite his biases, the will of the Committee shall prevail. He ended the meeting by saying, "Now, go home and think about why you came to Congress. The Democrats are going to attack you in the next campaign anyway. You might as well get something done."

The Republican Budget Committee caucus meeting adjourned around noon; later that day, the CPI issue exploded. Responding to pressure from organized labor, elderly citizens' groups, and liberal Democrats, Clinton took the advice of Senate Minority Leader Daschle and House Minority Leader Gephardt and announced his opposition to Senate Majority Leader Lott's idea of establishing another commission to recommend adjustments in the CPI. Liberals feared a commission would surely find what other studies concluded: the CPI was biased upward and a more accurate measure of inflation would require a reduction in the CPI. Clinton's announcement set off rounds of strong criticism from moderate Democrats, who were angry at the president for failing to assert leadership, and Republican budget makers, who felt betrayed in their negotiations with the White House.

Domenici and Kasich believed the Boskin Commission report on the CPI provided an opportunity to make significant reductions in entitlement spending with bipartisan support. Senate Democrats, including John Breaux (La.), Charles Robb (Va.), Bob Kerrey (Neb.), Kent Conrad (N.Dak.), and Daniel Patrick Moynihan (N.Y.), all endorsed a correction in the CPI. Blue Dog Democrats in the House, a coalition of moderate and conservative representatives, advocated an .8 percent adjustment. Behind closed doors in the budget negotiations, President Clinton endorsed the reduction and negotiators were discussing how to implement the change. The president could order the Bureau of Labor Statistics to make a technical adjustment in the CPI, or Congress could change the CPI by enacting legislation.

Yet support for adjusting the CPI ran shallow in Congress. Opposition came from members of both parties and reflected concerns about policy effects and political consequences. Liberal Democrats opposed any entitlement reforms that reduced benefits for government pensioners and senior citizens. Conservative Republicans opposed the idea because it would reduce the standard deduction for taxpayers, essentially raising income taxes for many Americans. Some Republicans also opposed changing the CPI for political reasons; they were worried the CPI could become the "Mediscare" of the 1998 congressional campaign. Those Republicans were unwilling to vote for legislation that would effectively reduce Social Security benefits without the president's clear commitment to sign it.

Clinton's opposition to another commission to study the CPI shook the foundations of the bipartisan budget negotiations. Lott said: "He doesn't have the courage to deal with it." Domenici and Kasich saw Clinton's decision as an indication he was not serious about developing a major budget agreement. The inconsistency between the president's public statements and the closed-door meetings brought back nightmares from 1995 for Domenici and Kasich. They had been promised several times by White House Chief of Staff Leon Panetta that the president was serious about reaching an agreement, only to turn on the television and hear the president's negotiators back away. Domenici's positive attitude about working with the White House turned sour: "The chances of getting a negotiated budget between Republicans and the president are finished."[25] Lott and Domenici began to consider changing strategies and negotiating with moderate Democrats to draft a congressional budget. Yet Clinton's rejection of the commission did not mean the White House was opposed to adjusting the CPI. Beneath the sound and fury, John Hilley tried to restore calm to the bipartisan negotiations and mend fences with Kasich and Domenici. He assured them the CPI was still on the table; Clinton was simply trying to quell an uprising from liberals in the Democratic Party.

Tax Cuts: To Be or Not to Be?

In his briefings with Speaker Gingrich, Kasich delivered the same message of a tax cut/CPI adjustment tradeoff that he brought to Budget Committee Republicans. Realizing that Republican members were concerned about voting on a budget resolution containing an adjustment in the CPI, party leaders began to consider a way to draft a balanced budget plan without tax cuts. On 12 March, Majority Whip Tom DeLay (R-Tex.) floated the idea of separating tax cuts from a deficit-reduction bill. Conservative Republicans responded negatively, and the issue seemed to subside until the following Monday, 17 March, when Speaker Gingrich took the House floor for Special Orders. Gingrich announced that tax cuts were a Republican priority, but under the circumstances a balanced-budget agreement with the White House might have to come before the tax cuts. Gingrich later told reporters: "We've said all along we think it's very, very important to balance the budget and get as large a tax cut as possible while balancing the budget. But we think that the moral imperative is to balance the budget." The best strategy might be to "take tax cuts away for a moment. Let's just talk about balancing the budget. Now what's the liberal excuse for not balancing the budget?"[26]

Gingrich's idea seemed to be a sensible and responsible way to move toward a bipartisan compromise. Holding off on tax cuts would make it much easier for Republicans to put together a credible plan. The idea received a favorable response from the White House, moderates on both sides of the aisle, and the public.[27] The day after Gingrich's floor speech, Republicans Michael Castle (Del.) and Fred Upton (Mich.), representatives of a group of Republican moderates called the "Tuesday Lunch Bunch," joined conservative Democrats Charles Stenholm (Tex.) and John Tanner (Tenn.) and dispatched a Dear Colleague letter that read in part: "We believe that considering tax cut legislation separately from the budget significantly improves the chances for an agreement to balance the budget by 2002." Seventy House Republicans, including twenty-two freshmen, signed the letter sent to Speaker Gingrich.

But the idea divided the party leadership and incensed conservative groups. The same day Castle was asking Republicans to support Gingrich's idea, Ralph Reed, executive director of the Christian Coalition, faxed an urgent letter to all members of Congress. The letter cautioned Republicans about "retreating" from their pledge to cut taxes:

> We strongly believe that any budget resolution passed by the Congress must provide for enough tax relief to accommodate a $500 per child tax credit. This has been our position since 1992, and we do not anticipate any circumstance under which it will change. Reluctantly, we could be forced to oppose a Republican budget resolution if it does not provide for significant and broad tax relief for American families.

Two days later the Family Research Council, a conservative group headed by Gary Bauer, faxed its *Daily Commentary,* which said flatly that Gingrich was "wrong to backtrack on tax relief for families and American entrepreneurs and investors." Luckily, said Bauer, Majority Leader Richard Armey (Tex.) is telling Newt to "Wait a Minute!" Twenty-eight conservative House Republicans, members of the Conservative Action Team (CATs), sent a letter to the Speaker expressing their strong preference for passing a tax cut early in the process. The letter read: "We can, and must, balance the budget and pass meaningful tax relief. That President Clinton chose to veto last year's Balanced Budget Amendment Act does not mean we should walk away from these important goals this year. It is unthinkable that President Clinton can offer a tax cut package in his budget and a Republican budget may contain none."[28]

At a 19 March party conference meeting, House Republicans hotly debated tax cuts and the CPI. Conservatives expressed their anger at Gingrich's suggestions to put off tax cuts. Gingrich tried to explain that the party was still committed to a tax cut and would include one in any budget they put together, but it was a matter of "sequencing." To take the heat off the tax issue, Gingrich announced that he was opposed to adjusting the CPI without Clinton's consent. Kasich plainly disagreed with Gingrich on the CPI, and their positions reflected the difference between a policy leader and a party leader. As a policy leader, Kasich sought major changes in entitlement spending and a way to pay for tax cuts; as a party leader, Gingrich needed to accommodate various factions in the party.

Later that day House Budget Committee Republicans met to discuss the party's first draft of the budget resolution.[29] Kasich floated the CPI issue again, telling his colleagues he was going to the White House that afternoon for another meeting. Kasich tried to convince them that despite press reports, Clinton wanted to adjust the CPI, and he sought their approval to negotiate a compromise. Kasich asked each member where he or she stood on the CPI. Only five of twenty members gave Kasich the leeway to negotiate for a CPI adjustment. Some of those who declined to give Kasich that flexibility thought it was a poor political strategy to show his hand early in the process; many didn't trust Clinton; and others said they would be uncomfortable explaining a CPI reduction to their constituents. Kasich listened attentively, joked occasionally, and finally accepted collective judgment of committee Republicans. But he could not resist one last attempt to persuade his colleagues. After each member expressed an opinion, he pointed out that despite all the negative attacks by organized labor and the Democratic National Committee during the 1996 campaign, the Republicans still held their majority in the House. Kasich pleaded: "The unions are going to attack you in the next election anyway; why not do something significant while we have the chance?" But the members were unmoved.

Budget Committee Republicans deliberated further on the options discussed the week before. They decided to cut discretionary spending below the current projected cost assuming the CBO's estimate of inflation (a "hard freeze"), adopt Clinton's Medicare cuts, and cut taxes by $90 billion, partly offset by a $30 billion airline-ticket tax and $20 billion in tax-loophole closings. Pete Hoekstra (R-Mich.), who had been working to improve the committee's communications strategy, said the message should be clear and simple: "No new spending, let families keep more." House Republicans had a budget they could live with, but one that would appall most Democrats.

Timeout

As the Easter recess neared, the budget process seemed in disarray. The president's tactics had Republicans thinking they were about to walk into a trap. Democratic leaders made every effort to convince the president there was no hurry to cut a deal and demanded that Republicans offer their own budget proposal as a condition for continuing negotiations. Despite efforts by policy leaders to negotiate in earnest, party politics were alive and kicking. President Clinton was about to depart for Helsinki, Chairman Kasich was off to get married, and members of Congress were headed home with only one thing to tell their constituents: the budget process was on hold and it was "politics as usual" in Washington.

But before the negotiators left town, Clinton called a cease-fire in the partisan war. Encouraged by Gingrich's vow to be "flexible" on the tax issue and suggestions by Domenici and Lott that the GOP would be willing to negotiate economic assumptions, on 19 March Clinton called Kasich, Domenici, Spratt, and Lautenberg to a meeting at the White House with Vice-President Gore, Bowles, Hilley, Sperling, Raines, Rubin, and Budget Committee staff directors. As a goodwill gesture, Clinton gave Kasich a wedding gift. Senate Budget Committee Staff Director Hoagland remembered the meeting as "a long, frank and careful discussion about the need to work together to achieve a bipartisan balanced budget." House Budget Chairman Kasich downplayed the meeting, saying that "it wasn't a turning point. The agreement was still uncertain."[30] The only certainty was that the negotiations would move on to a different stage. Both sides agreed to begin a series of high-level bipartisan meetings when members of Congress returned from Easter recess.

Principles, Politics, and Policy Change

The early stages of the budget process included bipartisan negotiations, partisan posturing, and bicameral differences. At times, the process appeared headed for partisan stalemate, as the inevitable gridlock model would expect in a divided government. Yet the process proceeded along an uncertain course, with a mixture of opportunities and constraints that permitted a range of possible governing patterns. The White House sought a bipartisan agreement, and Senate Republican leaders were receptive; House Republicans were less sanguine. In general, leaders recognized the potential for a bipartisan agreement and began to trust each other. They also saw opportunities to advance specific policy ideas, and they needed each other to achieve their separate policy goals: tax cuts and entitlement savings for Republicans and domestic spending initiatives for Clinton. Policy leaders like Kasich seized the opportunity to push major reforms in the hope of adding them to the mix of proposals discussed in the negotiations. Yet divided government places constraints on the degree to which either party can achieve its policy goals. Leaders must strike a balance between compromise and principle, feasible policy change and major reform. Searching for a coalition under uncertain conditions helps explain why party leaders like Speaker Gingrich suggest ways to break the logjam.

We also see how previous budget cycles affect decision making. The budget battles of the 104th Congress and the nasty Mediscare campaign in 1996 caused Republicans to limit Kasich's discretion in negotiations with the White House. While most House Budget Committee Republicans did not disagree with the rationale or the principle underlying Kasich's argument to adjust the CPI, they were fixated on political considerations and haunted by the previous campaign. Even though they were reelected in 1996, several won by narrow margins, and all were attacked for voting to cut Medicare. Most Republicans distrusted Clinton; they figured reducing the CPI was a losing proposition and feared the political backlash of "cutting benefits" to senior citizens. Under the conditions, it made sense for House Republicans to pursue a two-track strategy, though the party was internally divided over the importance of tax cuts. In the complex world of budgeting, deliberations reflected a variety of basic commitments to ideological principles, concerns about the fiscal implications of policy choices, and political considerations. Building a consensus may have been more difficult with opposite parties in control of Congress and the presidency, but gridlock was not inevitable. Despite the partisan posturing in the early stages of the process, leaders sought ways to avoid stalemate.

5

Bipartisan Deal Making under Divided Government

Members of Congress returned from Easter recess to a budget process that seemed much like the mixed blessings of spring weather in Washington. Bright colors bursting in bloom one day were overshadowed by gray clouds and thunderstorms the next. The budget process picked up with a ray of hope stemming from the President's plea for bipartisan cooperation, but members of Congress from both parties remained skeptical. White House and Republican budget negotiators took the process at a different pace than rank-and-file partisans. The principals and policymakers, hastened by deadlines in the budget schedule and a sense that the bipartisan goodwill might soon vanish, anxiously sought to conclude a deal quickly. When President Clinton and Republican leaders committed themselves to a compromise, they also accepted the limits of bipartisanship. Leaders had to set aside their grand designs and take incremental steps toward a shared goal of a balanced budget plus a mixture of Democratic and Republican priorities—and convince members to do the same. Yet liberal and conservative members of Congress returned with fresh reminders of constituent needs and strong commitments to their beliefs about the role of government. In contrast with the leaders, rank-and-file members were in no hurry to reach a bipartisan agreement; some even believed they were better off with no deal at all.

On 1 May, congressional leaders and key staff personnel from the White House reached a tentative five-year agreement to balance the budget. The plan also reduced taxes, extended the life of the Medicare Hospital Insurance (HI) Trust Fund for ten years, slowed the growth of discretionary spending, expanded health coverage for children, and funded several of the president's policy initiatives. The initial budget package also contained two bold and divisive initiatives: a cap on Medicaid spending and a reduction in the Consumer Price Index (CPI). This initial agreement clearly had a Republican cast. Yet even when the agreement was announced at two major media events the next day, the deal was not done. On the evening of 1 May, as White House negotiators John Hilley and Frank Raines briefed angry House Democrats on the particulars of the budget agreement, the process was rocked by sudden news of a windfall in revenues. Democrats had learned of an updated CBO analysis of economic projections that yielded an additional $225 billion in revenues above the estimates made in March. Liberal Democrats, already unhappy about the tax cuts, the amount of discretionary spending, cuts in Medicaid, and the CPI adjustment, demanded changes in the agreement. The CBO numbers caused negotiators to go back to the drawing board. In spite of the joyous celebration by leaders of both parties the next day, it took another two weeks to iron out the details.

This chapter reviews the major events of the budget process from the Easter recess to the conclusion of the budget negotiations (see table 5.1), focusing especially on how leaders develop a bipartisan agreement in a divided government situation. In private negotiations, leaders on both sides pushed *as far as possible* to achieve their objectives, but at the same time they accepted the limits of a bipartisan compromise. In public, leaders echoed the expectations of their electoral constituencies and their colleagues in Congress. Once negotiators resolved their

Table 5.1
Key Developments in the Budget Process: April–May 1997

High-level bipartisan staff meetings during Easter recess	24 March–4 April
Members return from Easter recess and negotiators resume talks	7 April
Formal deadline for passing congressional budget resolution	15 April
Senate Democrats meet with Hilley and Raines to complain about White House strategy	17 April
Domenici and Kasich meet secretly with Hilley and Raines to offer GOP plan	21–22 April
CBO reports $225 billion in new revenues to Budget Committee staff directors	30 April
White House negotiators reveal budget agreement to angry House Democrats	1 May
Initial budget agreement is publicly announced in separate press conferences	2 May
Final details of the budget agreement are completed after two weeks of bargaining	15 May

differences, leaders had to convince party loyalists that the budget agreement advanced their policy priorities and political interests. The events also demonstrate the complexities of the process and the many factors that affect decision making. As the process unfolds, the strategic ground shifts; first one party, then another, gains the upper hand. The deal never seems quite done as the process goes through an endless series of adjustments, and leaders weave their way through a thicket of obstacles and uncertainties.

Getting Started—Again: Details, Deadlines, and Priorities

Though negotiators talked for months about priorities and ideas, possibilities and limitations, they did not begin hard bargaining until after the Easter recess. Agreeing on the same economic assumptions was a major sticking point, and nothing could happen unless and until both sides agreed to start with the same projections. During the Easter recess, the House and Senate Budget Committee staff directors met in Senator Domenici's hideaway in the Capitol for about a week to work out the underlying economic assumptions. Though the economic projections had been a contentious issue since President Clinton proposed his budget in February, the parties were much further apart politically than economically. Once staff sat down to discuss the economic assumptions to be used in the negotiations, Republicans agreed that OMB was closer to the real numbers on wage growth and the effect of corporate profits on overall revenues. So an issue that seemed like a major hurdle was solved with a few technical adjustments. The staff directors spent the remainder of the two weeks identifying options for spending and tax cuts.

When Congress returned from Easter recess on 7 April, negotiations were pushed along by the budget schedule. Senate Majority Leader Trent Lott used the 15 April deadline for passing a congressional budget resolution as a way to stress the need for rapid progress. Lott suggested that an agreement be reached within two weeks. Specifically, Lott wanted the president to increase Medicare savings, reopen discussions of an adjustment in the CPI, and agree to cuts in capital gains and estate taxes. If the negotiations with the White House failed, Senate Republicans would seek a bipartisan compromise with moderate and conservative Democrats. House Republican leaders also worried about the budget timetable, though they had no plans to pursue a bipartisan strategy if negotiations failed. Clinton was widely distrusted within the House Republican Conference, and many members worried that the president might tie the Medicare savings in the budget resolution with the tax cuts, as he did in 1995. Thus they began to consider a strategy of passing separate bills for Medicare and taxes.

One thing was certain: the Republican budget resolution would include tax cuts. Republican Conference Chair John Boehner sent a letter on 4 April including a copy of reported results from a recent *USA Today*/CNN/Gallup survey. The survey showed that most Americans wanted tax cuts, and a majority believed Congress and the president could cut taxes and balance the budget at the same time. Moreover, after rumors began circulating about a possible attempt by conservative Republicans to oust him, Speaker Gingrich made a clear commitment to include tax cuts in the agreement. In his first news conference after returning from the Easter recess, Gingrich announced that his goal was to eliminate capital gains and estate taxes. He promised, "We will give Clinton a chance to veto a tax cut and show he is on the side of higher spending and higher taxes."[1]

In the first couple of weeks after Easter recess, the number of participants expanded. Domenici and Kasich held almost daily meetings with White House representatives Raines, Hilley, and Sperling, and congressional Democrats were regularly represented by Spratt and Lautenberg. If an agreement was going to win bipartisan approval in both houses, congressional Democrats had to be represented. At times, the group was joined by Donna Shalala, Secretary of Health and Human Services, and other White House staff. The main purpose of those meetings, according to Bill Hoagland, was to "slog through the numbers and details."[2] The principals on both sides gave the policymakers plenty of flexibility.

The first item on the agenda was Medicare, followed by discretionary spending and tax cuts. After the partisan war over Medicare in 1995 and 1996, the negotiators "took the politics out of Medicare," as Kasich put it, by agreeing not to attack the other side. Medicare was a litmus test for the negotiations. If the negotiators could settle the Medicare issue, then the prospects for an overall agreement were good. If they could not agree quickly on Medicare, however, then Republicans would be hard pressed to move much further. The president's original budget included about $100 billion in Medicare savings over five years, but the CBO scored the proposal as saving only $82 billion, and Republican negotiators insisted on additional savings. In an effort to reach agreement, the White House offered $18 billion more in Medicare savings by reducing payments to hospitals and other health-care providers. The White House was willing to do even more, but it was constrained by liberal Democrats. Before the week was over, Gephardt told Clinton that House Democrats believed the president was giving up too much and urged him to stop making concessions until Republicans offered a budget plan.

Sensing they had leverage over the president, Republican policy leaders pushed White House negotiators to cut entitlement spending further. Kasich announced that while he was encouraged with the latest offer on Medicare, the White House needed to go further. The following week, in a speech to general contractors, Domenici stated the White House would need to accept an additional $10 billion to $30 billion in Medicare savings in order to make a deal. Domenici and Kasich also wanted the White House to scale back its proposals for domestic discretionary initiatives. The hard line taken by Republicans was a rude awakening for Senator Lautenberg. Commenting on the 9 April meeting, Lautenberg concluded: "Today was the cold shower day. . . . The Republicans said discretionary spending was too high and the Republicans said entitlement spending is too high. It made each of us more aware of the magnitude of the job."[3]

Principle versus Progress

When tax day (15 April) arrived, both parties made popular appeals to reform the tax code and the IRS. The House voted on a constitutional amendment requiring a two-thirds majority to raise revenues and passed a resolution discouraging IRS officials from browsing through taxpayer files. At a tax forum sponsored by Empower America, Senator Lott predicted President Clinton would sign a bill containing a capital gains tax cut. President Clinton proposed a package of sixty items designed to simplify the process of filing taxes. Yet despite their differences, negotiators had already made progress in sketching the outlines of a package of tax cuts. Republicans conceded they could not expect to attain their ultimate goal of eliminating capital gains and estate taxes, but an agreement would include lower rates for capital gains, estate tax relief, and expanded individual retirement accounts (IRAs). In return, Clinton sought tuition tax breaks for higher education, and both sides wanted a child tax credit. Negotiators also reviewed ways of raising revenues to offset tax cuts, including airline ticket taxes, oil-spill excise taxes, the federal unemployment tax, the Superfund corporate income tax, and various loophole closings.

The formal deadline for passage of a congressional budget resolution was also 15 April, another reminder that the window of opportunity for reaching an agreement was closing. Negotiators realized that the longer it took to reach a compromise, the greater the chance of losing the goodwill they had established. They began to impose their own deadlines. First, the week of 14 April was considered a "make-or-break" week. When 18 April came and went with no deal, Senator Lautenberg said, "We're now approaching the time when we're going to have to do some fishing or cutting bait."[4] Senate Majority Whip Don Nickles (R-Okla.)

announced that if no deal was reached in a week, the Senate might have to pass a bipartisan budget resolution without the aid of the White House. On 21 April, Lott and Nickles announced they would suspend negotiations with the White House and develop their own budget if no "substantial progress" was made in the next couple of days.

Two more weeks would pass before the negotiators reached an agreement. During that time, leaders felt pressure from key members who opposed the negotiations, and factions of both parties began to stake out conditions for accepting an agreement. Liberal Democrats and conservative Republicans believed that any bipartisan deal would compromise their priorities. On 17 April, Senator Daschle and ten Democrats on the Senate Budget Committee met with Hilley, Raines, and Sperling to complain about the White House strategy. They insisted the Republicans were getting a free ride because they could negotiate without having to submit a balanced-budget plan. Daschle argued that Republicans were in disarray, and the White House was in a stronger position. Senate Democrats also complained that the White House was making concessions without consulting them. On 21 April, Daschle said a budget that cuts Medicare and taxes by more than $100 billion is "the limit beyond which we cannot go."[5]

Minority Whip David Bonior (D-Mich.) and Barney Frank (D-Mass.) sent a letter to Clinton, signed by seventy liberal House Democrats, stating "strong objections to any budget proposal which would maintain the current high level of military spending while reducing severely in real terms both discretionary spending on all non-military functions, and funding for Medicare and Medicaid."[6] Meanwhile, Senator Phil Gramm (R-Tex.), a staunch fiscal conservative, expressed concerns that the president and Republican negotiators were not focusing sufficiently on discretionary spending. Gramm told reporters: "I'm concerned not only about the president. I'm concerned about our negotiators. Spending money is popular; Republicans like to spend money as Democrats do."[7] Gramm, Sam Brownback (R-Kans.), and eight other Republican senators sent a letter to Majority Leader Lott saying they would oppose a budget agreement that violated five basic principles: a tax package including a cut in the capital gains and estate taxes and a $500 per child tax credit, steadily declining deficits, a freeze on discretionary spending at the current year's level, a plan using only CBO economic assumptions, and no legislative adjustment in the CPI. The letter stated: "We must not negotiate away the very principles that we were elected to defend. . . . A budget that violates our fundamental principles is worse than no budget deal at all."[8]

The public position taken by members of Congress resulted from the closed negotiation process. Kasich and Domenici believed the process failed in 1995 and 1996 because the White House made public statements that were inconsistent with the agreements worked out by negotiators. Democrats explained the inconsistencies as miscommunication, but Republicans saw them as violations of trust. This time, negotiators agreed to keep their deliberations as confidential as possible. Moreover, negotiators wanted members of Congress to focus on the big picture rather than the bits and pieces of the budget. They did not want interest groups and individual members of Congress raising objections to specific details that dribbled out to the press, so they tried to keep the most controversial decisions off the front pages. Members might be more willing to tolerate parts of the budget they disliked if they supported the general agreement. This approach could work as long as negotiations did not drag on too long. As negotiators worked behind closed doors, veterans of budget politics reminisced about the budget process of 1990, which lasted from June until September. As time went on, members became suspicious and were offended that they did not have a role in the process.

Politicians abhor a vacuum. Whether for policy reasons or political motives, conservative Republicans and liberal Democrats worried that leaders of their respective parties would rush to make a deal and sell out their party's principles. Negotiators and their principals were well aware of the problem, and they sensed that the likelihood of building support for a compromise in Congress would become increasingly difficult if members on both sides became more entrenched in their positions. On the heels of the Gramm-Brownback letter, Senate Majority Whip Nickles observed: "More and more sides are going to start saying, 'This is what we have to have.' If we are going to have anything wrapped up with the administration, it's important that we do it quick."[9]

As the White House negotiated secretly with Republican budget makers, President Clinton consulted with congressional Democrats on the House and Senate Budget Committees. Clinton solicited their input and reassured congressional Democrats he would not abandon party priorities and principles. After meeting with the Senate leadership and Senate Democrats on the Budget Committee on 18 April, Minority Leader Daschle commented: "We're walking out of this meeting as unified and optimistic as we've been in a long time."[10] Clinton began talking about the need to get at least a majority of congressional Democrats to support the agreement. Congressional Democrats encouraged the president to take his time. As the minority party in Congress, Democrats were not responsible for producing a budget resolution. In contrast, Republican leaders in both chambers felt the pressure to pass a budget resolution. With Clinton scheduled to leave the country the first week of May, Republican House leaders informed Kasich at the end of the week that they wanted him to schedule a markup of the budget resolution on 30 April, even in the absence of an agreement. On the Senate side, Lott said: "We're taking a risk by letting it go on much longer, because people are beginning to harden their positions on both sides."[11]

Final Offers

As the public ultimatums and bottom-line positions built up, negotiators narrowed their differences. On 17 April, the negotiators met one more time before the recess for Passover and scheduled to resume talks again on 23 April. But on 21 and 22 April, Domenici and Kasich met secretly with Hilley and Raines, and Domenici laid an offer on the table. The GOP proposal included $150 billion in tax cuts offset by $50 billion raised through the airline-ticket tax and loophole closings, compared with Clinton's $98 billion tax cut and $76 billion in revenue increases. It saved $125 billion in Medicare, compared with $100 billion in the president's budget. The proposal contained $15.5 billion in new spending for the president's priorities, about half of what the president wanted. The proposal also assumed an additional $50 billion in savings from a technical adjustment in the CPI made by the president without congressional approval.

When Republicans held their weekly whip meeting on 24 April, Chairman Kasich fielded questions about the emerging agreement.[12] Kasich used the occasion to quell rumors about the negotiations and to begin to sell the broad outlines of the agreement to House Republicans. Kasich announced that an agreement was "possible," despite the fact that members of his own conference had placed "obstacles" in his way. It would be a lot easier, Kasich explained, if he did not have to satisfy defense hawks, moderates concerned about education spending, and conservatives who wanted more cuts in discretionary spending and larger tax cuts. Kasich's main message was that the party must be willing to compromise and, if an agreement was reached, that members should learn about the details before denouncing it. He assured the members that any agreement would contain a capital gains tax cut, estate tax relief, a $500 per child tax credit, and significant entitlement savings. The chairman added that even though the bipartisan plan would not be his "ideal budget," he would not ask Republicans to support any agreement he did not believe in. "I am your agent," said Kasich. "My job is to represent the conference and negotiate on your behalf."

When Spratt and Lautenberg found out two days after their scheduled 23 April meeting with the president that they had been left out of key meetings involving just White House negotiators and Republicans, they "blew up," according to one person involved in the negotiations. House Minority Leader Gephardt complained: "The president mentioned nothing about this [Republican proposal] at the White House. This is all news to us." He voiced strong opposition to putting the CPI back on the table. "Our principles on this are the same as they've always been. We are not for hurting Medicare recipients in order to give a tax cut to the wealthiest Americans and for doing things other than saving Medicare. We are not for arbitrarily changing the CPI."[13]

On 26 April, a Saturday, Domenici, Kasich, and their two staff directors met at the home of OMB director Frank Raines to try to finalize the budget agreement. As Kasich later recalled, "Discretionary spending was the toughest part."[14] President Clinton wanted to spend an additional $43 billion on domestic initiatives in education, children's health, restoring welfare benefits for legal immigrants, and the environment, much less than the $15.5 billion offered by Republican negotiators. To close the gap they would have to adopt more optimistic economic assumptions or adjust the CPI, but neither option was palatable. Recent data from the Treasury Department concluded an unexpected increase in revenues from corporate profits would lower the deficit in the current fiscal year. Higher revenues would ease the pressure on negotiators to find additional spending cuts and make it easier to close the gap of savings required to balance the budget. Republican negotiators agreed to allow the CBO to study the Treasury report. In spite of objections from liberal Democrats, the president endorsed a change in the CPI on CBS's "Face the Nation" on Sunday, 27 April. He said, "I think most people—let's tell the story like it is, now—most people believe that the cost-of-living formula the government now uses overstates the real cost of living to the people who benefit from the programs."[15]

During the final week of negotiations culminating in a 2 May announcement of the agreement, the CPI became a hotly contested issue. Though Domenici, Kasich, and Clinton thought adjusting the CPI was the right thing to do, liberal Democrats and conservative Republicans were not on board, making Gingrich and Lott wary of supporting the idea. Lott said the issue was dead because the president was not forthright enough in his television announcement. Lott conceded: "It's going to be awfully hard for us to ask our people in the Senate to walk the plank. Time has come and gone on that issue. . . . People have hardened. I'm afraid it's not doable."[16] Domenici was confused by Lott's public posture; he still wanted to pursue a "technical adjustment" in the CPI by the Bureau of Labor Statistics so that Congress would not have to vote on a legislative change.

On Tuesday, White House officials met with Democrats in various meetings on Capitol Hill, and later that evening Democrats from the House Budget Committee visited the White House. Liberals urged the president not to accept a quick deal that contained large tax cuts and limited cuts in defense spending. House Democrats opposed tax cuts in general, but White House officials made it clear that tax cuts were part of the package. From that point, House Democrats urged the White House to make sure the tax cuts did not bring huge revenue losses and cause large deficits after they were fully phased in, and that families with low incomes received a fair share of the tax cuts. On the spending side, liberal Democrats expressed concerns about cuts in domestic discretionary spending and called for more cuts in defense.

On Wednesday, negotiators expressed hope that a deal might be concluded, yet they still needed to find sufficient revenues to fund Clinton's domestic spending initiatives, and they disagreed about the size and kinds of tax cuts. The president wanted to make sure the agreement incorporated his education tax breaks and mentioned the priorities of House Democrats. Bill Archer (R-Tex.), chair of the House Ways and Means Committee, insisted his committee was responsible for drafting details of the tax bill. Archer maintained that the purpose of the budget agreement was to establish the overall figures for the amount of the tax cuts and revenue increases and to identify the general kinds of tax cuts: a child tax credit, capital gains tax cuts, and estate tax reductions. Archer said the agreement must guarantee that "we have the freedom to write the tax bill in the Ways and Means Committee." He told the president any attempt to direct the committee would "jeopardize the passage of the entire package."[17]

Kasich appeared again at the House Republican whip meeting, physically exhausted by late nights of negotiating and long hours of individual conversations with confidants.[18] While he kept his word not to discuss the details of the negotiations, he gave a progress report and laid the groundwork for the final agreement. Kasich seemed delighted and amazed all at once about the prospect of an agreement that would advance Republican goals. Several members wanted more details. One member said he had heard the agreement would place an income cap on the eligibility for child tax credit; he said he would oppose the agreement on those grounds. Kasich answered: "Look, I'm not going to get into that level of detail; it will be up to Congress to decide the specifics of the tax bill." In response to critics, Kasich urged his colleagues, "Let me tell you, we all are going to have to agree to some compromise, but this is going to be a Republican agreement with tax cuts, spending restraints, real economic assumptions, and a balanced budget. Quite frankly, I'm astounded by how far we have come with this administration. We need to look at the big picture." Kasich said again, "This is not my budget. I will do my best to represent the conference. If the agreement is made, I will bring it back to the conference and I will tell you the good parts and the bad parts, and you can accept it or reject it."

On Thursday evening, with all but the precise details of the tax package complete, Raines and Hilley met with House Democrats to describe the budget and ask for their endorsement. The deal would likely include a net tax cut of between $80 and $90 billion, $115 billion in savings in Medicare (including $5 billion from an increase in the premium for physician care), $23 billion in savings in Medicaid by employing a per capita spending cap, and a .15 percent reduction in the CPI. At that point, negotiators were still squabbling over discretionary spending and taxes. Congressional Democrats continued to voice anger over the proposed agreement. In spite of President Clinton's attempt to assuage liberals by saying he would not accept an agreement unless a majority of Democrats could vote for it, at best, Democrats were divided on the budget deal. Moderates generally favored the agreement, while liberals were downright opposed to it. Liberals were clearly left out of the process, and they were dissatisfied with the results. The White House ignored their pleas for more cuts in defense spending, exacted no clear promises regarding the distribution of the tax cuts, failed to ensure that the tax cuts would not lead to huge revenue losses in the future, compromised too much on discretionary and entitlement spending, and agreed to a CPI adjustment.[19] One Democratic member described the reaction of his liberal colleagues:

> Well, I think you would have to say we were poorly served. It was sort of like, "I've decided to move you out of the house and you've got 15 minutes to pack your shit." What are we supposed to say? Why do you bother coming to us now? You didn't think it was important to come to us earlier. You cut the deal. There was no room to do anything. They hardly consulted John Spratt. House Democrats were left out of it totally.[20]

Another Democrat noted: "It was a pretty hostile caucus, because the members thought the White House had given in. A lot of members voiced frustration and they were distrustful of the White House. They didn't think the White House was forthcoming."[21]

After leaving the meeting, House Minority Whip David Bonior (D-Mich.) told reporters: "It stinks. It's not a good budget. It helps people at the top."[22] Bonior felt that the president "will not have the support of the majority of the Democratic Party. This deal does not speak to what the majority of Democrats are all about in this country."[23] Senior Democrat David R. Obey (Wis.) echoed Bonior's prediction: "I do not believe the majority of Democrats will vote for this turkey." Barney Frank (D-Mass.) said House Democrats tried to get the president to change his mind: "I sent the president a letter. . . . The problem was we addressed it to the Democratic president of the United States, and it came back addressee unknown."[24] Henry Waxman (D-Calif.) complained: "The combination of last year's welfare bill and the [proposed] cap on Medicaid will mean more harm will have been done by President Clinton to poor people than by President Reagan and President Bush. It's unworthy of a Democratic president."[25] Minority Leader Gephardt lamented that the White House "cut out a large part of the Congress. . . . Clearly the administration has to work with a Republican majority—I understand that. . . . But we have a pretty healthy minority."[26]

The reaction was much more positive at two House Republican Conference meetings on 1 May, where Kasich described the main components of the agreement. Republicans were happy to achieve three major objectives: a balanced budget, tax cuts, and a ten-year extension on the solvency of the Medicare Trust Fund. Billy Tauzin (R-La.), a former Democrat and cochair of the moderate Mainstream Republican Alliance, believed the deal would gain widespread support and praised the president for listening to moderate Democrats. Even fiscal conservatives looked favorably on the agreement. House Budget Committee deficit hawk Mark Neumann (R-Wis.) said: "I would believe we'd have taken the first step in moving in the right direction for our country."[27] Republican leaders were so enthusiastic about the agreement that on Thursday evening, before the agreement was completed, Republican Conference Chairman John Boehner (Ohio) faxed talking points to all members, entitled "A Historic Plan to Balance the Budget."

On 2 May, leaders from both parties celebrated the agreement with separate press conferences. Speaker Gingrich called the agreement "the completion of the Contract with America." Senator Domenici, making reference to the Sisyphus-like task he had labored over for years, announced: "The rock is to the top, the budget is balanced, and the American people are going to be grateful." President Clinton and Senator Lott were more reserved. Clinton said, "Everyone could find something that he or she wishes were in the budget. There is no perfect agreement." But he believed the agreement marked a "balanced budget, with balanced values." Lott said the agreement was an example of how the parties "listened to the American people" who wanted both sides "to work together to finish the job of balancing the budget."[28]

Not Quite Done

But the disappointment expressed by Democrats on Thursday and the hype reported on Friday were premature. A Republican staff person recalled:

> The staff were sitting in Domenici's hideaway in the Capitol trying to work out some details of the basic agreement. We still had not agreed on the deficit path (our members wanted declining deficits each year for five years) and we were not in agreement

on several other issues. Anyway, literally during the staff meeting, someone came in (it was around 1:00 or so) and said there is going to be announcement that afternoon that an agreement was made. So we looked at each other and said, "Well, we might as well end this meeting." We were not in balance at that point. But they went ahead and announced it before the deal was done.[29]

The remaining work stemmed from two sources: final details about what the two sides had agreed to in terms of taxes and discretionary spending and final spending, revenue, and deficit calculations in the light of a last-minute adjustment in economic assumptions. On 30 April, the CBO contacted budget committee staff directors Bill Hoagland and Rick May to explain how the improved economy had generated an estimated $45 billion in new revenues for the current fiscal year. Hoagland described their response:

> Before CBO reported, we had an agreement on paper, we had the estimates, we were there. Then we got the call that the new CBO numbers were in. I didn't want to hear that, because I felt strongly that as soon as members heard there would be proposals for less spending cuts or more tax cuts. It would make the job harder. I knew that even if we could get to balance in 2002, then no one should assume we have solved the fiscal problems of this country. So I thought anything additional we could do that could keep the pressure on would only be to our benefit after the 2002 window. Then word got out about the new estimates and we just needed to work through it.[30]

After the *Wall Street Journal* reported the story, John Hilley contacted Hoagland, and both men agreed the new information could be a "deal breaker."[31] During the Thursday night meeting with Democrats, Raines and Sperling were stunned to hear a rumor from a Democratic staff person that the CBO had underestimated annual government revenues by $45 billion.[32] Over five years, that amounted to $225 billion more in revenues than the CBO had predicted in March. In the light of the new revenues, liberal Democrats argued that it made no sense to adjust the CPI, cap Medicaid spending, and raise Medicare premiums, and they urged Raines to add spending for domestic programs.

The timing of the new revenue estimates generated speculation about the motives of the CBO and the authenticity of the calculations. Since the CBO was not scheduled to make a report on the economy until July, some believed the timing was purposeful. The new numbers presumably allowed the White House and congressional Republicans to resolve their differences over economic assumptions, balance the budget on paper without further policy changes, and make it easier for negotiators to complete the agreement. But this rumor was incorrect. Treasury Secretary Robert Rubin pointed out: "We had a deal even before the new CBO numbers. Coming as it did at the end like that . . . was useful, but not essential."[33] Hoagland made a similar point:

> Once the new data were made available, it did not change things that much. We had already begun in the Spring to look at an issue having to do with wages (income shares) to GNP. And we agreed that the OMB economists appeared to be closer to the real numbers than CBO. So we had already built into our plan a technical adjustment—it added up to something like $120 billion. All the CBO study did was validate an assumption we had already worked out with the administration.[34]

When White House officials and Republican negotiators met Thursday evening (1 May), they were lukewarm about changing the original agreement. Both sides feared they could never accommodate the interests of Democrats who wanted to spend the additional revenues and Republicans who wanted to cut taxes. Hilley later indicated to Kasich and Domenici that he did not want to change a thing, but something had to be done to placate House Democrats. Based on the Democrats' reaction to the original plan, Hilley was certain most Democrats would vote against it. Perhaps with a few compromises the president could make good on his commitment to get a majority of Democrats to support the budget agreement. In defense of the position taken by House Democrats, Vice-President Gore strongly advocated dropping the cap on Medicaid spending, the Medicare premium, and the CPI adjustment. Domenici and Kasich opposed removing those three provisions because they both wanted significant entitlement savings. But they were aware of concerns within their own party about the change in the CPI and the cap on Medicaid spending, so they went along. They also added some spending for transportation and defense, and the rest went toward deficit reduction (see table 5.2).

Agreeing to those decisions was easier than working out the details of how the changes affected budget calculations. The ambiguity surrounding the allocation of the $225 billion revenue windfall raised additional concerns about the precise nature of the agreement. The new CBO numbers opened up Pandora's box; it gave those who were not satisfied with the agreement an opportunity to press for more specific language in the agreement.

Table 5.2
Distribution of the $225 Billion in Additional Revenues
from CBO Revision of Economic Assumptions

$120 billion	Already assumed by negotiators as part of an agreement to use OMB estimates of income shares
$20 billion	By dropping from the agreement a .15 percentage change in the CPI
$18 billion	Spending increases over the original agreement for defense, Medicaid, and highway spending
$67 billion	Applied to the deficit as a result of changes in baseline estimates

Source: Rick May, "CBO's Revenue Estimates," *House Budget Committee Memorandum,* 15 May 1997.

The Devil in the Details

For two weeks, the bipartisan spirit display on 2 May gave way to hard bargaining and partisan rhetorical clashes. Each side immediately gave different and, in some areas, conflicting interpretations of the agreement. On 4 May, the Democratic staff of the House Budget Committee released a "Preliminary Summary of the 1998 Budget Agreement" including an extensive list of specific programs funded in the budget. On 5 May, the House Budget Committee issued a memo to committee Republicans classifying the major policy issues in the Balanced Budget Plan of 1997 into three categories: "assumed and agreed to," "not explicitly assumed," and "still to be determined." As table 5.3 (p. 88) illustrates, the two sides had very different understandings about what had been agreed to. Similar disagreements existed between Senate Democrats and Senate Republicans. In addition to the differences displayed in table 5.3, Democrats provided more specific information about spending and policy in Medicare benefits, Pell grants, the president's *America Reads Challenge,* expansion of Head Start, SSI benefits to legal immigrants, SSI coverage for children with disabilities, and cleanup of Superfund sites. Republicans refuted Democratic claims that the agreement contained specific commitments to increase Pell grants and accelerate cleanup of more Superfund sites. Republicans also pointed out that they did not agree to abandon efforts to prevent a future government shutdown with an automatic continuing resolution. Party leaders traded accusations almost daily until the details were finally settled. In one case, Gephardt charged: "We are still in the dark about the details of this budget." And "I think [Republicans are] trying to rewrite this agreement, in many important respects." Domenici responded, "That is not the case. Gephardt is looking for more time. We're going to get this done next week. To my knowledge, nobody's trying to change anything major in this, notwithstanding Mr. Gephardt."[35]

Table 5.3

Differences in Republican and Democratic Versions
of the 1997 Budget Agreement as of 5 May 1997 (selected items)

Taxes

Republican version	*Democratic version*
1. Net tax relief of $250 billion over 10 years.	1. Net tax relief of *up to* $250 billion over 10 years.
2. Assumes targeted tax relief for HOPE scholarships but the amount and the specific tax policy mechanism have not been finalized.	2. No specific details other than a tax cut of roughly $35 billion over 5 years for postsecondary education at the request of the president.

Spending

Republican version	*Democratic version*
1. Civil service: still to be determined.	1. Assumes the president's proposal to increase employee and agency contributions to the federal retirement systems. Federal employees would contribute more toward their retirement starting January 1999. The agreement also eliminates reimbursement to the U.S. Postal Service for the ongoing cost of pre–July 1971 workers' compensation liabilities. The budget agreement does not assume the three-month COLA delay for civilian retirees proposed in the president's budget.

Table 5.3 (Continued)

2. Veterans' benefits: still to be determined.	2. Accepts the president's proposal to the Department of Veterans Affairs (VA) to keep receipts it collects from private insurance companies for care that is unconnected with military service it provides to veterans. The VA would also retain copayments it collects. Currently, the VA retains only the portion of the receipts required to cover the administrative costs of collecting them.
3. Spectrum auctions: still to be determined.	3. The budget agreement calls for approximately $36 billion in revenue over 5 years. Sources of the new revenue include broadening and extending FCC auction authority, auctioning 120 MHz of nonbroadcast spectrum, auctioning some of the broadcast spectrum currently used for channels 60–69 (while reserving a portion for public safety uses), auctioning 78 MHz of spectrum currently used for analog television broadcasts, and auctioning toll-free vanity telephone numbers.

Sources: House Committee on the Budget, "The Balanced Budget Plan of 1997"; Majority Caucus, 5 May 1997; and Democratic Staff of the House Budget Committee, "Preliminary Summary of the 1998 Budget Agreement," www.house.gov/budget_democrats.

Democrats in Congress insisted that the White House procure a written summary of details. John Spratt (D-S.C.) diligently pursued more specific language because he knew Republicans would have a huge advantage once they began drafting the legislation to implement the agreement. Ben Cardin (D-Md.), a member of both Budget and Ways and Means, noted:

> I was not convinced of the budget agreement on the day it was announced. Spratt did an outstanding job throughout the whole process, but especially at the end. Democratic members said we need to nail down a lot of specifics. We were convinced we would be had if we didn't have the specific points in the agreement. I also think the explosion on Thursday night [1 May] convinced the White House we needed specifics.[36]

The partisan wrangling about what was and what was not in the agreement overlaid an important institutional fact. Democrats understood that while the general priorities contained in the agreement were important, the most critical stage of the budget process came after Congress passed the budget resolution. During reconciliation, congressional committees reconcile the goals of the budget resolution with specific changes in existing law. Thus, once the agreement was finalized, the strategic situation would shift from presidential-congressional negotiations to Congress, especially congressional committees that write legislation. For example, it is one thing to agree that $35 billion in tax breaks will go toward tuition assistance for higher education; it is another thing to determine who is eligible, how much each person will be eligible for, how the tax credits will be structured, and the like. As the minority party in Congress, Democrats knew it was in their best interest to work out as many specific details as they could while the two parties were negotiating the budget agreement. Senate Minority Leader Tom Daschle remarked as the negotiations were drawing to a close: "I want to see the specifics of the tax cuts."[37]

Conversely, since Republican committee chairs were not directly involved in the negotiations, they wanted a general agreement so they would have more discretion over the legislative details. Here is a sample of how committee chairs reacted to the agreement:

- Congressman Bill Archer (R-Tex.), chair of the House Ways and Means Committee: "Crucial tasks lie ahead. The Ways and Means Committee will write the policies and determine the details necessary to carry its part of the budget resolution."[38]

- Congressman Bud Shuster (R-Pa.), chair of the House Transportation Committee, in a letter to Republican leaders: "I am shocked to learn that specific funding levels were agreed to for transportation *without any consultation with me*. In fact, my staff was told by the leadership staff the exact opposite—that there were not specific agreements regarding transportation."[39]

- Congressman Robert L. Livingston (R-La.), chair of the House Appropriations Committee: "There are programs they have on a wish list that would have difficulty passing. We have to go through the regular appropriations process. The budget agreement sets the parameters. You're setting the goal posts. You can get to the goal line many different ways."[40]

Republican leaders also came to the aid of the committee chairs. Senator Lott indicated, "We're keeping our cool" about the "false claims" made by Democrats regarding a 9 percent increase in spending for EPA enforcement, increases in spending for several national parks, $668 million for energy efficiency, and $330 million for solar energy. Lott noted, "You can't get to that degree of specific-ity in a budget resolution." As for taxes, Lott was satisfied with a general agree-ment: "We did not and we cannot tell the [Senate] Finance Committee that, okay, you've got to do 'x' amount. The president cannot expect to get every dotted 'i' and crossed 't.'"[41]

By 7 May, the rumors and conflicting press reports led Chairman Kasich to convene a meeting of Republicans on the House Budget Committee to explain the current situation and reassure his colleagues.[42] Kasich entered the meeting late, visibly exhausted from long meetings, tense conversation, and sleep depriva-tion. His remarks clearly reflected realist expectations of the budget process. He began by saying: "Some stuff is not done. Some stuff Newt and Lott have to do." He explained how the new CBO estimates of future revenues were worked into the budget agreement and concluded: "This is the only town in America where you get cursed by good news." Then "I understand some people are worried the deficit goes up the first year, and I know the deficit path is important, but let's not get hung up on that. Look, this is a Republican deal; it has $600 billion in entitle-ment savings over ten years, $250 billion in tax cuts, the largest Medicare savings in history." On discretionary spending: "When you take Section 8 housing out, which frankly this committee has struggled with for three years, and add in the education and environmental pieces the president wanted, the rest is a freeze." Moreover, "The alternative is worse. If we did it alone, the Senate would never have gone for our committee budget [which froze discretionary spending]. Medi-care would be $100 billion tops. And, we would be fighting among ourselves." Then Kasich explained the fallout from the CBO revenue estimates:

> Let me tell you what happened [1 May]. The per capita cap on Medicaid was dropped; it is opposed by the governors, including Republicans, and probably would have been knocked out with an amendment in the Senate. And, the CPI was a problem. I knew that from talking with you on this committee. Most of you didn't support it. . . . Besides, the leadership wanted it out. The votes aren't there on the CPI. So when the CBO numbers came in, we dropped the CPI and the per capita cap. We spent a little more for defense and transportation, which came from on high. Most of it went to fill the hole in the deficit. By the way, this is not the end of the day. I'm glad everyone realizes we have not solved the problem with the baby boomers. The plan is to get this much banked. Then we can begin to push the envelope. My understanding is the Democrats on the left are going bonkers.

Some members expressed concerns over parts of the agreement or the process. Kasich confidently responded, though at times he lost his patience. Other members complimented Kasich and stressed the positive aspects of the agreement. David Hobson (R-Ohio), Kasich's closest confidant on the committee, ended the meeting: "This has been a positive meeting. I just wanted to say, we seem to be having a hard time being winners. It's gonna work out. Let's focus on what is right."

As negotiators were working through the details of the bipartisan agreement, Republicans in Congress were passing legislation that clearly reflected the distrust that goes with divided government. On 8 May, the Senate passed an "emergency" supplemental spending bill providing aid for flood victims in the Midwest and support for troops in Bosnia. The bill also contained a provision that guaranteed an automatic continuing resolution (CR) in case some of the appropriations bills for the upcoming fiscal year were not passed by Congress and signed into law. The idea of an "automatic CR" emanated from the crisis of 1995, when the government shut down after President Clinton vetoed appropriations bills passed by congressional Republicans. Republicans wanted to avoid that situation again by allowing government agencies to continue receiving funds at 2 percent less than the amount they received the previous year until the Congress and the president passed a new appropriation. On 15 May, the House passed the emergency supplemental appropriations bill, along with an amendment by Congressman George Gekas (R-Pa.) to provide funds automatically for programs and agencies at 100 percent of the previous year's level of funding if no appropriations were approved by the beginning of the fiscal year. Clinton promised to veto any legislation that included an automatic CR. Ironically, later in the evening of 15 May, negotiators settled the final details of the budget agreement.

The Consequences of Bipartisan Negotiations

This chapter illustrates several key points about the realist expectations view. First, bipartisan negotiations exposed internal party tensions. Liberal and conservative members with strong principles opposed the agreement because it went too far in compromising their beliefs about tax and spending priorities. Liberal Democrats also believed the White House strategy of compromise diffused responsibility and would limit their ability to campaign effectively in the 1998 midterm congressional elections. Internal party differences are an important consequence of bipartisan policymaking. Leaders attempted to quell the differences and broaden support for the budget agreement by dropping the most controversial entitlement reforms. Accommodating competing factions within the parties limited the extent of policy change.

Second, the bipartisan goodwill developed by the negotiators could not erase the underlying policy differences and the distrust between the parties. Despite the confidence Republican policymakers had in Hilley, Raines, and Bowles, Republicans in Congress continued to worry that Clinton would back away and blame Republicans for taking extreme measures to balance the budget. Congressional Democrats, realizing that the budget agreement was just a framework for key legislative changes that ultimately would be decided by Republican-dominated committees, wanted the agreement to include very specific language about government programs and the dollar amounts to be allotted to those programs. Adding the automatic CR provision to the supplemental appropriations bill, an insurance policy that anticipated gridlock at the end of the session, also reflected the deep lack of trust between the parties.

Third, while divided government did not prohibit negotiators from reaching an agreement, it did affect strategy, policy decisions, and institutional prerogatives. Leaders understand how the institutional differences affect their leverage in the process. Once the White House signaled they wanted an agreement, Republicans had an advantage and liberal Democrats were left out of the process. The CBO disclosure of additional revenues changed the policy situation and made it possible for liberal Democrats to have their way with the CPI and the Medicaid cap. With loose ends dangling from the agreement, the strategic situation shifted again so that Democrats assumed the advantage at the end of the negotiations. Since the deal had already been publicly announced, Republicans had almost nothing to gain by prolonging the process. But the White House benefited from responding to the concerns of liberal Democrats. Ultimately, the compromise diluted the most significant changes in entitlement policy, but it made the agreement acceptable to more members.

Finally, the chapter highlights a major theme of the book: the budget process and budget policy outcomes cannot be explained with a neat, simple model. The process provides multiple opportunities for adjustment, amendment, and revision, and the budget pie can be sliced in a thousand different ways. Meanwhile, the basis for support is in flux as some demands are accommodated and others are foiled, and the budget process moves from executive-congressional bipartisan negotiations to a congressionally dominated venue and back again. When the bargaining finally ended, the process produced a plan that no one believed was perfect, but a majority thought was acceptable.

6

"Don't Let the Perfect Be the Enemy of the Good"

After five months of negotiating, bargaining, and compromising among the principals and policy leaders, the budget agreement faced its toughest test: winning the approval of majorities in the House and Senate. In Congress, the budget agreement had to be translated into a congressional budget resolution and approved by the House and Senate budget committees and passed by the House and Senate. Leaders consulted members throughout the negotiations to find out if there were any issues that might cause them to vote against the budget agreement. But they could not possibly anticipate, much less accommodate, every member's budget priorities. Thus the agreement was about to undergo careful scrutiny in the clear light of day and face challenges from powerful members of Congress who were not directly involved in negotiations. The plan could be amended in the committees or on the floor of the House or Senate, upsetting the delicate bipartisan balance struck by the negotiators.

After the details of the agreement were completed, though no one believed they had developed a perfect budget, it was a reasonable compromise. Bipartisan majorities on both the House and Senate budget committees effortlessly passed the budget resolution, and it appeared bound for smooth passage in the House and Senate. The day the House of Representatives debated the budget resolution, John Spratt (D-S.C.), the ranking Democrat on the House Budget Committee, explained why his colleagues should vote for the budget:

> We have a choice between gridlock and compromise. And what we have before us is just that, it is a compromise. It is not a perfect solution. It is the art of the possible. But if we let the perfect be the enemy of the good, we will not get anything good done on the deficit this year.[1]

Spratt, a seasoned legislator, made impeccable sense at the moment. Yet in a process where "perfection" is unattainable, members of Congress seek to represent their principles and advance their interests by choosing among competing goods. Who was to say that the compromises struck by high-level negotiators behind closed doors were the best that members of Congress could do for the country, for their respective parties, or for their constituents?

The debate over the 1997 budget agreement in Congress produced another round of uncertainty and close calls as members attempted to alter the budget to suit their values and priorities. In the House, Kasich and Spratt, the two defenders of the budget agreement, fought a classic battle of national interests versus local pork barrel, as members were tempted by the lure of transportation projects for their districts. In the Senate, transportation was also at issue, but the more formidable challenge was posed by the unlikely duo of liberal Democrat Edward Kennedy (Mass.) and conservative Republican Orrin Hatch (Utah). Kennedy and Hatch normally disagreed on virtually everything, but they both passionately supported increasing the tobacco tax to provide more health coverage for uninsured children. In both chambers, various obstacles could be overcome only with effective leadership. Party leaders presented a realist case for the budget agreement and used what political scientist Doug Arnold calls "strategies of persuasion" and "procedural strategies" for building coalitions in the legislature.[2] In both the House and Senate, leadership made the difference.

The Budget Committees

The House Budget Committee met on Friday morning, 16 May, to mark up the budget resolution.[3] Chairman Kasich's opening remarks spoke of the "long road that led to this day," reflecting the notion that balancing the budget had been a long-term process. Kasich recalled his work with former Congressman Tim Penny (D-Minn.), credited Democrats for passing the 1993 budget deal and Republicans for cutting discretionary spending in 1995, and applauded Congress and the president for enacting welfare reform in 1996. He then acknowledged the integrity of John Hilley and Frank Raines and the trust he developed in them. Kasich noted that he personally preferred more entitlement savings and larger tax cuts, but that the agreement "moves the ball forward." He highlighted several key elements of the "historic" plan: discretionary spending growth at an annual rate of less than .5 percent, the largest entitlement savings in history, and the first tax cuts in sixteen years. He emphasized the important changes in Medicare that would extend the life of the program for ten years, though he cautioned that more needed to be done as the baby boomers approach retirement. He noted that with the exceptions of Section 8 housing increases and the president's initiatives in education and the environment, the rest of the discretionary budget was frozen for five years.

Spratt also touted the merits of the plan. He praised the Clinton budget of 1993, which raised taxes on the wealthiest income earners and boosted revenues to unexpected levels over the past couple of years. Spratt conceded, "Maybe each side gave too much, but both sides agreed to get something done. It is better to do it sooner rather than later." In Spratt's view the agreement was balanced in two ways: (1) it brought the budget into balance for the first time in thirty years and (2) it was not so fixated on the deficit that other programs and priorities were forgotten.

After Spratt made his remarks, several Democrats on the Budget Committee offered amendments that reflected their principles and priorities. Jim McDermott (D-Wash.), a staunch liberal Democrat who served on both the Budget and Ways and Means Committees, introduced an amendment that "ensures tax cuts paid for in the federal budget are distributed equally to American taxpayers."[4] The amendment reflected a major concern liberal Democrats had with the budget agreement and an issue that would be raised later in the budget process when the House debated tax relief. Congressional Democrats urged the White House to use income distribution tables during negotiations with Republicans and incorporate them into the agreement. Democrats used the same tactic in 1990 after the House voted down the original budget summit agreement. But Bill Archer (R-Tex.), chairman of the House Ways and Committee, insisted that his committee should have jurisdiction over the details of the tax bill. Republicans made the same argument against McDermott's amendment, and it was rejected on a straight party-line vote, 19 yeas and 22 nays. Committee Republicans voted in unison to defeat several other Democratic amendments aimed toward increasing spending for a variety of social programs. The House Budget Committee approved the budget resolution by a vote of 31–7; all the Republicans voted for it, 11 Democrats voted for and 7 voted against.

The Senate Budget Committee marked up the budget resolution on Monday afternoon, 19 May, with little dissent.[5] Domenici and Lautenberg praised the bipartisan spirit of the negotiations and asked for the support of their colleagues. Domenici said the budget represented a response to the message voters sent in the 1996 elections for the parties to work together. Lautenberg agreed: "While no one should see this as a perfect agreement, everyone should see it as a good agreement."[6] After passing a few nonbinding "sense of Senate" amendments, the Senate Budget Committee approved the document by a vote of 17–4. Unlike the House Committee vote, where Republicans unanimously supported the budget, in the Senate two conservative Republicans, Phil Gramm (Tex.) and Rod Grams (Minn.), voted against it. Gramm was an outspoken critic of the budget agreement all along and Grams opposed the budget because he said it did not "shrink" the federal government, the tax cuts were too small, and it did nothing significant to reform Medicare. Democrats Paul Sarbanes (Md.) and Ernest Hollings (S.C.) also voted against it.

All Politics Is Local—Sometimes

The smooth passage of the budget agreement through the House and Senate budget committees belied the potential obstacles it would face on the floors of the House and Senate. In the House, the budget resolution faced a formidable foe: pork-barrel projects. The former Democratic Speaker of the House, Tip O'Neill, was fond of saying, "All politics is local." Political scientists have written widely on the subject of satisfying the "folks back home" with good constituent service, frequent contact with the voters, and of course, securing federal projects for the district.[7] Pork-barrel politics have been around forever and show no signs of ending.[8] The attraction of additional transportation spending for district pork-barrel projects posed a serious challenge to the 1997 budget. In the end, after a vigorous effort by Republican leaders, the House rose above local politics and supported the budget resolution by the narrowest of margins.

Weighing the Choices: Kasich, Shuster-Oberstar, and CATs

The procedural rule for considering the House Budget Committee's budget resolution (H.Con.Res. 84) on the House floor allowed five substitute amendments: three sponsored by Democrats, one by conservative Republicans (CATs), and a bipartisan substitute offered by Bud Shuster (R-Pa.) and Jim Oberstar (D-Minn.), the chair and ranking members of the House Transportation and Infrastructure Committee. Kasich, the sponsor of H.Con.Res. 84, was mildly concerned with the conservative alternative offered by the CATs, but it turned out that the Shuster-Oberstar substitute was the bigger threat to H.Con.Res. 84. The cosponsors contended, among other things, that the "budget deal is a bad deal for transportation," and the "will of the House is ignored" because it does not allow the Congress to use a $24 billion surplus in the transportation trust fund for highway projects.[9] The Shuster-Oberstar substitute increased outlays for highway spending by $12 billion over five years and paid for it with an across-the-board reduction in all discretionary spending and tax cuts. Why $12 billion? The CBO estimated that the Transportation Trust Fund surplus would grow from $25 billion to $37 billion over the next five years, and "honest" budgeting dictated that the additional money should be used for transportation projects, not deficit reduction.

While the Shuster-Oberstar substitute changed only $12 billion in the budget agreement, the political ramifications of shifting priorities toward transportation were potentially devastating. If the Shuster-Oberstar substitute passed, the delicate balance of Republican and Democrat priorities reached over four months of negotiations would be upset by the first act of the whole House. The president could easily withdraw support because the substitute cut his spending priorities in exchange for transportation funding he opposed. Moreover, the Senate would have license to change the terms of the budget agreement when it took up the budget resolution later that week. In the words of supporters of the budget agreement, Shuster-Oberstar was a "deal breaker." Kasich commented later on the ramifications of losing the vote on Shuster-Oberstar: "Almost lost the whole deal. I think it would have devastated the whole process. The whole thing would have been obliterated."[10]

Though it was hard to tell how many House Republicans would support Shuster-Oberstar, it was clear that Shuster meant business. In a letter to Speaker Gingrich on 6 May, after the budget deal was originally announced, Shuster emphasized that the numbers allotted to funding transportation projects were "UN-ACCEPTABLE" and would make it "virtually impossible" to meet transportation needs.[11] Ideally, Shuster wanted to increase annual spending for transportation from $20 billion to $32 billion in fiscal year 1998 alone. The next day, at a Republican conference meeting, Shuster complained vehemently about how the constraints of the budget agreement undercut the nation's transportation needs. At Gingrich's request, budget negotiators marginally increased the amount of spending for transportation as they worked through the details of the budget agreement, but neither Kasich nor Clinton saw transportation as a priority. The budget agreement ultimately assumed an increase of $8.8 billion in outlays above current spending levels over five years, well below Shuster's expectations.

Numbers, politics, and the urgency of passing a reauthorization bill to provide federal funding for transportation projects gave Shuster and Oberstar the capability of upsetting the budget resolution. The Transportation and Infrastructure Committee, with seventy-three members (forty Republicans and thirty-three Democrats) is, by far, the largest committee on Capitol Hill. The committee's task for the 105th Congress was to draft a reauthorization of the 1991 Intermodal Surface Transportation and Efficiency Act (ISTEA). Funds for transportation projects under ISTEA were due to expire on 30 September 1998, just before the next midterm congressional elections. Reauthorization of ISTEA was a powerful magnet for members of Congress seeking federal funds for their districts. By March, at least 388 out of 435 members of the House submitted to the committee over 1,500 requests for projects, and 181 members presented a case for their projects in person at hearings held by the Transportation and Infrastructure subcommittee on surface transportation.[12] Obviously, Shuster was well positioned to do favors for a lot of members.

The contrast between Kasich's budget resolution and the Shuster-Oberstar alternative offered a tailor-made case study for theories of legislative politics that rely on the reelection motives of individual members of Congress. One Budget Committee staff person described the sharp contrast in the political value of the two alternatives:

> When you look at Shuster-Oberstar, the most important thing you need to realize is that members are concerned about representing their districts. And they weighed the choice. "Here is this theoretical budget deal that's got all of this stuff in it. I don't know what it means to me politically. Am I gonna get beat up for cutting Medicare? And here is Shuster. He can build a bridge in my district, or he can give me a road. Now, when I go back home, what is going to be more important, me standing in front of a ribbon cutting ceremony, or me talking about some budget deal?"

> And members make the logical choice. "My constituents have wanted this bridge for ten years, I'll be a big hero if I can get them this bridge!" No one cares about the budget. These are human beings who want to be liked by people. You hear some members who come up here and say, "Well I came here to make the tough choices, and I'm going to do what is right, and I don't care if I get beat up." In most cases, that's bull. The fact is the whole place is designed to get them reelected. Members are going to respond to what is in the members' best interests.[13]

Shuster and Oberstar devised an aggressive strategy for passing their budget resolution. Shuster met with transportation lobbyists on 19 May, and committee staff assigned lobbyists to contact members with whom they had close ties. Lobbyists arranged for national- and state-level alliances of transportation contractors to call members' offices and send letters urging support for Shuster-Oberstar. In addition to scores of transportation groups, Shuster had the backing of the National Association of Manufacturers.[14] In some cases contractors called members to express their worries that if the congressman voted against Shuster-Oberstar, Shuster would retaliate by denying projects they requested from the authorization bill. Committee staff ran a whip operation calling members' offices to find out whether they planned to vote for the substitute.

House Republican Party whips met on 20 May to discuss the budget resolution and its alternatives.[15] Ernest Istook (Okla.) made the case for the Conservative Action Team's (CAT's) budget substitute. Istook said he did not want to be the "skunk at the garden party," but the CATs opposed the budget agreement because the deficit would grow in the first year, spending would increase, and tax cuts were too small. The CAT's budget cut an additional $109.3 billion from nondefense, nontransportation discretionary spending over five years and shifted the savings to tax relief. John Doolittle (Calif.) sponsored the CAT's budget, and it received the active support of Istook, David McIntosh (Ind.), and Matt Salmon (Ariz.). CATs had the support of Gary Bauer and the Family Research Council, an ultraconservative organization, and won the endorsement of the *Washington Times*.[16]

Several Budget Committee members defended Kasich's budget resolution by pointing out that the entitlement savings and tax cuts were real, and that no alternative would get Clinton's support. One member almost perfectly described the political advantage of a diffusion of responsibility:

> I am behind this for political reasons as well as policy. We need to sell this. You know I thought about how this might be different if Dole were president. Just think about it, $115 billion in Medicare savings, which they would have called "cuts" and $135 billion in tax cuts. Can you imagine what they would be doing to us if this was a Republican-only plan? They would be killing us. Clinton gives us the cover we need to do some things. I think this is better than if Dole were president.

A few skeptical members wanted to hear from the party leaders. Majority Whip Tom DeLay (Tex.), a staunch conservative Republican, made a strong speech in favor of the agreement and provided a counterweight to the CAT's budget. "When I came here in 1985, I didn't think this type of budget was possible. I have heard people say the tax cuts are too small, but anytime I can get a tax cut, I'm going to take it."

Kasich continued to emphasize the Republican aspects of the budget agreement (entitlement savings, conservative economic projections, and slow growth in discretionary spending) and the necessity for compromise. Despite criticisms from conservatives, Kasich said: "Republicans should be elated about this budget." He also did not pass up the chance to defend his own record as a fiscal conservative. "You know, I hear about conservatives saying they want to cut more spending, but every time I go to the floor, we can't get 100 votes for spending cuts. I say to those who want to cut more, let's do it. I'm with you. There is nothing in this budget that says we can't cut more, but that means we have to do it, we have to work hard every day to cut appropriations." He added, "My only regret was that we dropped the CPI out of the original plan. But, you know what? All the people who talk about being fiscal conservatives who want to cut spending didn't want the CPI changes."[17] Finally, "Is this all of it? No. Of course, there is more to do. But this is a beginning."

Then Kasich defended the budget agreement against the alternatives. With respect to the Shuster-Oberstar substitute: "I'd be astounded if people are going to let this deal unravel to get a few tons of asphalt poured in their districts." As far as the CATs budget, "If it passes, you have to keep in mind, we'll get nothing—no tax cuts, no entitlement savings, no balanced budget." Finally, he returned to his original point: "I just hope everyone will stop and look at the positive accomplishments of this budget. Recognize that it contains an average of .5 percent growth in nondefense spending, but that you want to do more. It has tax cuts, but you want to do more. It cuts entitlement spending, but you want to do more. I want to do more, but this is what we can do today."

Debate and Amendment in the House

The debate on the rule for debating and amending the budget resolution began at 2:00 p.m. on Tuesday, 20 May, and the final vote on the budget resolution was not done until 3:00 a.m. the next morning. Under the rule, if any one of the five substitute amendments were adopted, the House would immediately vote on final passage of the budget resolution. Since Kasich's budget (H.Con.Res. 84) was scheduled last, all the substitutes would have to be rejected in order for the budget agreement to have a chance of winning the endorsement of the House. Doolittle's budget and the three Democrat substitutes sponsored by Maxine Waters (Calif.), George Brown (Calif.), and Joseph Kennedy (Mass.) reflected the contrasting principles and priorities within and across the two parties and gave nearly every member a balanced-budget proposal to support.[18] All four substitutes produced a balanced budget, but they did so in different ways, with the Democrats providing liberal alternatives and CATs representing the most conservative position. All substitutes were defeated easily, but the Shuster-Oberstar substitute presented a major challenge.

During general debate on the budget resolution, Minority Leader Gephardt made the signature address in opposition to the budget agreement. Gephardt said he was not opposed to balancing the budget, and he praised the efforts made by Democrats in 1990 and 1993 to make the tough choices in taxes and spending that made a balanced budget possible. But he disagreed with the priorities in the agreement and the way it balanced the budget. "In my view, this budget agreement is a budget of many deficits: a deficit of principle, a deficit of fairness, a deficit of tax justice, and worst of all, a deficit of dollars."[19] Though Gephardt spoke from the heart, he had political reasons for opposing the budget agreement as well. The minority leader made no secret of his differences with the White House over the strategy of working with Republicans, and he frequently expressed his dismay about being shut out of the negotiations. Moreover, Gephardt was seen as the only major potential challenger to Vice-President Al Gore in the Democratic field of presidential contenders for the 2000 presidential election. By opposing the budget agreement, Gephardt could draw a line between himself and Gore and solidify his credentials with labor union leaders, who also opposed the agreement. Gephardt's opposition to the agreement was important because it meant the Democratic Party leadership would not work to defeat Shuster-Oberstar, the biggest threat to the budget agreement.

Meanwhile, Shuster's lobbying strategy apparently was working. Ray LaHood (R-Ill.), a member of the Transportation and Infrastructure Committee, indicated that the pressure to vote along with Shuster was intense: "Shuster has made it very clear this is a defining vote for every member's project, road, or bridge. I'm telling you, this is a big vote for a lot of members. There is a lot of heartburn and anxiety around here."[20] As the House debated the various substitute amendments, Republican Party leaders met at about 4:00 p.m. and surmised that Shuster was going to win by a healthy margin.

Gingrich called the White House and told them they needed at least sixty Democrats to defeat the Shuster-Oberstar substitute. Raines faxed a letter to all House Democrats stating that the administration "strongly opposes" the substitute. "If adopted, this amendment would be a breach of the Bipartisan Agreement and would, therefore, significantly reduce the chances of balancing the budget."[21] But Raines also informed Gingrich that House Democrat leaders were not interested in working to defeat Shuster-Oberstar, and he could not guarantee that sixty Democrats would vote against it.

Republicans held a conference around 10:00 p.m. and did a whip check.[22] At that point, they were about fifty votes shy of defeating Shuster-Oberstar. Kasich reminded members how far they had come in the negotiations, warned them that if Shuster-Oberstar passed, the process would unravel, and asked them to rise above district interests. Speaker Gingrich, Majority Leader Dick Armey, and Majority Whip Tom DeLay pleaded with members to vote against Shuster-Oberstar. They said the Democrats were going to throw their support behind Shuster-Oberstar and, even if it passed, it would not go anywhere in the Senate. They also called the vote a test of the party's ability to govern.

Kenny Hulshof (R-Miss.), president of the freshman class, also spoke. Hulshof explained that he was as vulnerable to electoral defeat as anyone in the room, having been elected in 1996 with 49.5 percent and less than 6,000 votes to spare. A piece of the transportation bill would certainly improve his chances of getting reelected, but Hulshof argued that this vote is bigger than a transportation project. He asked his colleagues to think about the country and the message that voters sent in the 1996 elections that they wanted the parties to work together to balance the budget.

Republican leaders knew they needed more than fine speeches to turn around the vote. According to one staff person involved in the whip operation, "They whipped the vote hard. Sometimes members from marginal districts are left alone, but not this time."[23] The strategy was to rely on personal contacts, integrity, and protection against retribution for voting against Shuster-Oberstar. After the conference, party leaders enlisted all committee chairs and party whips with close personal ties to members leaning in favor of Shuster-Oberstar and prepared them to make the case for the budget agreement. There were no threats or promises, just a compelling argument for the budget resolution. They explained to members that Shuster-Oberstar was a deal breaker because the president would not accept its terms, and all the progress made in the negotiations would be squandered if it passed. DeLay later commented, "We asked them to really think about the big picture [of the budget deal] and not to think about getting a road or a highway" in their district.[24]

For protection against retaliation from Shuster, the leaders told members they would use a House rule to undercut Shuster's main source of power. A House rule concerning the Transportation and Infrastructure Committee states, "it shall not be in order for any bill providing general legislation in relation to roads to contain any provision for any specific road." Applying this rule would prohibit Shuster from drafting legislation containing specific transportation projects. Of course, a majority of the House could vote to waive the rule, but party leaders told wary members that if Shuster retaliated against them for opposing his substitute amendment, they would work to defeat the waiver.[25]

While the threat of Shuster-Oberstar rested on the political appeal of pork-barrel projects, Shuster framed the issue in national and moral terms. "All across America, our infrastructure is crumbling," he said. He articulated the national need for more highway spending to lower traffic fatalities, reduce congestion in cities, expedite commerce, and keep up with global competitors.[26] Finally, he asserted the prerogative of members of Congress to shape the budget priorities the way they liked.

> I would respectfully suggest that it insults the intelligence of the members to say that one-third of 1 percent cut over 5 years is going to break this deal when the bottom line remains the same. What are we, potted plants? Can we not, as members of Congress, make a very modest adjustment so long as the bottom line

numbers stay the same? . . . I believe we have every right as duly elected members of Congress to make such a modest perfecting amendment.[27]

Spratt tried to appeal to Democrats by emphasizing that the "adjustments" from Shuster-Oberstar did considerable damage to hard-fought Democratic priorities contained in the budget agreement. Spratt defended the negotiations process and emphasized to Democrats that the budget agreement was a balanced package that contained initiatives they "could not have accomplished on our own as a minority party in this House and in this Congress." Spratt calmly, carefully, and meticulously pointed to a chart prepared by Budget Committee staff that listed the spending reductions that would ensue as a result of the across-the-board cuts in the Shuster-Oberstar substitute. Spratt pointed out: "We are talking about deep and disruptive cuts here. And here they are individually, and I ask my colleagues, particularly those on my side of the aisle, to bear these reductions in mind." Spratt emphasized cuts in education ($980 million) and income-support programs, such as Section 8 housing and WIC ($860 million).[28]

The debate on the budget resolution came to a dramatic end as Oberstar and Kasich delivered dueling speeches which captured the tension between particular interests and the national interest. The hour was late, and most members remained in the House after the previous vote to listen to the last few speakers. Oberstar addressed the House with an indignant tone to his booming voice:

"A deal is a deal," intoned our colleague from North Dakota a few hours ago. "Do not break the deal," says a panicked White House. "Stick to the deal," says the Committee on the Budget leadership on both sides. Whose deal, I ask my colleagues? Who was part of this deal? Not me, and not very many in this Chamber. We did not have much to say about the deal, so why are we being asked to stick with it?

Our deal is with our constituents. Our deal is with America's future. Either we want to be part of this process, either we want to be relevant in America, or spend the next 5 years with an oil can filling potholes in the road that we refused to rebuild, in the bridge decking that needs to be torn down and rebuilt. . . .

Tonight you are going to make a choice about the future of America. About whether we move ahead, whether that bridge to the 21st century the president talks about has some concrete and asphalt on it, whether it has some bike lanes on it, whether it has some transit buses on it, or whether it is just a chimerical bridge that exists out there in nowhere.[29]

Oberstar's speech was met with both cheers and jeers. He was followed by Spratt, who made another appeal for the budget agreement, then by Sherwood Boehlert (N.Y.), a moderate Republican on the Transportation and Infrastructure Committee, and Shuster, both of whom spoke in favor of the substitute amendment.

Finally, Kasich addressed a full House. It was now almost 3:00 a.m., and the exuberant manner that characterized the speech Kasich gave to start the debate had given way to a restrained, sober tone. The chairman was visibly exhausted and worried. Months of hard work on a bipartisan budget agreement were in jeopardy. Kasich's speech took the high ground in the debate:

> This is not about highway funds. . . .This is not about roads. This is about a team. . . .

> And, it's not about a deal. I am sorry, but it is not about a deal. It is really about an agreement. It is about a bunch of people who got sent by their troops to go and try to bring something back that could put us together for once in this House. The gentleman for South Carolina [Spratt] went to those meetings and he stood up for his colleagues. And I went to those meetings, and I stood up for my colleagues. And I remember . . . when I thought it was going to collapse, I looked at Gene Sperling and I said, "Gene, you have to reach toward me, and I am reaching toward you, because we cannot walk away from this. We cannot let this fail. Our generation owes this to the country that we will stay here and we will work it out. And we will reach an agreement, and it will be based on one thing: that it will not violate your principles and it will not violate our principles."

> Mr. Chairman, what I think this is really all about is what the country wants. They elected a Democratic president by a wide margin. They elected a House and Senate made up of the other party, and they said, put the country first, put the politics second. Pitch in and move America forward.

> Look, I respect anybody who comes to this floor. That is why I have so many friends on the other side of the aisle. I have high regard for them. I would not question their commitment to this project, or that road or this priority. But I think that our leadership has brought us something that represents an agreement that the country wants, the country supports, and something we can be proud of marching together, reaching across the aisle and holding onto one another and looking at our districts and saying, yes, I am here to represent the district, but the country, the

country wants us tonight to look beyond our district, to look to
a degree beyond our own priorities and be part of America's
team.

Kasich's speech was greeted with thunderous applause, and the House, acting in the Committee of the Whole, proceeded to vote on the Shuster-Oberstar
substitute. The atmosphere was filled with anticipation and tension as members
watched the vote tally on the electronic board. One member described it as "the
most tense day I have seen on the floor." Another said, "The tension was so thick
you could cut it."[30] The margin of yeas to nays flipped back and forth. When the
count reached 212–214, Majority Whip DeLay motioned to John Boehner, who
was presiding, to drop the gavel. Boehner looked quickly to his right and left,
hammered the gavel down, and announced, "The vote is 214–216, the amendment in the nature of the substitute is rejected." Supporters of the budget agreement celebrated, DeLay reached over and hugged a smiling Kasich, and a few
moments later Shuster shook Kasich's hand. The House rose and passed
H.Con.Res. 84 with a large bipartisan majority, 333–99; the budget agreement survived to see another day.

Explaining Shuster-Oberstar: Politics, Member Goals, and Leadership

The House's decision to reject the Shuster-Oberstar substitute poses an intriguing
problem for political theories that explain congressional decision making in terms
of "special interests" or the particular needs of members' constituents. Members
of Congress are obviously concerned about reelection, and they can improve their
electoral prospects by claiming credit for delivering federally funded projects to
their districts. At least in terms of interest-group pressure and direct benefits to a
member's constituents, the cards were stacked in favor of Shuster-Oberstar. Since
many Democrats were predisposed to vote for Shuster-Oberstar, and Republicans
held only a small margin in the House, Republican leaders had to overcome significant obstacles to defeat the substitute. So how did the House reject a budget
substitute that promised particular benefits to individual members so that a bipartisan budget resolution with general benefits could succeed?

Political scientists offer two plausible explanations. Both assign leaders a key
role in the process, and both assume that budget decisions are based on a complex mix of interests and goals. First, though members of Congress seek to improve their chances of getting reelected, reelection is not the only motive that
affects their behavior, and it is not the primary motive on every roll-call vote.[31]
Particularly on roll calls with national consequences, such as the budget resolution, members may decide on the basis of public policy or principle. Instead of

asking, "How will voting on this bill affect my chances of reelection?" some members ask, "Is this a good budget?"

In this case, party leaders recognized that appeals to party goals, national interests, or good public policy resonate with members, and certain members clearly voted against Shuster-Oberstar for those reasons. Kasich constantly talked about the broad benefits of a balanced budget and tax cuts, and he appealed to members on the grounds that the budget agreement was good for the country. Spratt pointed out that Democrats should oppose the cuts in domestic spending that resulted from Shuster-Oberstar. Hulshof's speech at the Republican conference meeting on the night of the vote reflected the perspective of members who set aside particular constituency interests on an issue of national importance. After the vote, Tillie Fowler (R-Fla.), a strong advocate of defense spending and a member of the Transportation and Infrastructure Committee, pointed out, "I just felt this country could not afford a cut in defense."[32]

A second explanation for the failure of Shuster-Oberstar is based on Douglas Arnold's theory of the "logic of collective action." Arnold is particularly interested in explaining why members of a representative body predisposed to serving particular constituent interests sometimes pass economic policies aimed toward attaining broad, national goals. Arnold assumes that members always consider the electoral consequences of voting for or against a bill, but that does not mean they will always favor particular interests over general interests. Their choices depend on whether members see a substantial difference in the electoral benefits of choosing one over the other. As Arnold explains:

> I assume that when legislators have to make a decision, they first ask which alternative contributes more to their chances for reelection. If they see a significant difference, they choose the alternative which better serves that cause. If they see no difference, they base their choice on any other criteria they find relevant—perhaps they believe one policy is more effective or desirable than another, or they wish to curry favor with the president or a party leader, or they wish to repay a past favor.[33]

Thus Arnold's theory differs somewhat from the notion that members will sometimes ignore their reelection goals in the first instance. Nevertheless, under the logic of collective action, members can ultimately choose on the basis of various goals or criteria, and they might vote in favor of general interests over particular interests.

Leaders play a key role in Arnold's theory because leaders are responsible for developing policies that are politically feasible for members to support and selling the electoral benefits of one alternative over another. By shaping the terms of the debate and making effective use of House rules, leaders can persuade members that choosing a budget that aims to produce general goods is just as politically beneficial as legislation that promises particular goods. Thus in addition to appealing to party goals and national interests, party leaders tried to convince wary members that voting against Shuster-Oberstar could help them achieve their electoral goals. Party leaders also vowed to use the rules to protect the electoral interests of members who voted against Shuster-Oberstar. In sum, as one aide working for Majority Whip DeLay pointed out: "We argued on the merits of the budget. We said this is a deal breaker, we've come too far to bust the budget, and we will protect you against retribution from Shuster if necessary."[34]

Since the party leadership estimated they needed forty to fifty votes to defeat Shuster-Oberstar at 9:00 p.m., the leadership's effective lobbying operation in the couple of hours prior to the vote—including appeals to policy and political interests, protection under the rules, and reminders of past favors—certainly swayed some members.[35] Yet the successful last-minute lobbying should be viewed as part of an ongoing strategy begun a month before the vote, when Kasich and party leaders began laying the groundwork and building support for the budget agreement. Once the general framework of the agreement was in place, Majority Whip DeLay started to "grow the vote," a term he uses to describe the process developing support for a bill. Beginning 15 April, DeLay, Chief Deputy Whip Denny Hastert (R-Ill.), and Kasich started having "listening sessions" with Republican members. They met with groups of ten or twelve members organized in various ways: regional blocs (members from the Northeast and West), issue blocs (members concerned about Medicare or civil service pensions), ideological groups (the Tuesday Lunch Bunch and CATs), and classes (sophomores and freshmen). This gave the members some input and let the leadership know about the "land mines" in the agreement. In addition to those smaller meetings, Kasich persistently tried to shape expectations about the accomplishments of the budget agreement in whip meetings and party conferences. Over and over again, he tried to convince members about the positive aspects of the budget agreement, the realities of divided government, the need to compromise in order to govern effectively, and the importance of building a successful legislative record. Undoubtedly, those efforts paid off.

Showdown in the Senate

Floor deliberations over the budget resolution in the Senate were different from those in the House. House members could only offer substitute amendments (wholesale changes in the budget resolution), and only five were voted on; the Senate permits unlimited debate and amendment for up to forty hours. Debate lasted for three days, during which time the Senate voted for over fifty amendments. Transportation funding was also an issue in the Senate, and an amendment by John Warner (R-Va.) to increase funding for transportation by $12 billion was narrowly defeated, 51–49. But the main challenge to the bipartisan budget agreement was a tobacco tax sponsored by Orrin Hatch (R-Utah) and Edward Kennedy (D-Mass.). This time the White House played a crucial role in the process, first by indicating support for the additional tax, and later by lobbying against it.

Senators Domenici and Lautenberg began general debate on the budget resolution with accolades for the bipartisan negotiations that produced the agreement. Both senators recognized the central goal of balancing the budget and preserving Medicare, and each highlighted strengths of the budget from different perspectives. Domenici praised the entitlement savings, the tax cuts, and the slower growth in discretionary spending. Lautenberg highlighted the domestic priorities funded in the budget: larger Pell grants and tax credits for higher education, Head Start, and expansion of children's health care. Both senators also pointed out their concerns with particular parts of the agreement, but they reconciled their concerns with the need to compromise. Lautenberg noted: "I don't think there's anyone who is entirely happy with this agreement. But while nobody sees it as perfect, everyone should see it as a good compromise."[36]

The agreement was opposed by the most liberal and conservative senators. Senator Paul Wellstone (D-Minn.) raised concerns about the dangers of tax cuts, the limited spending on social programs, and the fairness of the spending reductions. He closed his speech by saying that the budget "is a raw deal for too many children in America, and that makes this budget unfair and that makes this budget wrong and that makes this budget not the best we can do for our children in America."[37] Phil Gramm (R-Tex.), the most outspoken conservative critic of the budget agreement, argued that the budget spent too much, depended on the economy to come into balance, and failed to deal adequately with the future costs of Medicare.

Joe versus Joey

As the Senate proceeded to debate amendments, Hatch and Kennedy developed support for their popular amendment, which coupled the peculiar interests of a social conservative Republican from Utah with a liberal Democrat from Massachusetts. The Hatch-Kennedy amendment raised cigarette taxes by 43 cents per pack and allocated the expected $30 billion in new revenues for two purposes: $20 billion for expanding children's health coverage to uninsured children and $10 billion for additional deficit reduction. The budget agreement already included $16 billion in new spending to cover up to 4 million uninsured children, but Hatch and Kennedy contended that was not enough because it left another 6 million uninsured. The day the budget agreement came to the floor, the Hatch-Kennedy amendment had 25 cosponsors, 18 Democrats and 7 Republicans.[38]

On the morning of 21 May, as members of the House rebounded from a late night of high drama, Majority Leader Trent Lott announced the schedule for debating the budget resolution, including several key amendments by Senators Gramm, Warner, and Kennedy and Hatch. He reminded his colleagues:

> There are going to be a lot [of] appealing amendments offered today. It will be difficult to resist those. But this is a very delicately crafted budget agreement that the Republican leadership signed onto and that the Democratic leadership has agreed to.
>
> So I hope that we will continue to hold the line. If we start down the trail of changing the mix, where will it end?

Of course, members of Congress see the budget process as the means of deciding the mix of national priorities and defense of their principles. This is the perspective Senator Hatch took as he introduced the amendment: "The amendment that Senator Kennedy and I offer today addresses what I consider to be a top priority of this Congress: making sure America's kids are healthy." Hatch proceeded to frame the debate as a moral decision over whether to support the tobacco companies or children, and at the same time reduce the national debt: "Senators, who do you stand with? Joe Camel, or Joey? That is what it comes down to. What the Senate must do today is decide whether we are going to protect Joe Camel, or whether we are going to protect Joey." He also noted the practical consequences of the amendment: "The Hatch-Kennedy healthy kids amendment benefits American families, working families, so that they can get health care. The healthy kids amendment helps reduce the deficit and reduce our debt service requirement."[39]

Hatch recognized that the budget agreement contained $16 billion to deliver more health coverage to uninsured children, but he told his colleagues, "It's just not enough." Hatch noted, "As a conservative, I am generally opposed to tax increases," but he argued that the combined advantages of providing health insurance and reducing the debt were more important. Hatch cited a *Wall Street Journal* poll that showed 72 percent of Americans favored the proposal.

Senator Kennedy followed Hatch and gave a passionate and substantive speech about the "crisis" of uninsured children in working families. Kennedy argued:

> Passage of this amendment, combined with money already included in the budget agreement, can end this crisis and make this the Congress in which we guarantee every child the opportunity for a healthy start in life that should be the birthright of every child.
>
> A budget is about setting priorities. There is no more important priority than health care for our children.[40]

Republican leaders knew the amendment had a strong moral and political appeal. Moderate Republican cosponsors of the amendment believed it was the right thing to do. Other Republicans worried that voting against the amendment would make them vulnerable to the charge of siding with Joe Camel over Joey in their next campaign. Moreover, two effective senators representing entirely different constituencies were pushing the amendment. To make matters worse, rumors were circulating that Minority Leader Tom Daschle was actively lobbying for the amendment, and Vice-President Gore was prepared to cast the tie-breaking vote in favor of the amendment if necessary.

Senator Domenici's main approach was twofold: (1) to emphasize the provision in the agreement that expanded health coverage for children and (2) to stress the point that Hatch-Kennedy violated the terms of the budget agreement by lowering the net tax cuts in the plan. In response to statements by Hatch and Kennedy that their amendment was consistent with the budget agreement, Domenici said:

> Mr. President, fellow Senators, there can be no more frontal attack and violation of this agreement than this amendment. Now let me make it clear. It says that the tax cut to the American people is reduced by $30 billion. And, it also says we will spend $20 billion of that. So we are going to reduce the tax cut and spend more money. And we already cover the children in this agreement.[41]

Majority Whip Don Nickles took an even tougher stand on the effects of the Hatch-Kennedy amendment:

> I will tell you I do not think everything in this budget package is perfect, but I am absolutely certain if we pass an amendment

that increases taxes $30 billion and increases spending $20 billion over what is already in this package we don't have a deal. We just killed the budget.[42]

As the heated debate continued, Lott worked behind the scenes. He could see the pendulum swinging in favor of Hatch-Kennedy, but his outrage stemmed from news that Gore and Daschle, who had pledged support for the budget agreement, were lobbying against it. Lott called Clinton and strongly urged him to help defeat the amendment. He reported to his colleagues that while President Clinton supported the concept of Hatch-Kennedy, he had committed to working to try to get Democrats to vote against it. The majority leader explained: "I signed in on the deal and I have taken criticism for it. The President signed in on the deal, and he is going to take some criticism for it. . . . But this is clearly a deal-buster."[43]

One way to mitigate the potential adverse political consequences of voting against Hatch-Kennedy was for Lott to offer a second-degree amendment in place of Hatch-Kennedy. This amendment allowed the Senate to take a separate vote on the provision of the $16 billion for children's health coverage already contained in the agreement. If the amendment passed, it would essentially wipe clean the provisions for adding $20 billion to that original amount and would be an affirmation of support for children's health insurance. Voting for the second amendment prior to Hatch-Kennedy would insulate senators from criticism that they opposed more health care for children.

Lott told his colleagues he would continue to offer a "series of second-degree amendments, and let me assure you, each one will get hairier and more difficult for senators to vote against, more uncomfortable." Lott said he had no problems with the Senate voting on Hatch-Kennedy, as long as he knew it would be defeated. Then, in the clearest instance of "hardball politics," he guaranteed that if he was not sure the amendment would be defeated, he would pull the budget resolution off the floor.

As Lott was about to offer his amendment, Minority Leader Daschle joined the fray and heightened the tension on the Senate floor. First, Daschle pointed out problems of negotiating an agreement with just a few senators and the pitfalls that might ensue from that approach. Second, he disputed Lott's claim that Hatch-Kennedy was inconsistent with the budget agreement because it strengthened the provision in the original agreement expanding children's health insurance, it did not alter the total amount of tax cuts, and it did not increase the deficit. Finally, he said he was willing to abandon the budget agreement over this issue: "I hope we can find a way to work through this disagreement, but . . . if it means bringing down the budget resolution, as some of our colleagues have threatened, then so be it."[44]

When Daschle finished, Domenici offered the second-degree amendment that replaced the provisions in Hatch-Kennedy with the proposal adding $16 billion for children's health coverage as specified in the original agreement. Then Domenici angrily responded to Daschle's suggestion that Hatch-Kennedy was consistent with the budget agreement. He called into question the commitment of the White House and the minority leader after they had pledged to support the agreement.

As senators hotly contested the amendment, the president's team of Hilley and Raines, along with several cabinet officials, called fifteen Democratic senators to tell them the budget agreement would fail if the Hatch-Kennedy amendment passed. Meanwhile, Lott worked on several moderate Republicans who previously pledged their support for the amendment. Floor speeches by Senators John Breaux (D-La.) and Dianne Feinstein (D-Calif.) in favor of preserving the budget agreement and urging the Senate Finance Committee to take up the cigarette tax separately were clear signs that the momentum was swinging away from Hatch-Kennedy. The Senate paused from the intense debate long enough to pass Domenici's second-degree amendment, 98–2, confirming the proposal contained within the budget agreement to expand children's health coverage by $16 billion. The Senate then proceeded to defeat the Hatch-Kennedy amendment, 55–45.

As was true of Shuster-Oberstar in the House, the ground of support for Hatch-Kennedy seemed to shift at the last minute. Hatch blamed the White House for lobbying against the amendment and turning several "yes" votes to "no" votes, and he contended that the amendment would have passed if it were voted on earlier that day. He concluded: "I think the President and the people in the White House caved here, people who we had every reason to believe would be supportive of kids' health."[45] White House lobbying may have been important for three of the eight Democrats—Feinstein (Calif.), Herbert Kohl (Wis.), and Joseph Lieberman (Conn.)—who voted against the amendment. But the other five—Breaux (La.), Max Cleland (Ga.), Wendell Ford (Ky.), Hollings (S.C.), and Chuck Robb (Va.)—were either conservative or had tobacco interests in their states. It is interesting to note that four Republican cosponsors of the amendment—Ben Campbell (Colo.), Susan Collins (Me.), Olympia Snowe (Me.), and Ted Stevens (Ark.)—all voted against.

In the final analysis, Lott effectively undermined Hatch-Kennedy, first by scheduling a second-degree amendment, and then by threatening to take the budget resolution off the Senate floor. Lott was able and willing to use his scheduling powers as majority leader to force the choice between Hatch-Kennedy or the children's health provision in the budget agreement; senators who wanted both the budget agreement and more health coverage were not going to have their way. Once the budget resolution made it to the Senate floor, the strategic ground had shifted, and even senators who supported additional children's health coverage had to face the reality of the choices before them. Senator Lieberman, a supporter of expanding children's health coverage who nonetheless voted against Hatch-Kennedy, rationalized his vote this way:

> The vote I cast today was not on children's health coverage. It was not on the tobacco tax. The vote I cast today was on whether to make substantial changes in critical elements of an arduously negotiated bipartisan budget agreement. On . . . the issue of whether to risk the resolution, I felt that the amendment threatened to undo the careful balancing and months of negotiations represented by the budget compromise. In the end, the effort to increase spending, threatened the children's health care coverage that we had achieved through the negotiations.
>
> Compromise is never perfect, but perfection is rarely possible.[46]

The Senate proceeded to reject every major amendment to the budget resolution, except a few minor nonbinding "sense of the Senate" amendments, and pass the budget resolution with a large bipartisan majority, 78–22. Since there were very few differences between the House and Senate budget resolutions, after a pro forma conference with the committee chairs and ranking members of the two budget committees, each chamber voted for the conference version of the budget resolution by wide margins.

Leadership and Realist Expectations

Despite widespread bipartisan support for the budget agreement, the budget process enabled members to pursue their policy priorities and political goals in ways that could have undermined the agreement. Members are bound to take every opportunity to advance their individual priorities through the budget process, and the mix of political motives and principles posed serious obstacles for party leaders and placed the fragile bipartisan compromise in jeopardy. Leaders from different parties attempted to overcome those obstacles by taking a realist perspective. They appealed to the interests and policy goals of members in their party—Spratt reminding Democrats of how the budget agreement advanced domestic programs and Kasich highlighting the Republican achievements in the deal. They also argued that a bipartisan compromise could not possibly meet everyone's needs and that amendments to the budget resolution would unravel the deal altogether. Thus leaders played key roles in defining the choices, explaining the implications of supporting alternatives, making effective use of the rules, and selling the budget agreement.

Theories of policymaking that rely solely on interest-group power or reelection motives cannot explain why the House defeated Shuster-Oberstar. When a roll call is decided by two votes, it is almost impossible to determine the deciding factor. One member noted, "It could be any combination of things—some arguments, like the agreement will fall apart and we would get no tax cuts or a balanced budget worked for some members; other arguments, like we will give you cover if Shuster decides to retaliate, were important to others."[47] Yet the final outcome of the vote on Shuster-Oberstar points to two conclusions. First, budget decisions are not easily explained by simple assumptions about how narrow, self-serving interests undermine general interests. Budget choices are based on a variety of political calculations, policy concerns, responsiveness to general public opinion, and basic principles. Second, leaders matter. Effective leadership is essential to crafting a favorable budget agreement and selling it to the members, especially when the outcome is decided by a close margin.

In the Senate, Hatch and Kennedy made reasonable arguments for expanding children's heath coverage and presented a political challenge to those who sided with Joe Camel. Ironically, perhaps, the forces aligned with Joey, not Joe Camel, defeated the amendment. Thus despite President Clinton's commitment to a larger tobacco tax, he lobbied against the Hatch-Kennedy healthy kids amendment, thereby foregoing his ultimate policy objectives for a feasible outcome. Yet the passage of the budget resolution did not deter Hatch and Kennedy from pursing their tobacco tax. As the budget process moved on to reconciliation, the strategic situation changed again, giving Hatch and Kennedy and numerous other policymakers further opportunities to shape the terms of budget policy.

7

Reconciliation Medley

"That was the easy part" is a familiar Washington phrase that normally follows passage of a congressional budget resolution. It is hard to imagine the process getting any more difficult when one considers the arduous negotiations that produced the budget agreement and the drama in the House and Senate. But it does. The budget resolution provides a road map for the legislative process in Congress, a general plan of spending and revenue targets, estimated savings required to reduce the deficit, and policy assumptions and instructions to authorizing committees about how to achieve those targets and savings. Though the budget resolution is an important planning instrument, it is limited to being a planning instrument; it does not actually change legislation. Congress reconciles the goals and guidelines of the budget resolution with legislative changes through the reconciliation process. The budget resolution provides instructions to various congressional authorizing committees, and the committees draft legislative details to meet the goals of the budget resolution. After the committees complete their work, they send their proposed legislative changes to the House and Senate budget committees, which package all the changes into a reconciliation bill (see table 7.1 [p. 118] for key developments in the reconciliation process).

Committees normally conform to reconciliation instructions, but they often go beyond them and sometimes violate the specific terms of the budget resolution. Clay Shaw (R-Fla.), chair of the House Ways and Means Subcommittee on Human Resources, which had jurisdiction over welfare changes in the reconciliation bill, explained why legislation drafted by committees might differ from the budget resolution:

> One of the problems we are having in terms of putting this budget agreement into legislation [deals] with welfare and tax policy.

The people doing the negotiating for us were not the experts in the House on these particular subjects. And in doing so there were probably some subtleties that were missed that we needed to look at more closely.[1]

Tom Bliley (R-Va.), chair of the House Commerce Committee, made a similar point: "Under the terms of the agreement I had to reach certain targets and we did. But I was also very concerned with the policy. I wanted to advance Republican ideals."[2]

Thus reconciliation is more difficult than passing the budget resolution for several reasons. First, more is at stake when Congress changes entitlement and tax laws, so interest groups work hard to protect and promote their particular interests. Second, a new cast of leaders takes over during reconciliation. Key policy decisions move from the hands of budget committee chairs to the hands of chairs of authorizing committees and their subcommittees. Those "policy leaders" may initiate policy ideas they think are best for the country or their party, regardless of their political consequences or whether those ideas are consistent with the bipartisan budget agreement. Finally, reconciliation bills provide individual members with an opportunity to advance their policy goals through the budget process. Reconciliation bills are vehicles for attaching amendments that affect government policy but do not necessarily change spending levels or tax revenues. Put simply, the reconciliation process brings another round of adjustments and policy changes.[3]

In 1997 Congress passed two separate reconciliation bills—one for taxes and one for spending. This chapter describes the variation and complexity of the reconciliation process with respect to the spending bill, lending further evidence of the realist expectations view of governing. The process reflected the complex mixture of principle, politics, rational policy analysis, and public responsiveness that underlie spending choices. In some cases, committees easily complied with the budget agreement; in others, they either violated or went beyond the terms of the agreement. Some committees engaged in a partisan process, others developed legislation through a bipartisan process, and still others reflected a mixture of partisan and bipartisan responses to the reconciliation instructions. Leadership styles of committee chairs, partisan priorities, and the ideological preferences of committee members help to explain the variations across legislative committees. In the end, reconciliation produced an unusual result: House Republicans veered further from the bipartisan process that produced the budget agreement, but the Senate actually made more dramatic legislative changes than the House.

Table 7.1
Key Developments in the Reconciliation Process

House and Senate approve conference version of the budget resolution	5 June
Ways and Means Committee reports reconciliation recommendations for Medicare to the House Budget Committee	9 June
Ways and Means Committee reports reconciliation recommendations for welfare and SSI programs to the House Budget Committee	10 June
House Committee on Education and the Workforce reports reconciliation recommendations for welfare to the House Budget Committee	12 June
House Commerce Committee reports reconciliation recommendations for Medicaid, Medicare, and Children's Health to the House Budget Committee	12 June
Senate Finance Committee reports reconciliation recommendations for Medicare, Medicaid, and Children's Health to the Senate Budget Committee	18 June
House passes reconciliation spending bill	25 June
Senate passes reconciliation spending bill	26 June

Reconciliation Overview

A brief overview of variations in savings, spending, and tax changes from the reconciliation instructions in the budget resolution illustrates the complexity of the reconciliation process. As Table 7.2 (p. 119) indicates, reconciliation instructions called for $168 billion in entitlement savings out of the $306 billion in total budgetary savings in the five-year balanced-budget plan. Spending increases of $31 billion—mainly for President Clinton's children's health initiative and low-income programs—and tax cuts of $85 billion reduced the amount of net savings from policy changes to $190 billion. Lower interest costs from servicing the national debt would save an additional $14 billion, bringing the total package of net savings to about $204 billion over five years.

As table 7.3 (p. 120) illustrates, the allocation of expected reconciliation savings/spending from the budget resolution varied widely across eight committees in both the House and the Senate. For example, the House Commerce Committee was expected to save about $138.9 billion, whereas the House Committee on Government Reform and Oversight was expected to save only $3.1 billion, and the House Education and the Workforce Committee was expected to spend an additional $1.2 billion. The process is made more complex by the fact that some

Table 7.2
1997 Budget Agreement's Five-Year Balanced Budget Plan
Plus Spending Initiatives and Tax Cuts (in billions of dollars)

Spending reductions		Spending increases	
Discretionary programs		Domestic program initiatives	
Defense	76.8	Children's health	16.0
Nondefense	61.2	Reinstate SSI and Medicaid for legal immigrants	9.7
Subtotal	138.0	Welfare-to-work grants	3.0
Mandatory programs		Food stamps	1.5
Medicare	115.0	Environmental programs	1.0
Medicaid	13.7	Total	31.2
Other	39.6		
Subtotal	168.3		
Total	306.3	Net tax cuts	85.0
Total changes from savings less spending and tax cuts			190.1
Reduction in interest costs			13.6
Total deficit reduction (net savings)			203.7

Source: "Concurrent Resolution on the Budget: Fiscal Year 1998," *Report of the Committee on the Budget,* House of Representatives, 105th Congress, 1st sess., 18 May 1997, 132–33.

committees share legislative jurisdiction for certain programs. In the House, for example, the Commerce and Ways and Means Committees share jurisdiction over Medicare. Ways and Means shares jurisdiction over welfare-to-work programs with the Education and the Workforce Committee. When committees share jurisdiction over the same programs, the reconciliation instructions of the budget resolution are referred to more than one committee, and the committees may propose different legislation for meeting the goals of the budget resolution. We also see that the jurisdictions of House committees do not correspond directly with those of Senate committees. In the Senate, for example, the Finance Committee had jurisdiction over $100.6 billion in savings, whereas its counterpart in the House, the Ways and Means Committee, had jurisdiction over about $87.6

Table 7.3

Increases/Reductions Needed to Achieve Spending and Revenue Targets in Reconciliation Instructions: House and Senate Committees (in billions of dollars)

Committee Entitlement Reform Targets Specified in Budget Resolutions

House committees	1998–2002	Senate committees	1998–2002
Agriculture	1.5	Agriculture, Nutrition, and Forestry	1.5
Banking and Financial Services	-1.59	Banking, Housing, and Urban Affairs	-1.59
Commerce	-138.938	Commerce, Science, and Transportation	-26.496
Education and the Workforce	1.208	Energy and Natural Resources	-.013
Government Reform/ Oversight	-4.927[a]	Finance	-100.646
Transportation and Infrastructure	-.736	Governmental Affairs	-5.467
Veterans' Affairs	-3.796	Labor and Human Resources	-1.792
Ways and Means	-87.607	Veterans' Affairs	-2.733
	Net tax relief		
Ways and Means	84.973	Finance	85

Source: "Budget Reconciliation in the 105th Congress: Achieving a Balanced Budget by 2002," *CRS Report for Congress,* Library of Congress, 7 July 1997, CRS-5, 6.

a. Figure includes $3.098 billion from savings in direct spending and $1.829 billion in deficit reduction from increased employee retirement contributions.

billion. The House Commerce Committee had more in common with the Senate Finance Committee than with the Senate Commerce, Science, and Transportation Committee.

When the authorizing committees finish with reconciliation, they report their legislative changes to the House and Senate Budget Committees, which package them into an "omnibus" reconciliation bill. It is not unusual for party leaders to intervene at this stage of the process. If a committee violates the terms of the budget resolution or if the committees report conflicting policy recommendations, party leaders arbitrate the differences and, if necessary, overturn the committees' recommendations. The "postcommittee adjustments" are necessary to package all the committee recommendations into a single omnibus reconciliation bill.[4]

Budget Reconciliation in the House

Five of the eight House committees passed reconciliation bills with bipartisan support and complied with the terms of the budget agreement. The most significant and controversial issues related to instructions given to the Commerce, Ways and Means, and Education and the Workforce committees. On some issues, Republican committee chairs worked with Democrats, while other issues were mired in partisan conflict. The controversies centered mainly on philosophical or partisan differences over social policy, though each side also used practical arguments to support their positions. In several cases, the committees violated the terms of the budget agreement in pursuit of specific policy goals.

Welfare Issues: Ideological Principles and Party Politics

The Personal Responsibility and Work Opportunity Act of 1996 replaced Aid to Families with Dependent Children (AFDC) with Temporary Assistance for Needy Families (TANF) grants to the states, reduced eligibility for food stamps, and cut Supplemental Security Income (SSI) benefits to elderly and disabled legal immigrants. After signing the legislation, President Clinton vowed to restore some benefits and expand government programs designed to move welfare recipients to work. Clinton's FY 1998 budget contained these priorities, and they were included in the bipartisan budget agreement. The budget resolution added $3 billion for welfare-to-work grants to the states, $1.5 billion for food stamps, and $10 billion to reinstate SSI and Medicaid benefits to legal immigrants who were scheduled to lose eligibility in August 1997 under the Personal Responsibility and Work Opportunity Act. Reconciliation instructions for all these programs went to the House Ways and Means Subcommittee on Human Resources, and the welfare-to-work provisions were jointly referred to the Committee on Education and the Workforce.

When the Subcommittee on Human Resources met on 5 June to mark up Chairman Clay Shaw's (R-Fla.) welfare proposals, the bipartisan compromise in the budget agreement gave way to partisan clashes. The Human Resources sub-committee enacted two key provisions that provoked intense opposition from the White House and congressional Democrats. First, a proposal to allow states to use noncash benefits (e.g., food stamps and Medicaid) to offset minimum-wage re-quirements for individuals involved in welfare-to-work programs went beyond the budget agreement and directly overturned Clinton administration policy re-garding welfare-to-work rules. Second, Shaw's proposal to change eligibility rules for SSI benefits to legal immigrants directly violated the terms of the budget agreement.

Workfare and Minimum Wage

Under the Personal Responsibility and Work Opportunity Act of 1996, states and nonprofit organizations could use noncash benefits to offset wages for individuals enrolled in welfare-to-work programs. In effect, this meant that individuals re-ceiving food stamps, welfare assistance, and Medicaid could be paid less than the minimum wage. The Clinton administration later ruled, under the Fair Labor Standards Act, that individuals enrolled in workfare programs must be paid at least the minimum wage, regardless of whether they were receiving other non-cash benefits. Congressional Democrats agreed with Clinton because they wanted more government assistance to low-income workers. Labor organizations sup-ported the administration's ruling because they believed lower wage requirements would encourage states to hire workfare recipients over union workers. But gover-nors and state welfare officials argued that states could not afford to pay the min-imum wage plus noncash benefits to all workfare participants and still meet the welfare-to-work requirements. Shaw believed Clinton's ruling forced states to cut their welfare-to-work efforts and discouraged workfare recipients from seeking employment in the private sector. Shaw commented on the effects of the ruling, by saying, "The administration may have hit the poor right in the teeth."[5] In ad-dition to his concerns about the practical effects of Clinton's ruling, Shaw was philosophically opposed to federal control of welfare policies and preferred to give the states as much flexibility as possible.

During the subcommittee markup, ranking Democrat Sander Levin (Mich.) opposed the bill for practical and philosophical reasons. Levin contended welfare-to-work participants should be treated like all other workers, and he said Shaw's bill would push wages below a sufficient standard of living. Furthermore, he pointed out, "This was not part of the budget agreement, and they should not violate the spirit of it."[6] Ignoring Levin's plea, Republicans defeated an amend-ment by Democrat Fortney "Pete" Stark (Calif.) to strike Shaw's welfare-to-work provision from the bill.

The Committee on Education and the Workforce, which also had jurisdiction over workfare programs, contained the same minimum-wage exemption as Shaw's bill. Democrats raised even more intense opposition to the provision. William L. Clay (Mo.), the ranking Democrat on the committee, said that paying subminimum wage to workfare participants "reminds me of slavery's crucial exploitation of human labor."[7] Clay's amendment to the committee's bill was also defeated along party lines.

SSI and Medicaid Eligibility for Legal Immigrants

SSI provides cash benefits to poor individuals who are elderly or disabled. SSI spending for legal immigrants is one of the fastest growing entitlements in the federal budget.[8] In an effort to slow the rate of spending growth in the program, the Personal Responsibility and Work Opportunity Act cut SSI benefits for 500,000 legal immigrants beginning in August 1997.[9] Shaw explained the rationale behind the cuts:

> Welfare reform [in the 105th Congress] was written under a reconciliation bill. We were working under a strict dollar amount. We were faced with a program [SSI] which was totally out of control. Over 50% of the benefits being paid to the elderly were being paid to noncitizens. The noncitizen population for SSI was growing at five times the rate of elderly citizens of the United States. We were given numbers that forced us to reform the program. We needed to protect our own citizens.[10]

The public backlash against the benefit cuts led members of both parties to restore SSI eligibility for certain legal immigrants. At the urging of the White House, the bipartisan budget agreement favored *disabled* legal immigrants over *elderly* legal immigrants. The budget resolution aimed to "restore SSI and Medicaid eligibility for all *disabled* legal immigrants who are or become *disabled* and who entered the U.S. prior to 23 August 1996. Those disabled immigrants who entered the U.S. after 22 August 1996 and are on the rolls before 1 June 1997 shall not be removed."[11] The agreement still allowed states to cut off benefits to legal immigrants who are *elderly* but not *disabled*.

Chairman Shaw disagreed with the policy. He also maintained that policy reforms should be aimed toward slowing the growth of spending in the SSI program and shifting the responsibility of caring for legal noncitizens from the federal government to the families sponsoring immigrants to live in the United States. Thus,

Shaw's bill diverged from the budget agreement by extending SSI eligibility to all poor disabled *and* elderly citizens who were in the country on 22 August 1996, the date the welfare bill was signed into law. All legal immigrants, even those who became disabled after 22 August 1996, would not be eligible for SSI benefits in the future.[12] Shaw explained the rationale:

> This time under the budget deal we were given a figure that we could work with. What we did was different from the administration under the budget plan. I think to have given what they wanted under the budget plan would have been their worst nightmare, because it would have taken all of the elderly under SSI (because of age) off of SSI and then they would have had to reapply. About two-thirds of them would have been back because of disability. . . . So the administration came down on the side of the disabled from that point on. We said, "No, we really don't want to be throwing elderly people off of Medicaid (because it is related to SSI). We don't want to be throwing these people out of nursing homes." You can be 75 and not disabled, but still poor. How are you going to find a job? Who is going to hire you?
>
> What I am saying is if you're on SSI by 22 August 1996, we're not going to throw you off. But if you are not a citizen, whether you are here or not after 22 August and you were not on SSI, don't try to get on SSI because we're not going to cover you.[13]

Liberal Democrats disagreed. Ideally, they wanted to cover elderly *and* disabled legal immigrants whenever they became eligible and whenever they came to the United States. But on balance they preferred the budget agreement's arrangement because they estimated that 75,000 fewer noncitizens would be eligible for SSI over the next five years under Shaw's bill when compared with the budget agreement. Levin strongly opposed Shaw's legislation and predicted, "This bill is headed toward confrontation instead of bipartisan accord."[14] In a speech delivered to advocates of immigrants, Vice-President Gore used more strident rhetoric: "The Republican Plan is un-American. It is unworthy of a nation of immigrants, and it must be changed."[15]

Shaw contended that the administration's position was not morally superior and that there was nothing "un-American" about his policy. Shaw estimated that the budget agreement threatened 300,000 current recipients with losing benefits after 1 October 1997, and he maintained that "given the limited funds, the

House policy is simply better because *it protects more noncitizens who already depend on these benefits.*"[16]

Despite Levin's warnings, Republicans rejected a Democratic amendment to restore the language contained in the budget agreement regarding SSI benefits for legal immigrants and proceeded to pass the bill by a vote of 8–3. In response to the markup, OMB Director Raines informed Shaw: "We would be compelled to invoke the provisions of the agreement that call on the administration and the bipartisan leadership to undertake remedial efforts to ensure that reconciliation legislation is consistent with the agreement." But Shaw responded: "There is no way I'm gonna back up on this. I am going to stick with this position come hell or high water."[17]

Health Programs: Medicare, Medicaid, and Children's Health

Health-care programs took the largest amount of entitlement savings in the budget agreement. Recall that Medicare, the government health insurance program for the elderly, is divided into two parts: Part A, Hospital Insurance (HI) coverage for all individuals sixty-five and older, and Part B, Supplemental Medical Insurance (SMI), which covers physician services, diagnostic tests, and the like. Part A is funded though HI Trust Fund revenues derived from payroll taxes, and Part B is a voluntary insurance program financed by a combination of beneficiary insurance premiums and general tax revenues. The HI Trust Fund was scheduled to be insolvent in five years, prior to passage of the budget agreement. Medicaid is the government-funded health-care program for the poor, including the poor elderly who cannot afford to pay the insurance premium for Medicare Part B, and it is jointly funded by federal and state revenues. The bipartisan budget agreement called for $115 billion of entitlement savings from Medicare and $13.7 billion from Medicaid. The budget agreement also called for $16 billion in new spending to cover a new children's health program for low-income working families who were not eligible for Medicaid. The House Commerce and Ways and Means Committees both had jurisdiction over reconciliation instructions for health-care programs.

The greatest test of bipartisan cooperation came in the area of Medicare. The contentious partisan conflict over the Republican reforms in the 104th Congress spilled over to the 1996 campaign, leaving deep wounds and a reservoir of distrust. Yet changes in the policy situation and effective leadership made bipartisan reform possible. Both parties recognized that something needed to be done to restore the solvency of the HI Trust Fund. House Republicans leaders avoided two controversial issues that had sunk Medicare reform in the previous Congress: a cap on Medicare spending and premium increases for upper-income beneficiaries.

Medicare in the Ways and Means Committee

Leadership played a key role in carrying out a bipartisan approach in the Ways and Means Committee. Bill Thomas (R-Calif.), Chair of the Ways and Means Subcommittee on Health, took an early lead in developing Medicare legislation. In January 1997, Thomas worked with Michael Bilirakis (R-Fla.), chair of the Commerce Subcommittee on Health and Environment, and Ben Cardin (D-Md.), a key member of the Ways and Means Subcommittee on Health, to draft H.R.15, a bill containing preventive-care benefits for Medicare recipients. When they introduced H.R.15 on 7 January 1997, Cardin noted: "It is my hope that this bipartisan legislation will be used as a model for a preventive benefits package that should be added to Medicare. This proposal would result in large cost savings in the long run, as well as saving lives."[18]

Cardin's wish came true as negotiators incorporated the preventive-care benefits package into the budget agreement. Moreover, Thomas used the package as a foundation for negotiating a more comprehensive bipartisan Medicare reform bill in conjunction with Cardin and White House health policy adviser Chris Jennings. Republicans wanted structural reforms that gave Medicare beneficiaries more choices. The "MedicarePlus" package allowed beneficiaries to choose between provider-sponsored organizations (PSOs), preferred provider organizations (PPOs), and Medical Savings Accounts (MSAs). Democrats mainly wanted more consumer protections for beneficiaries enrolled in Health Maintenance Organizations (HMOs). By March they had a general agreement with a few issues outstanding, and negotiators used the package as a framework for the budget agreement. Cardin later commented, "Bill Thomas was critical to developing a workable package. He has been wonderful in giving Democrats a chance to work on Medicare reform."[19] Cardin said the main differences between the 104th and the 105th Congresses were that Clinton's budget contained a serious and credible proposal to begin with and Republicans did not attempt "extreme" measures, as they did in 1995. He noted that Thomas would have preferred to develop a bipartisan solution in 1995, but Republican leaders demanded more dramatic reforms.

Still, Thomas pushed for two conservative policy initiatives that went beyond the budget agreement: Medical Savings Accounts (MSAs) and a $250,000 cap on medical malpractice awards. MSAs enable Medicare beneficiaries to purchase health insurance policies with a lower-than-average premium and large deductible payments to cover catastrophic illnesses. The remainder of the premium would go into a tax-free savings account used to pay medical bills, and any money left in the account after all the bills are paid would go to the beneficiary. Republicans argue that MSAs help to control medical costs because they give consumers incentives to use less medical care. Democrats oppose MSAs on the grounds that healthy people will exit the insurance pool, leaving the sickest individuals with no healthy ones to offset the costs.

Just as Kasich, Domenici, and Spratt seized opportunities to push the envelope in their direction, Thomas waited until after the budget agreement was signed to seek a compromise on MSAs. On 3 June, just prior to the subcommittee markup of the Medicare reform package, Thomas met with John Hilley and Erskine Bowles at the White House. Thomas said he preferred a comprehensive plan that allowed any eligible Medicare beneficiary to enroll in an MSA, but he would be willing to accept a demonstration project if the White House agreed to compromise. Compared with the direct confrontational approach Shaw took on the welfare provisions, Thomas said if he went for a comprehensive MSA plan, "we would create a clear conflict with the White House" over the issue.[20] The White House agreed to a demonstration project that allowed 500,000 seniors to enroll in MSAs, and decided to take its chances that medical malpractice would be defeated in conference with the Senate.

Outspoken liberal Democrats were not pleased with the White House's compromise on the MSAs. Stark criticized the White House: "All they want is a deal so the president can talk about his budget deal instead of Paula Jones. It's the Paula Jones budget."[21] During the markup, Republicans defeated Stark's amendments to strike the MSAs and the cap on medical malpractice awards. Despite Stark's criticisms, the Medicare reform package that emerged from the Ways and Means Subcommittee on Health reflected politically feasible bipartisan principles and policy goals. The plan extended solvency of the HI Trust Fund, Part A of the Medicare program, for ten years, and it slowed the rate of growth in Medicare spending from an annual rate of 8.5 percent to 5.9 percent over five years. Those savings were used to help balance the budget and provide additional health benefits for seniors enrolled in Medicare. The subcommittee unanimously approved the Medicare bill on 4 June, and one week later the Ways and Means Committee passed the bill by a vote of 36 to 3.

Of course, someone must pay the price for a bill containing $115 billion in Medicare savings, the largest in history. As table 7.4 illustrates, the savings came mainly from reducing payment rates to hospitals and physicians and establishing new payment rates for nursing homes, outpatient and home health services, and rehabilitation hospitals. Hospitals serving Medicare beneficiaries were outraged by a one-year freeze on Medicare reimbursement payments. Home health groups and nursing homes were unhappy with the new payment system, which yielded $23 billion in savings.[22]

Table 7.4
Congressional Budget Office Estimates of Five-Year Savings
from Medicare Reforms (in billions of dollars)

Policy changes	Savings
MedicarePlus reforms, including reductions in the rate of growth in payments to HMOs	18.1
Formation of prospective payment systems for skilled nursing facilities, rehabilitation hospitals, outpatient hospital services, outpatient therapy providers, and home health services	23.1
Slower growth in payments to hospitals	37.1
Reducing payments for physician services, laboratory services, and durable medical equipment and maintaining the Part B premium at 25 percent of program costs	22.9
Reductions in home health payments, extension of Medicare's secondary-payer status for enrollee with employment-based coverage, and other miscellaneous changes	19.8
Medical liability reforms	.2

Source: Balanced Budget Act of 1997, *Report of the Committee on the Budget House of Representatives,* 105th Congress, 1st sess., Report No. 105–149 (Washington, D.C.: Government Printing Office, 24 June 1997), 1384.

Medicare and Medicaid on the Commerce Committee

The week after the Ways and Means Subcommittee on Health finished its work on Medicare, the House Commerce Subcommittee on Health and the Environment dealt with its portion of Medicare, Medicaid, and the children's health initiative. Like Thomas, Michael Bilirakis (R-Fla.), chair of the Subcommittee on Health and the Environment, took a bipartisan approach to drafting reconciliation legislation. But Bilirakis was unable to accommodate liberal Democrats on the subcommittee, and deliberations over the three bills turned up mixed results. The Medicaid and

Medicare bills reflected clear partisan differences, the children's health initiative received broader support from members of both parties, and the subcommittee produced a few surprises as wayward Republicans joined with Democrats on several key amendments. The final reconciliation bill reported by the Commerce Committee contained several items that contradicted the budget agreement.

Though the Commerce Health and the Environment Subcommittee's Medicare bill differed in a few ways from the Ways and Means bill, it contained the same MedicarePlus package.[23] Three Republican members sought to amend the subcommittee bill to give more patient protections to Medicare beneficiaries enrolled in HMOs. Two physicians, Greg Ganske (R-Iowa) and Tom Coburn (R-Okla.), and one dentist, Charlie Norwood (R-Ga.), aligned with subcommittee Democrats to pass a package of consumer protections that gave doctors more discretion in treating their patients. Most Democrats saw the protections as a way to improve the quality of care for Medicare and Medicaid patients.[24] Doctors and consumer groups had worked for years to improve beneficiary care and wrest control away from managed-care agencies, and the reconciliation process offered an opportunity for policy changes. Lobbyists for the HMO industry opposed the consumer protections, arguing the new regulations would increase the cost of delivering health services.

After approving the amendments, the Health and Environment Subcommittee passed the Medicare bill along party lines, 15–11, and the Commerce Committee voted 30–17, with all the Republicans and only two Democrats voting for the bill. Though many Democrats supported the increased patient protections added to the bill, they failed at several attempts to cut the MSAs and the caps on medical malpractice awards at $250,000. Unlike Democrats on the Ways and Means Committee, many Democrats on the Commerce Committee voted against the bill mainly because they opposed those two provisions.[25]

The Health and the Environment Subcommittee's Medicaid bill violated the terms of the budget agreement in several areas. First, while the budget agreement called for net savings of $13.7 billion in Medicaid over five years, the Health and the Environment Subcommittee bill cut $15.3 billion from Medicaid, mostly by reducing reimbursements to disproportionate-share hospitals. Second, the subcommittee passed an amendment along party lines to strike a provision in the bill that restored Medicaid benefits to disabled children who lost eligibility under the welfare reform legislation passed in 1996. Third, the bill failed to include higher federal matching funds for the District of Columbia and inflation-adjusted increases for Medicaid programs in Puerto Rico and other territories, both of which were specified in the budget agreement. Fourth, the bill allowed just $400 million to subsidize the Medicare Part B premium for low-income seniors, which was

$900 million less than the amount called for in the budget resolution. Finally, in a surprising development, the subcommittee passed an amendment by Frank Pallone (D-N.J.) to reinstate the Boren amendment, named after former senator David Boren (R-Okla.), which required states to pay hospitals, nursing homes, and other long-term care facilities "reasonable and adequate rates." The amendment was well intentioned, but governors complained that lawsuits by hospitals and nursing homes drove up the cost of nursing home care under Medicaid and limited states' capacity to fund other Medicaid services. The White House supported the repeal of the Boren amendment, and it was part of the budget agreement, but liberal Democrats with the backing of nursing homes effectively passed the subcommittee amendment. After voting to overturn the Pallone amendment, the Commerce Committee approved the Medicaid bill by a vote of 28 to 18. All the Republicans and only two Democrats voted for the bill.

KidCare

One of President Clinton's key priorities was to expand health-care coverage to uninsured low-income children who were not eligible for Medicaid. The budget agreement called for $16 billion over five years with a goal of providing additional coverage for up to 5 million children. The budget resolution stated the funding could be used for expanding state Medicaid programs or providing grants to states to finance health insurance coverage, or some combination of both. The Commerce Subcommittee on Health earmarked $2.5 billion just for Medicaid, and the rest went to a Child Health Assistance Program, also known as KidCare. Under KidCare, states would provide matching funds for a federal grant, and the states could choose how to serve the health-care needs of low-income children. The states could add more children to the existing Medicaid program, enroll uninsured children in the health plans offered by private insurers, or spend the money directly on health services for children (including immunizations, well-child care, and services provided by disproportionate share hospitals).

The main concern raised by Democrats was that the KidCare grants could be used for "services," as opposed to guaranteeing "insurance," as specified by the budget agreement. They also opposed inserting the Hyde amendment into the children's health bill. The Hyde amendment, named after Congressman Henry Hyde (R-Ill.), prohibits Medicaid from paying for abortions, except in cases of rape or incest, or to save the mother's life. Since eligibility for the new health plan included individuals under nineteen years of age, without the Hyde amendment states might cover abortion procedures for pregnant teens. Nevertheless, most members supported the general goal of expanding children's health-care coverage, and the Commerce Committee passed the children's health initiative by a vote of 39–7, with four Republicans and three Democrats voting against.[26]

Tying up Loose Ends

Several loose ends obviously remained when the committees reported their legislative changes to the Budget Committee. Once again, the bipartisan budget deal was in jeopardy. The Commerce and Ways and Means Committees reported back conflicting versions of Medicare; Ways and Means violated the terms of the agreement regarding SSI beneficiaries; Commerce failed to comply with several Medicaid instructions; Commerce produced only $10 billion in savings of the $23.6 billion specified in the budget agreement from spectrum auctions; and Republicans took the liberty to adopt several controversial policy measures opposed by Democrats.[27]

The Budget Committee's job at this point is to package all the legislative measures passed by the committees into a large reconciliation bill. Yet, under the circumstances, Chairman Kasich's job went beyond mere packaging. With the support and advice of Speaker Gingrich, Kasich negotiated with John Spratt and Republican committee chairs for several days to work out contradictions with the budget agreement and differences between committees. Since the Budget Committee lacks the authority to amend legislative actions taken by authorizing committees, the postcommittee adjustments resulting from those negotiations must be approved by the House acting in the Committee of the Whole.[28] The Rules Committee, at the recommendation of the Speaker, packages the postcommittee adjustments to the committees' reconciliation reports into a floor manager's amendment to the rule for debating the reconciliation bill on the House floor. Once the House passes the rule, called a "self-executing" rule, the contents of the manager's amendment become part of the bill. Table 7.5 lists some of the key policy changes incorporated in the manager's amendment that resolved some of the problems with the committees' reports.[29]

Passage on the House Floor

On 20 June the Budget Committee reported out the reconciliation bill, and on 25 June the House passed the rule, thereby incorporating all the contents of the manager's amendment into the reconciliation bill. Republicans strongly supported

Table 7.5
Selected Key Changes in Reported Legislation Adopted in the Manager's Amendment

---

Low-Income Medicare Premium Protections. Adds $1 billion over 5 years for low-income Medicare premiums, raising the total to $1.5 billion as specified in the budget agreement.

Minimum-Age/Welfare-to-Work Participant Protections. Counts only Temporary Assistance for Needy Families [TANF] and food stamp benefits as compensation under minimum wage for workfare participants.

Medicaid. Drops language in Medicaid section that allows only physicians to decide appropriate hospital stays. This language was added to bring the Committee on Commerce closer to its reconciliation instructions.

Children's Health Care. Modifies the children's health block grant to ensure that it complies with the Bipartisan Budget Agreement's proposed spending $16 billion over the next 5 years.

Medicaid Coverage for SSI Children. Provides $100 million to allow states the option of maintaining Medicaid benefits for children currently on the Medicaid rolls who would otherwise lose Medicaid eligibility because of stricter SSI eligibility standards.

Spectrum Auctions. Increases from $9.7 billion to $20.3 billion over 5 years the receipts due to spectrum auctions. Drops or relaxes numerous conditions specified in the Commerce Committee's reported legislation that restricted the Federal Communication Commission's ability to auction spectrum. Also specifies additional spectrum to be made available for auction.

Budget Enforcement. Adjusts and extends statutory discretionary spending limits through FY 2002. Extends the pay-as-you-go (PAYGO) requirements, which provide that entitlement and tax legislation must be fully offset, through FY 2002.

Source: "Manager's Amendment to Be Self-Executed in the Rule on Reconciliation," Report of House Committee on the Budget, 24 June 1997.

the reconciliation bill, but Democrats were split. The White House urged Democrats to support the House bill and move it along to the conference, where the president would try to correct violations of the budget agreement. Many moderate Democrats recognized the changes made in the manager's amendment and agreed to vote for the bill under the condition that it would be "improved" in the conference. Yet despite the White House's pleas and the corrections already made in the manager's amendment, liberal Democrats were dubious about the prospects of the reconciliation bill. Henry Waxman (Calif.) explained the dilemma for liberal Democrats: "The bill has gotten better under the pressure of the administration, but even they say they don't think it is ready to sign. The question is should Democrats vote for it to get it into conference or vote against it because it's a bad bill and doesn't meet the terms of the agreement?" Pete Stark (Calif.) expressed the views of Democrats who had less confidence and trust in the White House: "They are going to sell out the House and Senate Democrats, period."[30]

Budget Committee Chairman Kasich introduced the reconciliation bill and asked members to look at the achievements in the bill rather than its specific parts. Kasich pointed out the incremental but important developments embodied in the bill: "What we have done is to take the first step to show the country that we can, in a responsible way, begin to get a handle on entitlement programs, balance the budget, transfer power from this city into the hands of individuals who are the recipients of these programs."[31]

John Spratt, the loyal Democrat soldier who worked hand-in-hand with Kasich to defeat Shuster-Oberstar and to help pass the bipartisan budget resolution, spoke in a more somber tone. His speech confirmed the proposition that partisan differences over budget policy are strongly related to principle and priorities and are not just a matter of politics. Spratt noted that 138 Democrats voted for the budget resolution, but many of them would not support the reconciliation bill because "this bill does not fully realize the goals that we set out in the balanced budget agreement. It is still a work in progress, very much something that is yet to be realized." Spratt mentioned the "bitter pills added by people who are ardent proponents of various projects that have nothing to do with reconciliation," including a new medical malpractice code, the Hyde amendment, and MSAs. If some Democrats who supported the budget resolution voted against the reconciliation bill, Spratt said, "It is not because they do not want to balance the budget, it is because they think the deal that they supported just a few weeks ago has not been upheld and has been actually breached." Yet Spratt said he would vote for the reconciliation bill because he had developed trust in Kasich and he believed the outstanding problems would be solved in conference with the Senate.[32]

Liberal Democrats had much less faith in the process than Spratt, and they used the House debate to articulate their principled, political, and policy differences with Republicans. Minority Whip David Bonior (D-Mich.), who voted for the budget resolution, spearheaded the charge from the left: "Mr. Speaker, this budget bill that we have on the floor breaks the deal, and it does so not in one or two places, it does so in about 12 different areas, major areas of the law."[33] One Democrat after another invoked themes of fairness, class warfare, injustice, and violations of the budget agreement. Lloyd Doggett (D-Tex.) summed up the Democrats' views by holding up a sign that read WRECKONCILIATION.

By splitting off from the bipartisan coalition that passed the budget resolution, Democrats presented Republican leaders with the dilemma of having to secure nearly all Republicans or hope enough moderate Democrats would endorse Spratt's approach. The bill was put in jeopardy when a coalition of fiscally conservative Republicans, led by Joe L. Barton (Fla.), and moderate Democrats, led by David Minge (Minn.), threatened to vote against the reconciliation bill unless Republican Party leaders ensured them a vote on a package of budget enforcement reforms.[34] Minge's main concern was to control the effects of tax cuts on revenue losses into the future. Barton, along with Zack Wamp (R-Tenn.) and John Sununu (R-N.H.), agreed to caps on revenue losses if Minge would agree to enforce caps on entitlement spending. On 23 June, Minge, Barton, Wamp, and Michael Castle (R-Del.) asked the House Rules Committee if they could offer a substitute reconciliation bill that included the enforcement language. But House Rules Committee Chairman Gerald Solomon (R-N.Y.) turned them down at the urging of Kasich and Gingrich, who were still smarting from the close vote on Shuster-Oberstar that nearly undermined the budget resolution a month before. Barton and Minge exerted more pressure, threatening to vote against the rule for debate on the bill if the leadership did not allow them a vote on the enforcement package. About an hour before the debate on the rule, Republican leaders realized they would lose the vote unless they granted the budget reformers their wish. Gingrich promised to give Barton and Minge a vote on a separate budget enforcement bill on 24 July in exchange for support for the reconciliation bill. The House passed the reconciliation bill 270–162, mainly along party lines; 219 Republicans voted in favor and only 7 voted against, while just 51 Democrats voted in favor and 154 voted against.

Senate Finance Committee: Major Entitlement Reform

Most of the major reconciliation action in the Senate took place in the Finance Committee. Unlike the House, where Ways and Means shares jurisdiction over health programs with Commerce and over welfare issues with Education and the Workforce, in the Senate, the Finance Committee handled all those issues. Chairman William V. Roth Jr. (R-Del.) drafted the Medicare and Medicaid provisions and the children's health initiative, and the committee considered an alternative children's health plan by Senators John H. Chafee (R-R.I.) and John D. "Jay" Rockefeller IV (D-W.Va.). The Finance Committee took a more bipartisan approach to drafting reconciliation language, reflecting the style of the chair and the prefer- ences of committee members. Roth sought the input of Republicans and Demo- crats, and several fiscally conservative Democrats joined Republicans to push major entitlement reforms.

Roth's Medicare bill contained the general framework of the bills passed by the House committees—$115 billion in savings, mostly from reducing payments to doctors and hospitals, and more choices for beneficiaries, including MSAs. But he diverged from the House and the budget agreement on several policy issues. Roth took a bold step by proposing policy changes that imposed direct costs on beneficiaries—a $5 copayment for home health visits and a gradual increase in the eligibility age for Medicare coverage. Roth's proposal opened the door to fur- ther amendments by a committee stacked with fiscal conservatives and entitle- ment reform advocates from both parties. In 1995 Senator Chafee teamed up with Bob Kerrey (D-Neb.), cochair of the Bipartisan Commission on Entitlement and Tax Reform, to offer an amendment that would to apply a means test to deduct- ible payments for Medicare Part B services.[35] Senator Kerrey emphatically stated: "Taxpayers should not be asked to subsidize those who do not need a subsidy."[36] The amendment passed by a vote of 18 to 2.

With respect to other controversial issues in Medicare legislation, the Fi- nance Committee took more moderate positions compared with the House bill. For example, Roth's bill contained no caps on medical malpractice awards. During the markup, the committee narrowly passed an amendment by Chafee and Bob Graham (D-Fla.) to reduce the size of the MSA demonstration project from 500,000 to 100,000 by a vote of 12–8. The committee also adopted an amend- ment by Rockefeller to place lower caps on the deductible costs and maximum out-of-pocket expenses of MSA enrollees by a vote of 11 to 9.[37]

Roth concluded that the bill passed by the committee was a compromise "between differing political philosophies; between deeply held views. . . . I doubt that anyone is entirely satisfied with it."[38] But some individuals and interest groups were more dissatisfied than others. OMB Director Raines complained that the $5 copayment, increased retirement age, and means-tested deductible went beyond the budget agreement. The Medicare reforms were opposed by groups rep- resenting different parts of the political spectrum. The American Association of Retired Persons (AARP) claimed the means test was "unworkable," the increase in the eligibility age left retirees between 65 and 67 with no health insurance, and the $5 copayment for home health visits was prohibitively expensive for poor elderly widows.[39] Horace Deets, executive director of the AARP, claimed, "We need to find equitable ways to curb rising health care costs rather than these red meat pro- posals that endanger Medicare, sharpen dissent among the economic classes and undercut America's social pact to protect the basic health care needs of people who've contributed to this nation."[40] The Seniors Coalition, a conservative group that supports free-market alternatives to traditional government entitlement programs, also opposed the means test as a "fundamentally unfair way of attempting to solve Medicare's financial troubles."[41] Two major business advocacy groups, the U.S. Chamber of Commerce and the National Association of Manufacturers, opposed raising the eligibility age for Medicare because many employer retirement plans cover health costs until employees become eligible for Medicare.

The Senate Finance Medicaid bill also failed to live up to the budget agreement. Roth's bill reduced Medicaid by $13.6 billion over five years, the amount projected by the budget agreement. But it failed to include two key provisions of the budget agreement: the $1.5 billion to subsidize the Medicare Part B premium for low-income seniors and assurance that Medicaid coverage would continue for 30,000 disabled children who lost eligibility for SSI payments under the 1996 welfare reform legislation. OMB Director Raines sent a letter to Roth stating that if those provisions were not changed, "we would be compelled to invoke the provisions of the agreement that call on the administration and the bipartisan leadership to undertake remedial efforts to ensure that reconciliation legislation is consistent with the agreement."[42]

KidCare on Senate Finance Committee: The Limits of Bipartisanship

KidCare legislation on the Senate Finance Committee reflected the limits of bipartisanship, as Roth led opposition to a bill sponsored by Senators Chafee and Rockefeller. Roth supported a bill by Senator Phil Gramm (R-Tex.) that allotted the $16 billion in new children's health spending to states in the form of block grants, very much like the House Commerce Committee plan. The Chafee-Rockefeller plan, which received the support of the White House and two Republicans, James Jeffords (Vt.) and Orrin Hatch (Utah), allotted $12 billion of the $16 billion in children's health initiative to Medicaid, and the remaining $4 billion to block grants for the states. Supporters of the Chafee-Rockefeller bill argued that funneling most of the money through Medicaid was the most cost-effective way to cover the most children and guarantee that the states used the money for insurance rather than medical services.

But conservatives wanted to give discretion to the states in the form of a block grant, and many governors contended the plan was too costly. Senator Gramm characterized the philosophical difference between conservatives and moderates in the Republican Party: "Senator Chafee and I disagree profoundly. He has faith in the Federal Government to decide these matters. He thinks Uncle Sam knows best. I believe Federal mandates are inefficient because they stifle innovation. With a block grant, we'd get much more innovation."[43]

Roth supported Gramm's approach, but he allowed the committee to work its will in deliberations over the Chafee-Rockefeller bill. The governors lobbied against the Chafee-Rockefeller alternative, and the Finance Committee defeated the bill by a vote of 9 in favor and 11 against. Despite White House concerns, the Finance Committee unanimously approved a package of the Medicaid and KidCare provisions.

Senate Floor

The Senate spent two days debating the reconciliation spending bill (S.947), the Balanced Budget Act of 1997. Before the bill came to the Senate floor, party leaders made one important postcommittee adjustment on the means-testing provision for Medicare. In response to arguments that applying a means test to deductible expenses was too difficult to administer, Roth, Moynihan, and Kerrey agreed to replace the provision with a means test on the Medicare Part B premium instead.[44] Still, the biggest question was whether the most controversial Medicare reforms would survive on the Senate floor. Liberal Democrats were opposed to raising the eligibility age for Medicare, requiring a $5 copayment for home health visits, and applying a means test to Medicare beneficiaries. Senators Edward Kennedy (Mass.) and Paul Wellstone (Minn.) led opposition to the $5 copayment for home health services. Kennedy called it a "cruel and unexpected provision, which was not debated or voted on in the committee and is not necessary to meet the committee's reconciliation targets, and will fall primarily on the oldest, poorest, and sickest Medicare beneficiaries."[45]

Roth responded by pointing out that home health costs under Medicare have been exploding at a rate of 30 percent per year, as the number of beneficiaries and the number of visits per beneficiary steadily increased, and the number of agencies providing care increased. "Obviously, that kind of increase cannot be permitted if we are going to salvage and strengthen the Medicare Program."[46] The $5 copayment was necessary because the payment system failed to control the utilization of home health-care. Roth also pointed out that Medicaid would pay the home health care costs of elderly citizens with incomes up to 100 percent of poverty.

Proponents of the Medicare reforms—led by Democrats Kerrey and John Breaux (La.) and Republicans Roth and Pete Domenici (N.Mex.)—made their case mostly on grounds of generational fairness, long-term solvency of the Medicare program, and simple demographic realities. They explained that raising the eligibility age for Medicare was one way to stem the rising tide of Medicare costs in the future as the baby boom generation moved into retirement and the proportion of sixty-five-year-olds doubled over the next thirty years.[47] Opponents—led by Wellstone, Tom Harkin (D-Iowa), and Senate Minority Leader Tom Daschle—charged that raising the eligibility age posed an undue burden on blue-collar workers, did nothing to address the long-term pressures of rising Medicare costs, went beyond the budget agreement, broke the contract with Americans who were promised health-care coverage in old age, and would increase the number of the uninsured.[48]

When all was said and done, Republicans overwhelmingly supported the Senate Finance Committee's recommendations to add the $5 copayment for home health, raise the eligibility age for Medicare, and means test the Part B premium, while a minority of Democrats voted for those provisions. By voice vote, Senators also accepted an amendment by Moynihan and Roth to provide $1.5 billion in funding to subsidize low-income beneficiaries' Medicare Part B premiums, resolving one of the major concerns raised by the White House. The final reconciliation bill passed by a vote of 73–27; Republicans voted 52–3 and Democrats voted 21–24.

A Mix of Policy Decisions

House and Senate deliberations over budget reconciliation reflected several themes associated with the realist expectations view of governing: the fragile nature of the budget agreement, the variations in policymaking patterns, the multiple factors that affect budget decisions, and the role of policy leaders in shaping budget policy. By the time the House and Senate finished work on reconciliation bills, key elements of the bipartisan budget agreement had been violated or substantially amended. Congressional Republicans had a strategic advantage in the reconciliation process. With the White House on the sidelines, the committee chairs pushed several parts of the reconciliation legislation in a Republican direction.

A comparison of the floor votes for the budget resolution and the reconciliation bill in both chambers provides evidence of shifting coalitions stemming from policy changes adopted under different strategic situations. Party leaders used postcommittee adjustments in the House to attempt to restore the priorities embodied in the budget resolution and approved by majorities of both parties. But the final roll-call votes reflected a shift in priorities. Only 25 percent of Democrats voted for the House bill, and just under a majority of Democrats voted for the Senate bill. By the time the process was completed, the House reconciliation bill contained more contentious partisan issues in the areas of welfare policy and Medicare. Those issues provoked the most debate and helped explain why a large majority of Democrats opposed the bill.

Of course, party was not the only factor at work in the process. In the House, Democrats on the Ways and Means Committee voted differently than their colleagues in the Commerce Committee, mainly for philosophical reasons. In the Senate, moderate Democratic Senators joined hands with Republicans to push major entitlement reforms opposed by powerful interest groups. Committee leaders and reform advocates ignored conventional arguments about political feasibility and electoral vulnerability. The Medicare reforms in the Senate were justified as practical steps to address a major problem, and they were rooted in principle and policy analysis, rather than politics.

The variation in policymaking patterns and policy outcomes typifies the realist view of the budget process. Institutional and political differences across committees and chambers help explain some of the variation. The Senate, in particular the Senate Finance Committee, is better suited for bipartisan policymaking than the House. The leadership styles and policy goals of committee and subcommittee chairs also affect the reconciliation process and its outcomes. Thus, after each chamber passed its reconciliation spending bill, significant differences remained between the House and Senate bills. On the other hand, policy leaders who used the reconciliation process as an opportunity to advance their priorities could be expected to hold their ground in conference negotiations over final legislation. The strategic situation was about to change again. Democrats who opposed the reconciliation bill in both chambers looked to the White House to play a crucial role in deciding final aspects of the conference bill between the House and Senate.

8

The Politics of Tax Policy

Just before the House of Representatives voted on the Taxpayer Relief Act of 1997, Ways and Means Committee Chairman Bill Archer spoke pointedly to Democratic members of the House:

> It is clear from this debate that the Democrat caucus remains a liberal caucus. The overwhelming majority of the Democrat party . . . insists that the government in Washington remains the only solution and represents the best hope of how to solve our problems. . . .
>
> To my friends across the aisle I have a simple message: Let it go, let it go, let it go. We have tried your way. For 30 years we raised taxes and we increased spending.[1]

Archer's speech typified the partisan differences that defined the Ways and Means Committee's markup and the House debate on the tax bill.

The scene was very different in the Senate, where Democrats praised the bipartisan efforts of Senate Finance Committee Chair Bill Roth. Roth began the Senate floor debate of the tax bill, saying:

> Tax relief is no longer a partisan issue, and I was encouraged by the spirited cooperation that was exhibited in the Senate Finance Committee as we deliberated and then reported this bipartisan bill out of committee. And because of our efforts to ensure bipartisan cooperation, the Finance Committee bill we consider today contains a balanced and fair package of tax relief measures. It includes proposals important to both Democrats and Republicans, and it is structured to provide major tax relief— relief to America's hard working and overburdened families.[2]

Archer and Roth, the chairs of the House and Senate committees with jurisdiction over tax policy, took very different approaches to fulfilling the instructions of the budget resolution. In addition to distinctions related to party, the committees handled constituent and interest-group pressures differently as well.

This chapter traces the development of the House and Senate tax bills and explains the House-Senate differences with reference to institutional differences between the chambers, policy constraints, and the leadership styles of the two committee chairs (see table 8.1 for key developments in the process). The budget resolution gave Roth and Archer considerable discretion to shape the details of the tax bill, but it also constrained their ability to satisfy the various policy preferences of individual members and the competing priorities of the interest groups who wanted tax cuts. The chapter also illustrates how policy constraints and internal feuding threatened to undermine party unity among House Republicans and how Republican leaders managed to build support to pass the bill in the House.

Table 8.1
Key Developments in the Reconciliation Tax Bill

House Ways and Means Chairman Bill Archer announces his tax relief bill	9 June
President Clinton vetoes the disaster relief bill	9 June
House Ways and Means Committee passes tax bill along party lines	13 June
Senate Finance Committee Chairman Bill Roth announces his tax relief bill	17 June
Senate Finance Committee passes tax bill with bipartisan support	19 June
House passes Ways and Means tax bill after several postcommittee adjustments	26 June
Senate passes Finance Committee tax bill	27 June

Institutions, Policy, and Leadership

The House Ways and Means and Senate Finance Committees have traditionally wielded significant power over tax policy, though their control over legislation varies with institutional and political circumstances, policy constraints, and leadership styles. In 1997 both Senate Finance and House Ways and Means operated in a divided government that created the potential for partisan conflict. Furthermore, the instructions guiding tax policy in the budget agreement limited the policy options of both committees, though the terms of the agreement were broad enough to grant the committees plenty of discretion to shape the details. The committees differed in terms of individual goals, members' policy preferences, and the role of the party leadership.[3] Those factors plus the personal styles of the two chairs explain the different legislative strategies and policy outcomes of the two committees.

The budget resolution reduced some of the partisan differences over tax policy by providing general instructions to the two tax-writing committees. But the general terms masked important differences between Republicans and President Clinton over tax policy and did not guarantee that congressional committees would write bipartisan tax bills. The budget agreement called for a five-year plan containing $135 billion in tax cuts, offset by $50 billion in revenue increases, for a total net tax cut of $85 billion. The agreement also specified the tax package would include a $500 per child tax credit, a capital gains tax cut, reductions in estate taxes, expansion of Individual Retirement Accounts (IRAs), and higher education tax breaks.[4] During the budget negotiations in the spring, Archer and Roth insisted that their committees would decide the details of the tax bill, which explains why the budget agreement contained very general guidelines. For example, the committees could decide who received the $500 per child credit and when it would take effect, and they would determine the size, timing, and eligibility of the education, capital gains, estate tax, and IRA provisions.

While divided government had the potential for conflict between the parties, the policy constraints of the budget agreement led to disputes within the Republican Party. A net tax cut of $85 billion over five years was not enough to accommodate the priorities of all Republican groups.[5] Social conservatives wanted full and immediate funding for the $500 per child tax credit. Small business organizations wanted to abolish estate taxes; and corporations, realtors, and investment companies sought a large cut in capital gains taxes. The money allotted for tax cuts seemed meager compared with the demand, so that Senator Phil Gramm predicted a "destructive" intraparty battle over which kinds of cuts to include in the package.[6] In addition to dividing a small pie among hungry groups, the tax-writing committees had to find revenue offsets of $50 billion by extending existing taxes, adding new ones, or eliminating subsidies in the tax code.[7]

Though both tax-writing committees faced similar external constraints, they operated under different internal conditions. As table 8.2 (p. 143) illustrates, ideological differences between Democrats and Republicans were stronger on the House Ways and Means Committee than on the Senate Finance Committee. The first column of the table measures ideology in terms of average Conservative Coalition (CC) support scores for Republicans and Democrats on the two committees.

Scores range from 0 to 100, with 100 being the most conservative and 0 the most liberal. While Republicans on both committees have about the same scores, Democrats on the Senate Finance Committee are far more conservative (CC = 66) than Democrats on the House Ways and Means Committee (CC = 28).

Party-unity scores indicate that Republicans and Democrats on the Ways and Means Committee are both more likely to vote with the majority of members from their respective parties than either Republicans or Democrats on the Senate Finance Committee. Senate Democrats were the least partisan of all four groups of committee members. Moreover, the general issue of tax cuts has provoked greater partisan differences on the House Ways and Means Committee than on the Senate Finance Committee. House Republicans wanted a tax bill that would give individuals and businesses as much discretion as possible to spend and invest their incomes, and they were less concerned about how tax cuts were distributed across income levels. Ways and Means Democrats were not interested in cutting taxes, and if tax cuts were necessary to reach a budget agreement, they wanted the cuts to be targeted toward middle- and lower-income earners. By contrast, several Senate Finance Committee Democrats had sponsored bills aimed toward encouraging individuals to save and invest. Thus the preferences of the members made it more feasible for Roth to work with Democrats in drafting the tax bill.

Table 8.2
Party Unity and Conservative Coalition (CC) Support Scores
for the House Ways and Means and Senate Finance Committees

Senate Finance Committee	CC support	Party unity
Republicans	83	82
Democrats	64	75
Difference	19	—
House Ways and Means Committee	**CC support**	**Party unity**
Republicans	85	88
Democrats	28	87
Difference	57	—

Source: *Congressional Quarterly Weekly Report,* 3 January 1998.

In addition to the policy preferences of committee members, political scientists have emphasized the importance of individual member goals in terms of explaining committee politics and policy decisions.[8] Norms regarding individual goals on the House Ways and Means changed significantly after the 1994 elections. Traditionally, members sought to serve on Ways and Means because of its prestige and influence in the House, or to pursue specific policy interests, rather than to serve constituent needs or pursue reelection.[9] Party leaders supported those goals by either appointing or enabling the chair to appoint members who were collegial, loyal to the party, and electorally safe. Thus, the committee was able to operate more independently from the pressures of interest groups and constituent needs, and if necessary, take unpopular positions on fiscal issues.[10] After Republicans won a majority in 1994, party leaders deliberately appointed members who were elected by small margins so that they could raise more money and increase their chances for reelection.[11] As table 8.3 illustrates, all seven Republicans appointed to the Ways and Means Committee since the 1994 election were freshmen or sophomores who won with 52 percent of the vote or less. Only one Republican appointed prior to the 1994 elections, Jim Nussle (Iowa), represented a marginal seat when he joined the committee, and not a single Democrat on Ways and Means won with less than 55 percent of the vote in 1996. Those freshman and sophomore Republican members from marginal districts were bound to consider how the tax bill affected their electoral chances, and they might limit Archer's capacity to persuade them to act independently of constituency needs and group pressures.

Table 8.3
Electoral Margins of Freshmen and Sophomores Appointed
to the House Committee on Ways and Means after 1994 Elections

		Percentage of the Vote	
Republicans	Year appointed	1994 elections	1996 elections
Phil English (Pa.)	1994	49	51
John Ensign (Nev.)	1994	48	50
John Christenson (Neb.)	1994	50	57
J.D. Hayworth (Ariz.)	1996	55	47
Jerry Weller (Ill.)	1996	61	52
Wes Watkins (Okla.)	1996	—	51
Kenny Hulshof (Mo.)	1996	—	49

Since Speaker Gingrich played a large role in committee appointments, the presence of Republicans from marginal districts reflected his indirect influence on committee decision making. Yet while Gingrich and the dictates of the Contract with America directly influenced decision making on Ways and Means in the 104th Congress, the Speaker was not expected to intervene as much in 1997. Though the Speaker could make adjustments after the tax bill passed the Ways and Means Committee, Archer acted more independently from the party leadership and had more leverage over the committee's legislative product in 1997. The Senate Finance Committee, in contrast, was top heavy with party leaders; Majority Leader Trent Lott, Majority Whip Don Nickles, and Republican Conference Chair Connie Mack had joined the committee within the past two years. This limited Roth's independence, and it turned out that Lott played a direct role in developing the tax bill in the Senate Finance Committee.[12] Most importantly, Lott's presence made the committee more sensitive to the preferences of senators who were not on the Committee. As a party leader, Lott was interested in striking compromises in the Finance Committee and shaping a bill that could pass on the Senate floor with as few amendments as possible. In contrast, Archer's distance from party leaders left him free to decide whether Ways and Means should develop a bill that would win easily on the floor or one that suited the policy goals of the majority party on the committee.

The institutional circumstances and policy constraints under which the committees operated certainly affected the strategies of the committee chairs and the policy decisions of the committees. The conditions encouraged Roth to consider taking a more bipartisan approach than Archer. Yet each chairman had leeway to define policy priorities and develop policymaking strategies.[13] Roth, a conservative Republican with a bias toward tax policies that stimulate growth and investment, cosponsored the Kemp-Roth tax cut, championed by Ronald Reagan in 1980. Roth typically dodged the public spotlight and was respected more for his mild manner, studious work ethic, and general competence than for his strong intellect, political skill, or forceful leadership.[14] Many colleagues described Roth as "unassuming," "thoughtful and patient," and a "low-key consensus builder."[15]

Ways and Means Committee members generally viewed Archer as a good legislator who was knowledgeable about the tax code, and committee members on both sides respected Archer's honesty, determination, and candor.[16] Archer fashioned himself as a conciliatory leader who sought to reach out and consult individually with committee members. Yet Archer had a reputation for being stubbornly independent, and some committee members wondered if he had the political savvy to broker the competing interests and constituency needs of committee members.[17] Archer was more concerned about advancing conservative policy than appeasing various political interests. He did not have a strong record of working with Democrats, and he often clashed with ranking Democrat Charles Rangel (N.Y.). Archer's independent style also annoyed Speaker Gingrich, who threatened to strip Archer of his chairmanship if he did not cooperate with party leaders.[18] Archer's conservative preferences, concern for policy over politics, and independent posture became evident in the formation of the House tax bill.

Tax Policy on the Ways and Means Committee

On 9 June, Archer unveiled his tax plan at a crowded news conference, saying it fulfilled the budget deal and "represents a solid first step toward a smaller government for bureaucrats in Washington and a larger paycheck for workers in the heartland."[19] As table 8.4 shows, the bill met the overall targets for net tax relief and specified the terms of the major tax provisions in the budget resolution. Yet each provision came with conditions designed to lessen or delay the impact of the tax cuts on total revenue losses. For example, the full $500 per child tax credit was available to families with children under seventeen and incomes up to $110,000 (unmarried individuals with incomes up to $75,000). But it would be delayed until 1998 and would be phased in, starting at $400 the first year and increasing to $500 in 1999. Moreover, Archer went beyond the terms of the budget agreement by proposing major changes in the alternative minimum tax (AMT). Archer's plan immediately exempted small businesses from the AMT and phased out the AMT for corporations for a total projected cost of $19.2 billion over ten years.[20]

Table 8.4
Highlights of Bill Archer's Tax Proposal, 9 June 1997

Tax cuts

Tax provision	5-year revenue loss/gain	Description
Child tax credit	-$71.3 billion	Applies to children under 17; phased-in beginning in 1998 ($400 first year and $500 thereafter); full credit available to families with incomes up to $110,000 (unmarried individuals up to $75,000); indexed for inflation beginning in 1998; nonrefundable; taxpayers receiving dependent-care credit would receive just 50 cents for each dollar beginning in 2002.

Table 8.4 (Continued)

Tax provision	5-year revenue loss/gain	Description
Postsecondary Education Tax Incentives	-$31 billion	HOPE tax credit equal to 50% of higher education expenses up to $3,000 for individuals with income up to $40,000 per year and couples up to $80,000; tax deduction of up to $10,000 for higher education expenses paid through state-sponsored education programs; penalty-free IRAs for postsecondary education expenses; education investment accounts to allow tax-free savings up to $50,000 saved.
Capital Gains Tax Relief	-$2.7 billion	Capital gains rate of 10% for individuals in the 15% tax bracket and 20% capital gains rate for individuals in the 28% or higher bracket; tax exclusion on sale of a home (up to $500,000 for married couples and $250,000 for single individuals); capital gains rate of 30% for corporations on assets held for more than 5 years; inflation indexation for individuals after 2000; depreciation recapture for real estate capped at 26%; new rates effective 7 May 1997.
Individual Retirement Accounts (IRAs)	-$33 million	American Dream Savings Account to $2,000 per year and withdraw the principal and interest tax-free so long as the account was held for 5 years or the individual was 59 1/2 or the withdrawal was for a first-time home purchase; indexed for inflation after 1998.
Unified Estate and Gift Tax Relief	-$3.6 billion	Increase the unified estate and gift tax relief from $600,000 to $1 million by 2015; indexed for inflation thereafter.
Alternative Minimum Tax (AMT)	-$8.9 billion	Increase the individual AMT exemption amount by $1000 every other year 1999–2007 and index thereafter; exemption of AMT for small corporations; phaseout of AMT for all corporations by 2006.

Table 8.4 (Continued)

Revenue raisers

Tax provision	5-year revenue loss/gain	Description
Airline-Ticket Tax	+$34 billion	Cut current 10% rate on tickets to 7.5%. But add a $2 per passenger fee on each segment of a domestic flight ($3 in 2002); increase tax on international flights from $6 to $31 dollars, including a new $15.50 passenger tax on international arrivals; extend expiring fuel and cargo taxes.
Ethanol Credit	+$1.2 billion	Phase out tax subsidy on ethanol by 31 December 2000.
Indian Gaming and Commercial Activities	+1.9 billion	Native American tribes pay income taxes on all earning on commercial activities, including gambling.

Sources: "Estimated Budget Effects of Chairman's Mark Relating to Revenue Reconciliation Provisions," Committee on Ways and Means, 9 June 1997; "Fact Sheet on Tax Provisions in Chairman Archer's Mark," Committee on Ways and Means, 9 June 1997; and Alissa J. Rubin, "Key Cuts and Revenue Raisers in Ways and Means Tax Package," *Congressional Quarterly Weekly Report*, 14 June 1997, 1358–59.

Anticipating criticism from dissatisfied Republicans, Archer took a realist perspective: "After all, it is better to deliver tax relief that people will actually receive than to raise false hope by making wishes that won't come true." Indicating that he intended to work with the White House, Archer said, "The tax package is a compromise. It's not big and it's not small. But unlike two years ago, this tax-relief package will, I'm confident, be signed by the president."[21] In a letter to Republican colleagues, Archer said the bill provided permanent tax relief "within the limitations imposed by the budget agreement, while preserving the important principles that are at the core of our beliefs. When this proposal is signed into law—and I expect that it will—we will have completed virtually all of the items in our Contract with America."[22]

Chairman Archer's tax bill was based on three general premises. Each had its advantages and drawbacks from the standpoint of meeting the diverse expectations of interest groups, Democrats, and Republicans. First, Archer employed a "divide and conquer" approach with respect to distributing tax cuts among Republican-leaning groups. The bill contained priority items sought by social conservatives, small businesses, and investment groups, but the specific conditions for implementing the tax cuts left groups unhappy and invited them to seek ways to amend the bill.

Second, Archer developed a decidedly Republican bill based on the assumption that he would have to compromise with the Senate and the White House later in the process. Archer consulted with every Republican member of the Ways and Means Committee, and Republican Committee members met several times to debate the priorities and tradeoffs in the tax bill. Though Archer met individually with Committee Democrats, they did not expect him to incorporate their ideas into the tax bill. One Ways and Means Democrat noted: "Archer met with everyone and he was sincere. But we didn't see it as an opportunity. We knew we could not affect the fundamental issues in the tax bill."[23] Archer's bill ignored Democratic concerns about distributing tax cuts to low-income individuals and distorted President Clinton's education tax incentives, setting up partisan clashes on the Ways and Means Committee and public relations battles with the White House.

Third, Archer focused on attaining realistic party goals and developing policy based on free-market principles rather than on the political interests of individual Republicans. Clay Shaw (R-Fla.) described Archer's approach:

> Bill Archer realized that a few members would have to leave his mark because of the constituents they represented. He was very clear that unless this was horribly important he didn't want us to change it. And I think we were disciplined in doing that. I think he was more than willing to lose ground on a few of these so long as we stuck generally to the chairman's mark.[24]

Overall, Archer solicited policy advice from Republicans, but he was not inclined to bargain or exchange policy preferences for votes. His independent style and commitment to market principles took precedence over political goals. Archer wanted to establish a solid Republican bill within the realistic constraints of the budget resolution, argue for it on the merits, and establish leverage in conference negotiations later in the process. In the short term, though, the bill faced immediate pressures from within the party, requiring Archer to give way to angry groups, Republican committee members, and party leaders on several controversial aspects of the tax package.

Pressure Points

White House officials complained that Archer's plan favored the wealthy, violated the terms of the budget agreement, and eventually would lead to huge revenue losses. White House officials were particularly critical about how Archer carved up Clinton's $35 billion package of education tax breaks. Archer's package offered only $22 billion for Clinton's education tax credits and deductions. The additional $13 billion went toward various Republican priorities not specified in the budget agreement: employer tax credits for investing in education and training for their workers, a tax credit for families who participate in state-sponsored prepaid tuition programs, and a tax-deferred education savings account similar to IRAs. The White House also assailed the $500 per child tax credit. Archer's bill applied the credit to children under the age of seventeen, compared with age twelve under Clinton's plan. But the child credit was "nonrefundable," meaning that low-income families with no tax liability were not eligible. Since working families with incomes between $16,000 and $25,000 already received the Earned Income Tax Credit (EITC), and had little or no tax liability, they would not receive the full child tax credit. In addition, families who deducted child-care expenses under the existing tax code were not eligible for full credit. In sum, Treasury Secretary Robert Rubin concluded: "In component after component . . . it seems to have moved the tax benefits away from the less well off, and even away from middle-income people, toward upper-income people."[25]

House Democratic leaders hammered away at the limits of the child tax credit. House Minority Leader Richard A. Gephardt said, "House Republicans have turned the effort to balance the budget into a ruse for delivering the Republican crown jewel," and the tax cuts "reward the corporate special interests who favor them with their support."[26] House Ways and Means ranking Democrat Charles Rangel noted: "Every part is skewed against low-income people . . . he has pushed this envelope as far to the right as he could."[27] Other Democrats issued warnings about the long-term revenue losses from the tax-deferred IRA and education investment accounts and indexation of capital gains, as well as the structure of the education tax breaks and the child tax credit.

Archer's divide-and-conquer approach attempted to strike a precarious balance among the competing interests of social conservatives, supplysiders, and small business advocates. Though the child tax credit consumed $70 billion over five years, more revenues than any other tax break in the package, social conservatives complained that the credit would not begin until 1998 and amounted to only $400 the first year. Family Research Council head Gary Bauer noted: "The child tax credit is better than some of the rumors we heard last week but it is still disappointing."[28] Small business groups were content with the AMT provisions, the capital gains tax cut, and a host of small business initiatives, but they were disappointed by the estate tax exemption. The bill raised the exemption from $600,000 to $1 million, to be indexed for inflation after it was fully phased in, but this would not be until 2014. Jack Farris, president of the National Federation of Independent Businesses (NFIB), a huge organization that heavily funds Republican Party campaigns, complained: "The death tax component of the House tax package is unacceptable to the nation's largest small-business organization and will do very little to help family-owned businesses survive to the next generation."[29] The day after Archer unveiled the tax bill, the Family Business Estate Tax Coalition, a group of more than 100 businesses and farm organizations, sent Archer a letter expressing their "extreme disappointment" with the estate tax provisions and urging him to "increase the death tax relief."[30] The investment sector applauded the capital gains provisions, which cut the rate of capital gains in half and indexed it for inflation after the year 2000, making the maximum rate of capital gains equal to 20 percent. Mark Bloomfield, president of the American Council for Capital Formation, said the capital gains tax was "very significant, very well crafted, and will have a maximum positive effect on economic growth."[31] But even investment companies paid the price for proposals to close several loopholes in the tax code related to financial transactions.[32] Meanwhile, realtors generally benefited from the tax exclusion on the sale of a home up to $500,000 and the lower rate of capital gains, but they lobbied against the bill because it taxed capital gains on investment real estate at a higher rate than other investments.[33]

Although Archer consulted each member of the Ways and Means Committee, the revenue increases in the bill ignored the constituency interests of several Republican members. Archer attempted to justify the provisions in terms of free market principles, but they were politically risky measures for several committee Republicans. Mac Collins (R-Ga.), representative of the 3d District of Georgia, which is bordered by Hartsfield International Airport and is the home of Delta Airlines, argued that the plan to extend and restructure the airline-ticket tax was too costly and would unduly harm the airline industry. About $27.2 billion would be raised from restructuring the airline tax and another $4 billion by increasing the international departure fee from $6 to $10 per person and levying a fee on international arrivals. The bill decreased the tax rate on domestic commercial flights from 10 percent to 7.5 percent, but extended the tax to domestic legs of international flights and added a $2 takeoff fee.[34] Archer justified the plan on the grounds of record profits in the airline industry in the past year, owing mainly to the fact that the airline-ticket tax had lapsed for ten months.

Large portions of new revenues also would come from a new tax on Indian gaming and commercial activities and repeal of the ethanol subsidy, both lightning-rod issues for several Ways and Means Republicans. Archer insisted the ethanol subsidy was "an anachronism in the [tax] code, and we have to do everything we can to eliminate it."[35] House members of the Alcohol Fuels Caucus planned to work with the Renewable Fuels Association and the National Corn Growers Association to defeat Archer's proposal to phase out the ethanol subsidy. Ways and Means Republican Jim Nussle of Iowa planned to offer an amendment to restore the subsidy in the committee's markup. Archer's proposal to raise $1.9 billion with a new tax on gambling and commercial activities on Indian lands was also based on market fairness. Archer said: "The problem is that as Indian gambling grows and grows and grows, it begins to compete with dollars in the outside sector that are taxed—other business entrepreneurs."[36] Opponents of the tax, including the White House, said it was unconstitutional based on federal court rulings that give Indian tribes the same legal status as states, and protects the tribes from taxation. The tax outraged Ways and Means Republican J.D. Hayworth, who represents the 6th District of Arizona, which includes the Navajo, San Carlos, and Apache reservations and where nearly one-quarter of the population is Native American.

Precommittee Adjustments

The Ways and Means Committee markup, originally scheduled for 11:00 on 11 June, was delayed several times as Archer attempted to manage the fallout from Republican objections to the tax bill. Archer met Republican leaders who expressed the concerns of conservative groups and questioned the political wisdom of eliminating the AMT at the expense of small businesses and families with children. Republican Conference Chairman John A. Boehner (Ohio), an ally of small business organizations, told Archer that phasing out the AMT was an obvious political target for Democrats. Boehner said phasing out the AMT is "just bad politics, and the Democrats will use it against us."[37] Republican leaders also worried that conservative Democrats might undercut their efforts to satisfy groups loyal to the Republican Party. Thus for strategic and policy reasons Republican leaders strongly urged Archer to shift some of the tax relief devoted to repealing the AMT and allocate more toward estate taxes and phasing in the child tax credit earlier than 1998.

Before the Ways and Means Committee's markup of the bill, Archer agreed to make some changes, but he held his ground on several controversial issues. He dropped the provision that repealed the corporate AMT by 2006 and delayed the phase-out of key aspects until January 1999. Those changes freed up about $13 billion additional revenues over ten years for other parts of the tax package. In a nod to small businesses and their allies in the Republican caucus, Archer sped up the schedule for raising the estate tax exemption.[38] The change still did not satisfy the NFIB, and committee Republicans pressed for an even larger estate tax cut in a party caucus meeting just prior to the scheduled markup. But Archer held his ground. According to one participant at the meeting, Archer told Republicans that if everyone kept pushing for their particular interests, the tax-writing process would be like a "shark tank," where "the big sharks will eat the little sharks until there is nothing left, and then they eat each other. It will be a political exercise regardless of policy. I think we are better than that."[39] Archer reduced the airline tax package by $3 billion by dropping the 10 percent surcharge on the domestic leg of an international flight. Again, Archer justified the change in terms of market principles: "The airlines pointed out to me, and I think it was a valid concern, that this would make them less competitive with foreign airlines."[40] Archer held firmly to his child tax credit proposal, insisting "there's nowhere to go" in the tax bill to start the credit in 1997.[41] He also refused to drop elimination of the ethanol subsidy or the tax on Indian commercial sales, though he said, "The bill is open to amendment—every amendment will get a full hearing."[42]

Ways and Means Committee Markup

As expected, the Ways and Means Committee markup featured more partisan strife. Democrats frequently referred to Treasury Department analysis of the tax bill, which showed that two-thirds of the benefits from the tax cuts would go to families with incomes over $93,000. They warned about long-term revenue losses from tax cuts, accusing the Republicans of favoring wealthy corporations and Wall Street at the expense of middle- and lower-income families. Democrats offered amendments to expand the education tax breaks, make the child tax credit fully refundable to families who received the EITC or the child-care deduction, and reduce the rate of capital gains for investment real estate. Republicans remained unified enough to defeat all but one Democratic amendment.

Archer's plans to repeal the ethanol subsidy and impose a tax on Indian gaming and commercial activities came under siege from members of his own party. Congress gave ethanol, a gas additive made from corn, special tax preference in 1978 to encourage development of alternative fuels during the energy crisis. The tax subsidy effectively reduced the federal excise tax for gasoline blended with ethanol by 5.4 cents per gallon. A General Accounting Office (GAO) study of the ethanol subsidy showed that it cost $7.1 billion through 1995 and had no positive effects on the economy, the environment, or energy independence. Archer called the subsidy "highway robbery."[43] But Archer was swimming upstream against powerful forces. The ethanol subsidy had the support of a powerful agribusiness lobby led by Archer-Daniels-Midland, which gave $1 million to both parties in the previous election and enjoyed strong bipartisan support from farm-state representatives and senators. The National Corn Growers Association framed the issue as a power grab by the oil industry and as a tax increase. President Clinton and Speaker Gingrich also expressed support for continuing the subsidy.

Nussle, a Republican from the largely rural 2d District of Iowa, made good on his promise to offer an amendment to kill the repeal of the ethanol subsidy. Despite the power and prestige of Chairman Archer, Nussle, who won his seat in 1996 with just 53 percent of the total vote and a margin of only 22,000, had a clear political interest in trying to salvage the ethanol subsidy. When he introduced the amendment, Nussle thought he had enough votes to win. But just before the vote was taken, Archer appealed to Republicans to support him and to think about making the right policy choice for the country instead of serving narrow political interests. The amendment was defeated by a vote of 17–21.[44] Still, Archer needed Democrats to win; the final tally was 9 Democrats and 8 Republicans voting for the amendment and 15 Republicans and 6 Democrats voting against it.[45]

Archer failed to garner enough support to defeat an amendment by J.D. Hayworth (R-Ariz.) and Barbara Kennelly (D-Conn.) to eliminate the tax on Indian gaming and commercial activities. Archer based the new tax on a GAO report that showed Indian tribes had experienced increased revenues from commercial activities since they began operating casinos. Most of the tax advantage went directly to casino business, though tribes also benefited from selling tax-free commercial products to the general population. Archer said, "They're competing with private entrepreneurs, and they're doing it without paying taxes." Failing to tax the tribes, Archer said, "creates an unlevel playing field and it's unfair. . . . It's a matter of fairness and justice and equity."[46] Hayworth directly challenged the chair, waving a copy of the Constitution and stating: "I want to accept the primacy of the Constitution over any GAO report." Secretary Rubin also said the tax would violate the "sovereignty of Indian tribes and their special status as domestic dependent nations."[47] Unlike Nussle's amendment, which split Democrats, the Hayworth-Kennelly amendment won the unanimous support of Democrats, and the amendment passed by a vote of 22–16, with 7 Republicans voting in favor.

After all the amendments were voted on, the committee took up the Democratic alternative sponsored by Rangel. The Democratic bill contained President

Clinton's HOPE scholarship credit, credits for local governments that issue bonds for school construction or improvements, a refundable child tax credit, targeted capital gains tax relief, targeted estate tax relief, and a host of other presidential initiatives. The substitute was defeated 22–15 along party lines. The committee proceeded to pass Archer's bill, as amended, with all Republicans except Nussle voting in favor, and all Democrats voting against. The votes on Archer's bill and the Democratic alternative foreshadowed several weeks of partisan conflict.

Senate Finance Committee

The Senate Finance Committee took a different approach to developing the tax bill. Roth consulted ranking Democrat Daniel Patrick Moynihan and several moderate Democrats on the Finance Committee to formulate his initial mark for the bill. After the bill was introduced, the committee deliberated in executive session behind closed doors, and the final product endorsed by the Finance Committee reflected the process that produced it: a patchwork of various Democratic and Republican priorities.

Bipartisan Policymaking

On 17 June, four days after the House Ways and Means Committee approved its tax bill, Roth unveiled his proposal. Though Roth's bill did not satisfy the White House, it clearly indicated an effort to compromise with Democrats on the Senate Finance Committee. Compared with Archer's bill, Roth's bill was much less susceptible to Democratic criticisms about pandering to corporate interests; it contained no reduction in the corporate capital gains tax and no indexation of capital gains, and it did not phase out the AMT. Though the child tax credit was not refundable, it cost $81 billion over five years, compared with $70.5 billion in the House bill; made the credit effective in 1997; and did not limit the credit to families who were also eligible for the child-care tax credit. The bill increased the estate tax exemption from $600,000 to $1 million over eleven years and immediately gave family-owned farms and businesses a $1 million credit. The bill's capital gains tax cut and IRA provisions were similar to Archer's bill.

With the help of Senate Democrats, Roth pared back the $35 billion in higher education tax breaks sought by Clinton in the budget agreement. The bill expended only $20.4 billion on a modified version of Clinton's HOPE scholarship program. Another $12 billion was used to finance student loan deductions, tax credits for employer-provided educational assistance, and an education IRA,

Roth's preferred mechanism for personal savings. Roth noted: "This tax relief package is a combination of some of the best ideas from both sides of the aisle, and both ends of Pennsylvania Avenue . . . Republicans, Democrats and President Clinton can all claim authorship."[48]

Compared with the near-general condemnation Archer's bill received from Democrats, Roth's bill managed to split the White House and Senate Finance Committee Democrats. Though Treasury Secretary Robert E. Rubin believed Roth's bill was closer to the budget agreement than the House bill, he said: "The bottom line is that Roth . . . has education proposals that are not consistent with the budget agreement . . . and in our judgment doesn't begin to meet the test of having a bill that in some way balances the benefits for middle-income and working Americans."[49] But Finance Committee Democrats took a different view. Moderate Democrat Senator John Breaux, who worked closely with Lott on several parts of the bill, commented: "We're on course to having a bipartisan mark. A lot of us would like to be on the inside helping to write the tax bill rather than on the outside criticizing."[50] Senator Moynihan, who opposed tax cuts in general until the budget was balanced, spoke to the reality of the situation: "The congressional leadership and the President have agreed that there will be tax cuts this year. And so given that reality, I joined with other Democratic members of the Finance Committee in working with Chairman Roth—in a bipartisan mode—to help shape the bill now before us."[51]

The Democratic reaction reflected clear differences in the leadership styles and strategies of Roth and Archer. Archer ignored the priorities of House Republican Party leaders, whereas Roth consulted extensively with Lott. Archer believed he needed to establish a Republican mark in the House and bargain later, whereas Roth believed the best approach was to compromise with Democrats early in the process. Archer never attempted to develop a working relationship with Rangel, whereas Roth started negotiating with Moynihan and other moderate Democrats a month before the Finance Committee markup. Roth noted: "I tried to include everyone in the mix, whether they were Republican or Democrat, senior or junior."[52] Roth also took advantage of the moderate leanings of several Finance Committee Democrats to neutralize criticisms from the White House and discourage Democrats from offering an alternative to his bill.

A key breakthrough came on the education tax breaks. Several Democrats on the committee believed the HOPE scholarships and income tax deductions in Clinton's tax package would do nothing to make university education more available and affordable to middle- and low-income families, or to increase personal savings for higher education. Roth endorsed a proposal advocated by Bob Kerrey,

Breaux, and Moynihan, who were more interested in using education tax initiatives as a way to generate savings than to give a tax break to parents of college-bound students. The so-called Kidsave proposal allowed parents with children under twelve the option of either claiming a $500 per child tax credit or placing the money in a tax-deferred account that could be withdrawn without tax penalty for college expenses. Only parents of children between the ages of thirteen and sixteen were eligible for the Kidsave accounts. The compromise opened the doors to further deals with Democrats and literally froze the White House out of the process. Senate Finance Committee Democrats rejected White House attempts to offer an alternative to Roth's bill.

Roth also took a different approach from Archer's in dealing with Republican-leaning groups. Rather than divide and conquer, leaving all groups dissatisfied, Roth's bill clearly sided with the small business and investment-oriented groups at the expense of social conservatives. The NFIB was generally pleased with the estate tax provisions, and supplysiders and the investment industry endorsed the capital gains tax cut and the bevy of investment opportunities in the Kidsave accounts, the new education IRAs, and the expanded eligibility for existing IRAs. On the other hand, the Christian Coalition and the Family Research Council opposed the requirement that the child tax credit must be used for education savings accounts or individual retirement accounts.

When the Finance Committee met to mark up the bill on 19 June, one Democrat after another praised Roth's leadership. Senator Conrad called the bill a "model of fairness." Even liberal Democrats "Jay" Rockefeller and Carol Moseley-Braun praised Roth's leadership. After opening remarks, the Finance Committee went into executive session, where members met secretly for hours and cut numerous deals to build the broad support of Democrats and Republicans. The key to contentment rested in an amendment proposed by Orrin Hatch to increase the cigarette taxes from 24 cents to 44 cents per pack. After the Senate defeated the Hatch-Kennedy amendment to the budget resolution, Hatch vowed to find a way to increase tobacco taxes to pay for more children's health insurance. Hatch argued that while he opposed raising taxes in general, increasing the tobacco tax was morally correct and politically wise.[53] Several other committee members planned to offer amendments to increase tobacco taxes to offset tax cuts in various areas: real estate, estate taxes, and airline taxes. Roth and Lott accepted the reality that the tobacco tax had momentum in the Senate. If the Finance Committee failed to adopt Hatch's amendment in committee, it was bound to pass on the Senate floor. Unlike in the House, where Republican leaders could restrict floor amendments to the bill, in the Senate the bill was open to amendments. Moreover, the reconciliation process had changed the strategic situation in terms of building a coalition to pass the tax bill. The tax bill moved so far away from Clinton's higher education initiatives that Lott could no longer make the case, as he had in the Senate debate over the budget resolution, that an amendment to raise tobacco taxes was a "deal breaker."

Roth used the additional revenues from the tobacco tax to placate several members concerned about his tax bill. The 20 cent increase in cigarette taxes was expected to raise $15 billion over five years. The committee agreed to parcel out $8 billion for additional children's health, enough to satisfy Hatch. The rest was used to reduce the airline-ticket tax, a major priority of Senator Mosely-Braun; cut the capital gains tax on investment real estate from 26 percent to 24 percent at the request of Alfonse D'Amato (R-N.Y.) and Gramm; accelerate estate tax relief by one year at the urging of Gramm; and allow more EITC recipients to benefit from the child tax credit, an initiative sought by Rockefeller and Moseley-Braun. The committee also approved several other amendments to satisfy the interests of particular senators.[54] Lott later called the tobacco tax "the glue that kind of pulled things together."[55] In contrast with the party-line vote in the House Ways and Means Committee, Roth emerged from executive session with the bipartisan backing of the Finance Committee. The committee approved the bill by a vote of 18–2; all Democrats voted for it, and only two conservative Republicans, Nickles and Gramm, voted against it.

The work of the Finance Committee made the Senate floor debate almost a formality. All but four of twenty-six amendments to the tax bill failed; the Senate defeated a Democratic substitute bill sponsored by Minority Leader Tom Daschle and proceeded to pass the Senate finance bill by a vote of 80–18.[56] Republicans voted 51–4 and Democrats voted 29–14 in favor of the bill. The nay votes came from the most liberal Democrats opposed to the distribution of the tax cuts and from conservative Republicans or senators from tobacco states opposed to the cigarette tax. Moynihan praised Roth and the Republican leadership and predicted, "We will now go on to a successful conference and write some history this year."[57]

A Test of Party Leadership in the House

As the Senate Finance Committee pursued a bipartisan approach to the tax bill, House Republican leaders had their hands full preparing to bring the Ways and Means tax bill up for a vote on the House floor. The partisan war of words that consumed the tax-writing process in the House during the week of 9 June was played out through the media for two more weeks after the Ways and Means

Committee approved the tax bill on 13 June. Democrats continued to stress tax fairness in staged news events, television talk shows, and speeches on the House floor. Behind closed doors, lobbyists representing social conservatives, small businesses, airlines, and the real estate industry pushed Republican leaders to incorporate changes in the tax bill before it went to the floor. The National Association of Realtors launched a public relations campaign targeting Republican members from marginal districts, Chairman Archer, and Minority Whip Tom DeLay.[58] Republican members also brought their concerns about how specific provisions in the bill affected their constituencies and urged the Speaker to intervene on their behalf. In the midst of it all, the Republican leadership faced a crisis of confidence and was thrown into disarray as a growing number of Republican members voiced concerns about several strategic blunders in handling the floor schedule and attempting to advance key Republican priorities.[59]

Trouble at the Top

Speaker Gingrich had been under fire since January after he admitted to violating House rules, was reprimanded and fined $300,000 as the result of an intensive ethics investigation, and scrambled to win enough support to be elected Speaker. Over the next few months, a handful of conservative members complained regularly at Republican Party whip meetings and to the press about the leadership's failure to advance a Republican agenda. They began to think seriously about ousting Gingrich from the Speaker's office in March when he suggested delaying tax cuts in order to reach a budget agreement with the White House. Gradually, the leadership team of Gingrich, Majority Leader Dick Armey, Majority Whip DeLay, and Republican Conference Chairman John Boehner drifted apart, failed to communicate, and quarreled about legislative strategies. After two signal events, doubts about the effectiveness of party leaders grew. First, some members viewed the last-minute heroics to defeat Shuster-Oberstar and salvage the budget agreement as indicators of poor planning and ineffective leadership. Armey blamed Gingrich for giving in to Shuster's demands for a vote on his budget alternative. DeLay, in turn, blamed Armey for discouraging him to act earlier to round up support for the budget resolution.

Following the passage of the budget resolution, the Republican leadership suffered an even more embarrassing setback over an emergency supplemental appropriations bill to provide disaster relief to midwestern flood victims. Conservative Republicans saw the bill as a vehicle to force President Clinton to sign legislation carrying two legislative riders: an automatic continuing resolution that prevented government shutdowns in case Congress and the president failed to enact all of the appropriations bills before the start of the fiscal year, and a provision that blocked the use of sampling techniques in the year 2000 census.[60] But on the afternoon of 9 June, shortly after Archer announced his tax package, Clinton vetoed the disaster relief bill. His veto message blamed the Republican leadership for including "contentious issues totally unrelated to disaster assistance, needlessly delaying disaster relief." He urged Republicans "to stop playing politics with the lives of Americans in need, and to send me a clean, unencumbered disaster relief bill."[61] Public opinion polls held Republicans responsible for delaying disaster aid.[62] Meanwhile, Democrat Minority Leader Tom Daschle, whose home state of South Dakota suffered from some of the worst flooding, conducted a masterful public relations campaign to promote federal aid for flood victims and vowed to stop all legislation in the Senate until the disaster-aid bill was passed.[63] After twenty moderate Republicans signed a letter to Gingrich asking him to honor the president's request, Gingrich and Senate Majority Leader Lott agreed to strip the two riders from the bill, and it easily passed Congress.

The event exposed internal divisions among party leaders that had lingered for months. In protest against Gingrich's decision to compromise, DeLay, Boehner, and Armey voted against the disaster-relief bill. Meanwhile, Armey had emerged as an ally of conservatives who had begun to explore procedural means to depose Gingrich. But even moderate Republicans were now beginning to express public reservations about the party leadership. Chris Shays (Conn.), a long-time ally of Gingrich, said: "As a rank-and-file member, I must say it's disconcerting to see the leadership in such public disarray."[64]

In the throes of dissension, Gingrich faced a challenging task, though the situation was not entirely bleak. In order to build a winning coalition to pass the Ways and Means tax bill, Gingrich needed to defend the bill from attacks by Democrats, strike a delicate balance among dissatisfied Republican groups, and appease anxious Republican members worried about representing their constituents and getting reelected. Two things worked to the Speaker's strategic advantage. First, Roth's bipartisan approach managed to split the Democratic Party. Though House Democrats railed against Archer's bill, Senate Finance Committee Democrats unanimously supported Roth's bill, leaving the White House stuck in the middle. If the president eventually wanted to sign a tax bill, he gained very little leverage by continuing to condemn Archer's bill. Instead, the White House and Senate Democratic leaders had to concede that the Finance Committee bill was an improvement on the House bill. The president would have a more constructive role in shaping the content of the legislation during the conference committee. So for the moment, Republican leaders were spared a major public relations campaign by a populist president who always seemed to win the public's favor in showdowns with Republicans over tax and spending issues. Second, tax cuts are the bread and butter of the Republican Party. All Republicans want to vote for tax cuts, and most were willing to overlook minor objections to the tax bill for the sake of passing tax relief in general. Tax cuts became the tonic the Republican Party needed to overcome the bloodletting and dissension that ensued from the disaster-relief bill. At a House Republican whip meeting on 18 June, several members spoke about the need to put the disaster bill behind them and work hard to pass the tax cut bill. As one member said, "This is our issue, we need to win on this issue."[65]

Thus the party leadership's main job was to ensure that Republican members and interest groups appreciated the opportunity to pass a tax cut bill and understood that this was the best they could do under the circumstances. In the week leading up to the vote on the House floor, party leaders worked relentlessly to communicate with members and mobilize support for the tax bill. The Speaker made postcommittee adjustments in the tax bill to avert potential opposition from Republican members, recruited Republican-friendly groups to endorse the bill, and conducted a media blitz to highlight the positive aspects of the tax bill and defend the bill against Democratic criticisms. In spite of the obstacles, Speaker Gingrich rose to the occasion and unified the party to pass the tax bill.

Postcommittee Adjustments: Ethanol Lives

As noted in the previous chapter, the Speaker can change parts of a bill reported out of a committee and incorporate those changes in a self-executing rule before the bill is voted on by the whole House. As the leader of the majority party, the Speaker must balance the prerogatives of the Ways and Means Committee chair with the general interests of the party. Archer ignored Gingrich's earlier warnings not to include the elimination of the ethanol subsidy in his package of revenue increases. After Nussle failed to defeat the amendment in committee, Gingrich told Archer in a closed-door meeting, "The House is not going to be the place that kills ethanol."[66] Gingrich proceeded to remove the provision to phase out the ethanol subsidy as part of a self-executing rule for debate.

By yanking the ethanol provision, Gingrich fulfilled two expectations of his role as Speaker: building a winning coalition on the tax bill and preserving a Republican majority. Since Republicans had only a slim majority in the House, if the Democrats voted unanimously against the bill, as they did on the Ways and Means Committee, and Nussle's vote against the committee bill indicated potential opposition by farm-state Republicans, Archer's bill was in jeopardy on the House floor. Removing the ethanol provision reduced the likelihood of a revolt from a cadre of Republican representatives sworn to support the ethanol subsidy. It also protected Republican members from corn-growing regions from having to face opposition on the ethanol issue in the next campaign. One Republican member of Ways and Means described the decision: "Archer met with Newt Gingrich, who was trying to be the Dutch uncle to these people who had great concerns about their own future and their constituents. Gingrich was trying to take some of the rough edges off so we don't lose these candidates in the next election."[67] Moderate Republican members expressed concern about the restrictions of the child tax credit, especially to taxpayers who filed for the child-care credit. Republican leaders worried the Democrats might win the public relations battle over "tax fairness."[68]

As the Ways and Means Committee was marking up Archer's tax bill, on 12 June President Clinton strongly criticized the bill for failing to provide the full child credit to low-income families who received the EITC or to families who deducted child-care expenses. Though he stopped short of using the word veto, Clinton announced, "I cannot let it stand."[69] The next week, Democrats pounded away at the tax fairness issue in one-minute speeches on the House floor and held several media events to denounce the tax package on the grounds that it was unfair to low-income taxpayers. As a compromise gesture, after Ways and Means passed the bill, Archer agreed to place a modified version of the child-care provision in the self-executing rule that would allow a full child credit for families who received child-care credit and made less than $50,000 per year. Archer hoped that Clinton would agree to raise the eligibility for the tax credit from children under thirteen to children under seventeen and stop insisting the tax credit be refundable. The White House countered by requesting that Archer do away with any changes in the AMT and provide a refundable child credit to all children under seventeen. Meanwhile, Rangel mocked Archer's compromise: "It seems the Republicans are having trouble fulfilling promises made to their wealthy constituents and still trying to look good to average, hard-working people."[70]

Public Relations and Class Warfare

The child tax credit had become a central issue in the Democrats' public relations strategy to defeat the tax bill and a major test of Gingrich's ability to keep conservative Republicans on board. In one news conference, House Minority Leader Gephardt asserted that Republicans had aimed their tax cut at the richest 5 percent of taxpayers, while the Democratic plan would offer average taxpayers "a helping hand." Gephardt said, "There is a different way to provide tax relief than rewarding traders of stocks and bonds for a bull market brought on by the Democrats' economic recovery."[71] Reflecting the views of conservative Republicans, Gingrich countered: "When you take out billions of dollars in tax cuts for working people and put in billions of dollars for people who pay no taxes, that's increasing welfare spending," he said. "That's sending the wrong message."[72]

Republicans also attempted to rebut Democratic criticisms with practical arguments about how the tax package benefited a wide range of people. On 19 June the House Republican Conference faxed memos to members to highlight how the Ways and Means bill brought tax relief to college students, teenagers, working women, mothers, and small-business owners.[73] At a Republican whip meeting on 24 June, Conference Chairman Boehner announced the leadership was putting on a "full court press," enlisting interest groups aligned with the party to lobby for the bill and staging several media events for the following two days.[74] Budget Committee Chairman Kasich told the members that Bowles and Hilley assured him that the president wanted to sign a tax bill. He said that the White House would lobby for Rangel's alternative, but it would not oppose the Republican bill. Kasich finished his presentation by applauding Archer's efforts and asking his colleagues to ignore the parts of the bill they disliked and think about what the party had accomplished. "Just think for minute," Kasich said, "If I told you the day after the 1996 elections that Clinton would sign a capital gains tax cut, you would think I was crazy."

For the next two days, the Republican leadership supplied members with fact sheets to explain and promote the tax bill and bombarded the press with upbeat messages about how the tax bill helped middle-income families. One fax from the House Republican Conference, "Taxpayer Relief Act Helps Real Estate," included talking points about how the tax bill helped realtors and a letter signed by ten real estate associations that urged Republicans to vote for the tax bill.[75] On 25 June the Republicans held a news conference featuring Kay Granger (Tex.), Gingrich, Archer, and Kasich, who had become the party's most effective salesperson for the budget agreement. Archer explained how the bill helped Americans "from the childhood years to the education years, from the savings years to the retirement years." Kasich followed with a campaign-style speech about how the Republican tax bill represented freedom and returning power and opportunity to people. On 26 June, the day the House would debate the tax bill, party leaders held a tax-relief rally with the help of major small business, investment, and socially conservative groups who had a stake in the tax bill. The leadership managed to win the endorsement of nearly every group that backed the Republican Party, who sent letters to Republican members urging their support for the tax bill.[76] Party leaders continued to make the case to those groups who objected to parts of Archer's initial bill that some tax relief was better than none, and that the conference committee would decide ultimately the final details of the tax bill.

Debate on the House Floor

The debate on the House floor was filled with talk about fairness, class differences, and partisan politics. The Democrats focused mainly on the child tax credit and the distribution of the tax cuts, using Treasury Department data on family incomes. After a Republican member spoke, a Democrat responded, citing the number of children from the Republican member's state who would not receive the child credit. The Republicans countered that their tax plan was targeted toward middle-class families who pay income taxes, not to welfare recipients, and referred to distribution charts prepared by the Joint Economic Committee.[77] Members from both parties referred to people in their districts who would benefit from the tax cut.

Minority Leader Gephardt chastised the Republicans for not making the child tax credit refundable:

> How dare anyone say that someone is on welfare who goes to work every day earning $17,000 and $20,000 and $25,000 a year. They are paying taxes. They are paying the Social Security tax. They are paying federal excise taxes, they are paying state taxes, they are paying local taxes, they are paying lots of taxes, and they need help. And they above everyone need the child credit.[78]

Ranking Ways and Means Democrat Rangel bemoaned the partisan process on the Ways and Means Committee and listed the provisions in the bill that were unacceptable to the President: the education tax cuts, the nonrefundable tax credit, and indexing capital gains.

> Bipartisanship means Democrats and Republicans working together with the President of the United States, and the President now says that this has moved so far away from the issue of fairness that he would not be able to sign the Republican bill.
>
> Even in the State of Texas they have so skewed and increased the number of people that will be ineligible for the child credit that half of the kids in Texas and over half of the kids in the State of New York will be ineligible for the family tax credit.
>
> Mr. Chairman, I think it is arrogant and all Americans ought to be indignant, when people do not even consider going on welfare and they work every day. . . . But we are saying, "We have to

pass over you because we want to make taxes lighter on the very richest of Americans."[79]

Archer responded to Democratic criticisms by saying that tax relief was overdue and that the American people were signaling that the "era of big government is over, and the era of big taxes is over." Archer emphasized that most of the tax breaks would go to the middle class:

> This plan is dedicated to America's forgotten middle-income taxpayers. Fully 76 percent of the tax relief in this plan goes to people with incomes between $20,000 and $75,000 a year.
>
> When it comes to taxes, my philosophy is simple. We must cut taxes because tax money does not belong to the government; it belongs to the middle-income workers of America who earned it, who made it and who are entitled to spend it in the way that they want to spend it. People in Washington, I think, sometimes forget that, but I never will.[80]

Rounding out the partisan battles, the House proceeded to defeat Rangel's substitute by a vote of 197–235, along party lines; not a single Republican voted for it, and only eight Democrats voted against it. The House passed the Republican tax bill 253–279, with only 1 Republican voting against and 27 Democrats voting in favor.

Tax Policy and Realist Expectations

This chapter underscores several aspects of the realist perspective. First, the bicameral differences in the tax bills illustrate how institutional and political circumstances, policy constraints, and individual leadership styles affect the legislative process and policy outcomes. The fact that the two institutions responded differently to the broad instructions of the budget resolution indicates the variability and flexibility in the political system. Second, leadership is crucial to policymaking and coalition-building both within and across party lines. If policy leaders like Archer decide to act independently, party leaders must intervene in order to ensure a winning coalition and protect the electoral interests of individual members. Third, divided government can facilitate policymaking by diffusing responsibility. Republican leaders told their colleagues, in essence: "This is the best we can do with a Democratic president." And "This is better than we might expect under the circumstances." Divided government enabled party leaders to take responsibility for the "good" parts of the bill and blame the White House for the concerns raised by wary members and GOP-friendly interest groups.

Finally, the debate over the tax bills once again confirms the notion that budget policy decisions are based on a complex mix of principles, political calculations, rational analysis, and public responsiveness. Principles form the broad contours of the policy debate, a debate about fairness, opportunity, risk, and reward. Members hold those principles because they define their perspective on governing, and leaders express them because they know their party's primary constituencies care about them. Indeed, a debate must be framed in terms of principles to engage the members and address the core needs of party loyalists. Party leaders must weigh principles and partisan priorities against practical concerns about how to advance their policy goals and political interests.

9

Conference Politics: Staking Out Positions and Restoring Bipartisanship

The House and Senate reconciliation bills produced a mix of partisan and bipartisan provisions, with the House tax and spending bills decidedly more Republican. In order for the bills to pass both chambers, conference committees had to resolve numerous differences between the House and Senate reconciliation bills. Conference committees consist of representatives and senators from the House and Senate committees that have jurisdiction over the bills passed by each chamber. Conference committees have always played a key role in the legislative process because they are positioned at the end and they must put together the final bill to be voted on by both chambers and, if approved, sent to the president.[1] Yet as political scientist Stephen Van Beek observes, conference committees have changed significantly over the years, especially when dealing with omnibus legislation.[2] They are more than "mopping up" operations that split the differences between bills passed by each chamber. Instead, party leaders play key roles in organizing conferences and facilitating compromises between contending parties, and the president participates indirectly by sending signals through the media and often directly by negotiating with congressional leaders. The president is especially important in divided government. Thus the conference presents another opportunity to adjust policy and introduces another round of uncertainty in the budget process.

Overview of the Conference Process

Formal conference proceedings began in a traditional fashion: members from House and Senate committees were assigned to the conference committee, and subconferences were established to deliberate over the two reconciliation bills, meeting from 10 July through 18 July to work through the differences in the House and Senate bills. By the end of the week, though, leaders recognized that a traditional conference committee was not going to work. The Republican-dominated legislation passed by the House, the bipartisan legislation passed by the Senate, and the divided-government situation set up a three-way bargaining arrangement. On some issues, the House and Senate disagreed and the White House favored one side over the other; on other issues, the White House disagreed with both chambers (see table 9.1, p. 170). The situation required the White House to play an active role in the process, but it was not clear at the outset with whom the White House should bargain. Meanwhile, Republican leaders realized that the unwieldy conference committee consisting of members from both parties weakened their bargaining position in relation to President Clinton—the person who had the ultimate power to accept or reject legislation passed by Congress. Thus, after one week, the formal conference committee essentially disbanded, and from 18 July to 23 July House and Senate Republicans met in Speaker Gingrich's office to develop "unified" Republican bills for taxes and spending. The unified plan took a decidedly conservative bent and was designed to improve the Republicans' bargaining leverage.

President Clinton's strategic advantage was anchored by institutional powers and bolstered by public opinion. Since House and Senate Republicans approved different bills, Clinton could play one chamber off the other and position himself as the "decisive" actor on several key issues. Clinton sided with the Senate on the tobacco tax, additional spending for children's health, applying federal labor laws to workfare recipients, restoring SSI benefits for legal immigrants who become disabled, and opposing indexation of capital gains. He sided with the House in opposing Senate proposals to raise the eligibility age and add a $5 copayment to home health services for Medicare beneficiaries. President Clinton also had the power to veto a bill if he strongly disagreed with some of its provisions. He had demonstrated his skillful use of the veto and his capacity to marshal public support in June when he forced Republicans to agree to his terms on the disaster aid bill. In addition to the president's institutional advantages, a *Washington Post* survey found that Clinton's public approval ratings reached 64 percent, the highest of his administration.[3] Even Republican surveys showed the public preferred Clinton's priorities on tax policy and believed they were more "fair" to the middle class.[4]

Clinton gained further advantage as Gingrich faced severe doubts among Republicans about his fitness to continue as Speaker. Just as conferees began to meet on 10 July, Republican leaders Armey, Boehner, and DeLay and Gingrich's special assistant, Bill Paxon (N.Y.), were entertaining a plan to oust the Speaker. While party leaders tried to quash rumors about an internal rebellion, Paxon resigned and the other three party leaders were forced to apologize to the House Republican Conference.[5] Speculation swirled around the Capitol about the effects of the "attempted coup" on the budget talks. Democratic leaders suggested that internal divisions among Republican leaders disrupted negotiations. With the party in turmoil, Republican leaders seemed undecided over whether to strike a quick compromise with the president or hold firmly to Republican priorities.

Yet the precise effects of the episode were unclear. Some observers argued that the plot reflected deep divisions within the Republican Party; others viewed it as a lack of confidence in Gingrich.[6] A House Republican budget aide said: "It's an absolute public relations disaster." In contrast, House Budget Committee Chairman Kasich, who was used to the ups and downs of the budget process, believed the incident was a "momentary snag" and drew parallels between the budget process and an adventure film: "This is like an Indiana Jones movie. I mean, you've got arrows, you've got boulders, you've got poisonous snakes, you've got everything—but we're going to get there. It's just part of the process."[7] Democrats argued that the Speaker's troubles caused Republicans to take more conservative positions than they normally would have, disrupted the process of compromise, and strengthened the president's hand in negotiations.

After party leaders presented the White House with the details of the unified plan on 23 July, congressional Democrats urged Clinton to resist a quick compromise. The tension between Clinton and congressional Democrats over negotiating strategies had been apparent since the outset of the budget process. While congressional Democrats benefited from pointing out differences between themselves and Republicans, Clinton wanted to make a deal, and there were risks in waiting too long. Gene Sperling, director of Clinton's National Economic Council, suggested that Clinton's motives differed from those of congressional Democrats: "For the president, this will be a legacy . . . that he was able to bring down the deficit, reform welfare and still show there was a significant role for a smaller but more effective government in investing in people."[8]

Negotiations also seemed impelled by a CBO report released in July showing that strong economic growth would raise enough revenues to balance the budget by 1998, even without the budget deal. Since tax cuts and short-term increases in discretionary spending actually boosted projected deficits for 1998, liberal Democrats and conservative Republicans argued the deficit would be lower if Congress and the president did nothing. Though negotiators on both sides refuted those claims, the optimistic projections pressured them to move quickly, as new revenues brought renewed demands by liberal Democrats for more spending and by conservative Republicans for larger tax cuts.

Table 9.1

Major Characteristics of Medicare, Children's Health, and Welfare Provisions of the House Bill, the Senate Bill, and the President's Position (Selected Issues)[a]

Medicare

Issue	House bill	Senate bill	President Clinton
Means test	None	Means test Medicare Part B	Open to a means test, depending on details
Eligibility age	No change	Phase in increase in eligibility age from 65 to 67 by 2027	Opposed to Senate
Home health services	No change	Add $5 copayment for home health services	Opposed to Senate
Medical savings accounts (MSAs)	Demo project to 500,000 seniors/Cap the deductible ($6,000)	Limit project to 100,000/Cap the deductible ($2,250)	Limit numbers and geographical area of MSA project

Medicaid

Issue	House bill	Senate bill	President Clinton
Fund Medicare Part B premiums	Less than budget agreement	Funds for 5 years	Prefers guaranteed funding after 5 years
Legal immigrants	Does not restore benefits	Restores some benefits for children of some immigrants	Opposes both chambers
Disabled children	Does not restore benefits	Does not restore benefits	Opposes both chambers

Table 9.1 (Continued)

Children's health care

Issue	*House bill*	*Senate bill*	*President Clinton*
Cost (5 years)	$16 billion	$24 billion	Supports Senate
Health services/ insurance	States choose to purchase services, insurance from Medicaid, or private plan	Requires states to purchase insurance under Medicaid	Supports Senate
Benefits package	No required package, states choose among options	Guaranteed comprehensive package of benefits equal to Blue Cross/Blue Shield for federal employees	Supports Senate
Tobacco tax	None	Increase cigarette tax by 43 cents	Supports Senate
Hyde amendment	Included in bill	Included in bill	Opposes both chambers

Welfare provisions

Issue	*House bill*	*Senate bill*	*President Clinton*
SSI for legal immigrants	Restores SSI to all legal immigrants as of 22 August 1996, but does not extend benefits to those who become disabled after that date	Restores SSI to all legal immigrants and provides benefits for those who were in the country after 22 August 1996 and later became disabled	Supports Senate
Workfare participants	Allows states to offset the minimum wage with other cash benefits (food stamps and welfare); workfare participants exempted from federal labor laws	Full eligibility for minimum wage and protection under labor laws	Supports Senate

a. The table contains only major differences. The House and Senate reconciliation bills contained hundreds of discrepancies in funding formulas and eligibility rules for those programs, though they were much easier to handle than the selected items in the table.

Staking Out Positions

The White House began to stake out positions on the reconciliation spending bills immediately after they passed the House and Senate. The president and his advisers cited major problems with the House-passed welfare provisions, the Senate-passed Medicare changes related to beneficiaries, parts of the children's health initiative, and various aspects of the two tax bills. The Medicare and children's health provisions split House and Senate Republicans, and President Clinton complicated matters with a third perspective on both issues. Meanwhile, Clay Shaw, chair of the Ways and Means Subcommittee on Human Resources, maintained an uncompromising position on SSI and workfare, items the president singled out as potential deal breakers. In the area of tax policy, on 30 June, less than a week after the House and Senate finished work on their tax bills, the president introduced a third alternative. Beginning on 10 July, conferees of both parties deliberated for about one week over the House and Senate versions of both bills. Yet aside from issues related to Medicare, they made only marginal progress toward resolving their differences. Republicans caucused separately and developed unified positions on the major issues before bargaining directly with the White House.

Medicare and Medicaid

As table 9.1 shows, the House and Senate disagreed on several aspects of Medicare policy. Yet the major question was whether the House and the president would accept the Senate's proposals to raise the eligibility age for Medicare, means test the Part B premium, and add a $5 copayment for home health services. President Clinton opposed raising the eligibility age and adding the copayment, but he seemed willing to go along with a means test for Part B premiums. Liberal Democrats, led by House Minority Leader Gephardt, strongly opposed all three proposals. House Republican leaders, still smarting from the Democrats' "Mediscare" campaign in 1996, were not prepared to go along without Gephardt's support. Ultimately, all three provisions were dropped from the bill as Democrats and groups representing the elderly raised concerns about the costs to senior citizens and House Republicans feared a political backlash from Democrats. The means test was also brought down by a dispute over administrative procedures that evoked political differences between the parties.

The Senate provision to raise the eligibility age from sixty-five to sixty-seven was an early casualty of the conference on the reconciliation bill. On 10 July, the first official day of the conference committee, Gephardt and Senate Minority

Leader Tom Daschle held a news conference with two dozen senior citizens to voice their opposition to the Medicare changes. Gephardt said of Republicans: "Their intent is to destroy Medicare." After meeting with House Democratic leaders later that day, Erskine Bowles told reporters: "From the president's viewpoint, we don't see how it makes any sense whatsoever to create a whole new class of uninsured people."[9] The same day, the House voted 414 to 14 to instruct conferees to reject the Senate's proposal to raise the eligibility age.

The public deliberations over means testing the Medicare Part B premium lasted a bit longer, as the White House and Republican leaders debated differences over how to administer the policy. The Senate plan called for a means test to begin with individuals earning incomes of $50,000 and to increase progressively, capping off at 100 percent for seniors with incomes above $100,000. President Clinton wanted the scale to begin at $75,000 and cap off at 75 percent of the total premium. Most importantly, Clinton thought the IRS should collect the premiums through income tax forms, but Senate Majority Leader Trent Lott wanted the Department of Health and Human Services (HHS) to administer the policy by deducting the premium from Social Security checks. Lott complained of the president's idea: "I think that is kind of a poison pill and turns it into a tax, which is not our goal."[10] On purely rational grounds, the White House position made more sense; according to the CBO, the government would save $5 billion more over five years if the IRS administered the policy.[11] But letting the IRS collect the premium increase sent up a red flag for Republicans, and the issue sank under the political weight of being labeled a tax increase.

A coalition of centrist senators, led by Kerrey and John Chafee (R-R.I.), urged leaders to look beyond the logistics of collecting the premium and take advantage of an opportunity to pass a significant Medicare reform. Yet any efforts to reach a compromise over how to implement the means test glossed over the fact that behind the scenes, House Republican leaders rejected all three Senate provisions from the outset of the conference. Though Kasich pushed for the reforms, Bill Thomas, chair of the House Ways and Means Subcommittee on Health, was lukewarm about the changes, and Ways and Means Chair Bill Archer was downright opposed. When conferees met, House Republican party leaders, led by Majority Leader Armey, immediately vetoed the Medicare initiatives. House Republicans had taken a beating by Democratic candidates on Medicare in 1996, and they voiced concerns about having to vote for a bill that would increase costs to seniors. Bill Hoagland, staff director of the Senate Budget Committee, described the situation:

> In the end, the politics dominated, mainly the politics of the
> House and presidential politics. When we first went to the

House with our reconciliation bill, from the beginning, the Speaker, the Majority Leader made it very clear, and so did Mr. Archer, that we weren't doing those provisions. Even when there was a hint the president was willing to go along with means testing, it was discounted rather quickly on the part of the House Republicans, particularly Mr. Archer, who believed this was a trap for taxes.

Then the big part of presidential politics. Mr. Armey said: "Until Dick Gephardt stands out front and says he supports the proposals, unless he makes a commitment, there is no way any Republican in the House of Representatives should support this because we will lose the House in the next election." So, this showed how dominating the Minority Leader was, even though he played no direct role in negotiations. So there was hardly ever a chance for those provisions. They passed the Senate but they weren't given 30 seconds in conference.[12]

Other key House and Senate differences over Medicare and Medicaid were worked out in the Republican unified plan, but the GOP proposals were opposed by the White House. For example, Senate Republicans agreed to accept the House proposal for a demonstration project that allowed up to 500,000 seniors to enroll in a Medical Savings Account (MSA); the White House wanted a smaller project. The White House strongly opposed portions of the House and Senate reconciliation bills related to restoring Medicaid benefits to legal immigrants and disabled children. Republicans agreed to the Senate position of allocating all of the $1.5 billion in Medicaid spending to pay for the Medicare Part B premium for seniors with incomes between 125 and 150 percent of the poverty line. Yet the Senate proposal guaranteed funding for only five years, the life of the budget agreement, whereas the White House wanted to extend funding beyond that.

Welfare Provisions

The main differences over welfare policy dealt with SSI eligibility for legal immigrants and rules governing welfare-to-work programs. The House bill took more conservative positions by denying SSI to legal immigrants who became elderly or disabled after 22 August 1996 and exempting welfare-to-work participants from federal minimum wage and labor laws. The Senate bill restored SSI benefits to all eligible immigrants who were in the country after 22 August 1996 and later became disabled, and it did not treat welfare-to-work participants any differently from other workers. President Clinton preferred the Senate's position, contending that Republicans should stick with the terms of the budget agreement regarding SSI eligibility and adopt the administration's ruling that workfare participants are treated like all workers. The president sent early signals that the House positions on both issues could result in a presidential veto.

Conferees made almost no progress. On the weekend of 19 July, just after the plot to remove Gingrich became public, the Speaker convened Republican conferees in his office to develop a unified Republican proposal on welfare issues. By then, President Clinton's strategic advantage could not have been greater, and Republicans concluded they needed bargaining leverage as they approached a final round of negotiations with the White House. In the closed caucus meetings, House and Senate Republican conferees decided to endorse the House's proposals on SSI and rules for workfare recipients. Senate Democratic Minority Leader Tom Daschle responded: "It appears that all of the talk and concern about revolution in the House has caused some of our Republican colleagues to attempt to placate the far right of their caucus in the House and that is not going to get us an agreement."[13]

Children's Health Initiative

Republicans took a similar tack as they formed a unified position on the children's health initiative. House and Senate versions of the children's health initiative differed in two major areas, with the House plan reflecting a more conservative approach. First, the House approved a $16 billion plan with no cigarette tax, whereas the Senate passed a $24 billion proposal with the remaining $8 billion funded by an increase in the cigarette tax. Second, while both bills distributed the bulk of funds to states in the form of block grants, the House bill did not require states to guarantee specific health benefits for children, whereas the Senate bill did. The president endorsed the Senate proposal to expand health coverage beyond the $16 billion specified in the budget agreement with additional funding from cigarette taxes, though he expressed reservations that even the Senate bill gave too much discretion to the states. The White House preferred legislation that directed states to use most of the funds to enroll uninsured children into the Medicaid program.

After little progress was made in the subconference on children's health initiative, Republicans attempted to develop a unified plan that would serve as a benchmark for negotiations with the White House. Once again, Republicans took a more conservative approach, reflecting demands made by most House Republican members. House Republican leaders knew they might have to compromise eventually, but many members opposed raising taxes and they wanted the leadership to take a strong position against the tobacco tax. House and Senate Republicans agreed to disagree on whether to endorse a cigarette tax, and House leaders maintained that such a tax should not be used to fund additional children's health coverage. They agreed to a $16 billion plan with at least 85 percent of the funds devoted to providing health insurance, but the proposal omitted guaranteed uniform benefits and allowed the states to decide among a variety of benefit packages. President Clinton insisted on more specific guarantees of health insurance and $24 billion in new spending.

Tax Alternatives

As table 9.2 (p. 177) illustrates, the House and Senate tax bills differed with respect to several items. The major differences were over the child tax credit, the alternative minimum tax, capital gains provisions, and the cigarette tax. In contrast with the Senate bill, the House version indexed capital gains for inflation, phased out the corporate alternative minimum tax, contained no increase in the cigarette tax, and offered no child tax credit for lower-income families who received the EITC and had no income tax liability. On capital gains, both bills reduced the rate of capital gains, but the House indexed capital gains for inflation.

On the surface, the differences were not insurmountable, but the two chambers pursued different paths, and policy leaders had already compromised on specific details of their respective tax bills. House Ways and Means Chairman Archer entered the conference with strong commitments to indexing capital gains, cutting the corporate AMT, and a nonrefundable child tax credit. Senate Finance Chairman Roth's main priority was the individual retirement accounts (IRA), which would have to compete with Archer's priorities and face White House criticisms about long-term effects on revenue losses. By opting for a bipartisan process in the Senate, Roth emboldened such Democratic conferees as Daniel Patrick Moynihan, the ranking member of the Senate Finance Committee. Senate passage of the tax bill legitimized the cigarette tax and diminished the importance of House proposals to index capital gains and limit the child tax credit.

Though the White House generally favored the Senate bill, Treasury Secretary Rubin complained that not enough of the tax benefits went to middle-class Americans, the education tax breaks swayed too far from Clinton's original proposal, and the IRAs threatened to cause large revenue losses in the long run. On 30 June, President Clinton introduced a third alternative. Clinton's bill represented a

Table 9.2
Major Components of the House and Senate Tax Bills (key differences in italics)

Child tax credit

Both the Senate and House would allow a nonrefundable credit, though the details of the two bills differed significantly. The House bill contained a $400 credit in 1998 rising to $500 the next year to each child under the age of 17. *The Senate bill gave parents with children age 12 and younger the option of diverting their credit into a tax-deferred education savings account. Those children ages 13–16 would be required to deposit $500 in such savings accounts to benefit fully from the credit. The credit began at $250 per child in 1997 and increased to $500 thereafter. Lower-income families receiving the EITC were eligible for a partial credit.*

Education tax incentives

Both the Senate and House bills include tax credits equal to 50 percent of up to $3,000 in out-of-pocket tuition expenses and books for postsecondary schooling for taxpayers with adjusted gross incomes of up to $40,000 a year and couples with incomes of up to $80,000. *The House bill provides a deduction for undergraduate college costs not offered in the Senate bill.*

Capital gains

Both bills cut the top tax rate on individuals' capital gains from 28 percent to 20 percent for those making more than $40,000 a year and 10 percent for those with incomes of less than $40,000. *The House bill indexes the tax cuts for inflation.*

Estate taxes

Both the House and Senate bills increase the estate tax exemption from $600,000 to $1 million. *The Senate bill phases in the exemption more quickly.*

Individual Retirement Accounts

Both bills expand IRAs by allowing individuals to contribute up to $2,000 without a tax penalty and make tax-free withdrawals on the principal and interest accumulated in the accounts when they retire. *The Senate bill expands tax-deferred IRAs by raising the income limits on taxpayers eligible to use them.*

Alternative minimum tax

Both bills reduce the alternative minimum tax for individuals. *The House bill also phases out the alternative minimum for corporations.*

Cigarette tax

The Senate bill increases cigarette tax by 20 cents and earmarks $8 billion for children's health beyond the $16 billion paid for in the budget agreement.

compromise that accommodated the basic priorities sought by Republicans, responded to the concerns of many Democrats on several details, sided with the Senate bill in a few controversial areas, and made room for his highest priority—education tax breaks. In making concessions to Republicans, Clinton's bill contained a capital gains reduction, estate tax reform, tax incentives for IRAs, and a child tax credit for children up to age seventeen, rather than age twelve. Yet in a nod to Democratic concerns about the distribution effects to lower- and middle-income taxpayers and long-term drains on federal revenues, the capital gains provision increased the exclusion from taxes rather than cut the rate of capital gains, the estate tax exemptions were targeted to family-owned businesses and farms, the IRA incentives were limited, and the child tax credit was refundable against an individual's entire federal tax burden, including payroll taxes. Clinton sided with the original Senate bill by including a 20-cent increase in cigarette taxes, allowing parents to use the $500 tax credit in a tax-free Kidsave account for higher education expenses and opposing the indexation of capital gains. Finally, Clinton retained his commitment to the HOPE scholarship credit for the first two years of postsecondary education, and he dropped the tuition tax deduction in favor of 20 percent credit for tuition in the third and fourth years on the first $5,000 until the year 2000 and the first $10,000 thereafter.

While Republicans warmly received Clinton's proposal, congressional Democrats were disappointed and puzzled. Archer said Clinton "deserves credit and praise for joining with Republicans in endorsing our approach to tax relief."[14] Ranking Ways and Means Democrat Rangel said that Clinton's plan "moves the budget negotiations in the right direction" but that it fell short of extending the child credit to all "working poor" families. Rangel expressed the concerns of many Democrats that Clinton's latest offer weakened the Democrats' bargaining position in further negotiations: "The president is trying to work with the Republicans, where they would not work with us in the House. . . . I would hope that the president wouldn't rush into an accommodation without the support of Democrats on the tax-writing committees. He still has the power of the veto and shouldn't give it up."[15] Yet Clinton did not threaten a veto, and White House officials privately told Republican negotiators the president was eager to sign a tax bill.[16] The day the tax bill was announced, Clinton told reporters: "We are committed to working with the Republicans, and this is a good-faith effort to do that, incorporating both their ideas for capital gains and some other things as well."[17]

Yet while Clinton's tax proposal included several Republican priorities, fundamental differences remained between the White House plan and the House and

Senate tax bills. Treasury Secretary Robert Rubin, the administration's point man on tax policy, claimed that a disproportionate share of the House and Senate tax bills went to the wealthiest Americans and revenue losses threatened to "explode" the deficit in the long run. While Rubin stopped short of promising a presidential veto, he contended that both bills failed to meet the administration's four "basic tests" of sound policy: fiscal responsibility, fairness, contribution to economic growth, and inclusion of the president's education package.

The issues raised by Rubin illustrated, once again, the complex mix of principles, politics, and policy analysis in the budget process. As a matter of principle, Democrats favor tax cuts that benefit lower- and middle-income Americans. Moreover, they believe that "fiscal conservatism" means raising enough revenues to keep pace with government spending. The political advantages of accusing Republicans of being unfair to the middle class were clear from polls that showed Americans believed Republicans favored tax breaks for the wealthy. As a policy matter, Democrats believed that the Reagan tax cuts produced large deficits in the 1980s and that restoring the revenue base, especially with tax increases in the 1990 and 1993 budget bills, had been a key element in the progress toward a balanced budget. Rubin also cited a Treasury Department study that showed how Clinton's tax plan conferred more benefits to the lower and middle classes (see table 9.3).

Table 9.3
Treasury Department Estimates of the Distribution of Tax Cut Proposals over Ten Years

	Clinton	**House bill**	**Senate bill**
Education and child credits (middle-income tax cuts)	83%	38%	43%
Savings, capital gains, AMT, estate taxes (upper-income tax cuts)	10%	55%	53%
Remaining tax provisions	7%	4%	4%

Source: Clay Chandler, "GOP Tax Plans Collide with Clinton's; Support Unlikely, Rubin Warns," *Washington Post*, 6 July 1997, A14.

Republicans based their arguments on policy, principles, and analysis. While Democrats pointed to a Treasury Department study that reported 67 percent of tax benefits from Clinton's plan went to the middle 60 percent of taxpayers, Republicans claimed that 75 percent of the benefits in their plans went to households with incomes of less than $75,000.[18] As a matter of principle, Republicans opposed giving the child tax credit to families who did not pay income taxes and in many cases already received a subsidy for payroll taxes for Social Security and Medicare. They also used political tactics, accusing Democrats of giving tax breaks to welfare recipients. Republicans relied on analyses made by the Joint Economic Committee (JEC) and the Joint Committee on Taxation (JCT) to challenge the methods the Treasury Department used to measure family income. Chairman Archer also complained that by adding the tobacco tax and extending the earned income credit to "welfare" recipients, the net tax cut of $85 billion in the budget agreement dropped to $60 billion.

For three weeks, the parties traded barbs. The battle was over principles, but the debate was complicated by the fact that the two sides relied on different methods and assumptions in calculating the effects of tax changes. Consequently, Democrats and Republicans talked past each other. The Treasury Department focused on ten-year effects, whereas the JCT used five-year projections of how tax cuts affected benefits and revenues. The White House and congressional Republicans also disagreed over whether to treat capital gains revenues as a tax cut, who qualified as middle class, who were welfare recipients and whether they deserved a tax cut, what happens to the relative tax burden as a result of the tax cuts, and whether each side met the terms of the budget agreement dealing with education tax breaks or total net tax relief.[19] Debates could have gone on forever. The reality was that the public favored President Clinton's tax cuts and considered his plan more "fair," and Republicans did not have enough time to change that perception.

In order to strengthen their collective position in relation to the president, House and Senate Republicans developed a unified package of priorities that could form the basis for final negotiations with the president. Replicating the strategy they pursued on welfare and children's health, Republican conferees took more conservative positions on several key aspects of the tax bill. The Republican unified plan endorsed the House provisions to index capital gains, cut the corporate AMT, make the child tax credit nonrefundable, and omit the 20-cent increase in the cigarette tax. When Republicans presented the plan to the White House on 23 July, Gene Sperling said, "We don't consider it a serious starting point." Commenting on the cigarette tax, President Clinton said, "I intend to fight to keep that money in the budget, and fight for our children."[20]

Restoring Bipartisanship and Closing the Deal

The Republican unified plan reduced House and Senate differences and gave Republican leaders more bargaining chips in negotiations with the White House.

But the hard line taken by Republicans provoked Democrats to fight back, and for several days after the Republican plan emerged on 23 July, the process was mired in partisan conflict and public wrangling. The outlines of the bipartisan budget agreement passed in May were still in place, but Republicans had violated parts of the agreement, Congress had added new items, and the legislative details of the tax bill became subject to negotiation. Both sides wanted a budget deal, but the endgame was unclear. Uncertainty over how far each side was willing to push on various terms of the tax bill increased tensions, and negotiations came to an abrupt halt on 25 July. But trust was restored, enabling Republican leaders to resolve their differences with White House negotiators over several high-profile issues.

Partisan Politics and the Threat of Gridlock

After Republicans presented their plan on 23 July, congressional Democrats and President Clinton once again weighed the virtues of compromising. Minority Leader Tom Daschle pointed out: "They moved in the wrong direction; they moved farther and farther to the right, rather than towards the middle, where we needed to be if we were going to make any real progress on many of the issues."[21] After meeting with congressional Democratic leaders, Daschle told reporters: "The president's last words to me were, 'I'm not going anywhere.' He's in no hurry."[22] Yet Clinton wanted to complete the budget agreement, and if he waited too long or provoked Republicans too much, he ran the risk of undermining the deal altogether. Thus the White House negotiating strategy was to use the president's advantage to secure the president's priorities and get as much as possible before compromising with Republicans.

White House negotiators initially viewed the unified Republican plan as an unnecessary step away from conciliation. In response to the unified plan, OMB Director Raines lamented to Republicans, "Looks like on every issue where you had a chance you went against us."[23] Clinton insisted that several key provisions must be part of a compromise: $8 billion more for children's health, labor protections for workfare participants, restoration of SSI benefits for legal immigrants, and a more limited demonstration project for Medicare beneficiaries enrolled in MSAs. Secretary Rubin took a hard line on the president's proposal to extend the child tax credit to more low-income families and stated strong opposition to indexing capital gains. After emerging from meetings with White House officials on 24 July, Republican negotiators expressed pessimism about reaching a quick resolution to partisan differences. Senate Budget Committee Chairman Domenici observed:

"We're not making any headway yet." House Budget Committee Chairman Kasich added, "There's nothing going on but talk."[24]

In an effort to expedite the process, the principal leaders agreed to reduce the size of the meetings. On 25 July, Republican Party leaders Lott and Gingrich met with Bowles, Hilley, and Rubin, and within a few hours, they resolved several differences over welfare policy and Medicare. Republicans agreed to a slightly scaled-down version of the MSA plan for Medicare and gave in to Clinton's demands to restore Medicaid for children who lost coverage as a result of welfare reform and to extend SSI coverage to legal immigrants who become disabled. The White House agreed to allow for private contracts between doctors and Medicare patients. Yet no progress was made on tax policy, and negotiations reached a boiling point on 26 July over the child tax credit. *Washington Post* journalists Clay Chandler and Eric Pianin described the encounter that nearly undermined the negotiations:

> The Clinton team had insisted the tax break [child credit] be extended to families earning as little as $18,000 a year. The demand infuriated Republicans, who complained this was really just a backdoor increase in "welfare spending." Finally, Gingrich made a major concession and agreed to what he thought was the White House proposal. "That won't work," said Gene Sperling, the administration's point man on the issue. Clinton was actually insisting on a formula that was much more generous. The speaker was dumbfounded—and began to suspect that he'd been had. Each time Republicans made concessions, it seemed, the Clinton team only raised the bar. Where would it end? "Forget it," he snapped with disgust, and stalked out of the room.[25]

The White House had pushed the delicate issue one step too far. Gingrich threatened to end negotiations, but Senator Domenici urged the Speaker to stay in Washington and work out the disagreements with the White House.[26] Gingrich agreed and sent copies of his book to Bowles and Hilley with "sincere inscriptions." Gingrich later commented: "Despite the fact that we were in a muddle, I refused to believe their intent was malign. I wanted to say, 'Look, guys, this is a roadblock, not an impossibility.'" Hilley insisted: "It was never a matter of us trying to screw them. . . . It was a matter of them not understanding the original proposal and thinking we were trying some last-minute [deception]." With trust restored, negotiators moved swiftly through their differences on 28 July.

Other participants in the process pointed out that the terms on which the two sides returned to negotiations were a matter of trust and necessity. Gingrich's decision to leave the room was based on more than a personal frustration with

Sperling. Gingrich had taken a strong stand against extending the child credit to families with no income tax burden, and there were limits to how far he could compromise and retain the support of House Republicans. The trust Gingrich had established with Hilley and Bowles went only so far, and when he returned to the bargaining table, Gingrich assured White House negotiators that the president would pay a price if they continued to undermine the budget deal for political gains. Republican House Conference Committee Chair Bliley recalled: "The Speaker made it clear to the President, 'Hey if we don't get agreement on this package, then it is going to be all out war. You won't get fast track on GATT, you will have a difficult time getting expansion of NATO, and we will cut to the bone all of the appropriations bills. You won't get any new money for the programs you want.'" Kasich pointed out: "It almost blew up at the end. But then they got a reality check. They were too greedy, and you can't get too greedy."[27]

Final Decisions

As he summed up the final meetings with the White House, Senate Majority Leader Lott concluded: "We gave ground, and the administration gave ground, and we found common ground."[28] More specifically, negotiators applied one or more of three decision rules to reach final compromises. First, the leaders of each party had an informal veto over provisions that either went against their basic principles or violated the terms of the bipartisan budget agreement approved in May. Second, on spending or tax provisions that went beyond the budget agreement, negotiators opted for what might be called a "rule of two-thirds"—negotiators agreed to the position taken by two of the three institutions prior to the unified Republican plan, as long as the two proponents could agree on the details. Third, negotiators traded off the funding, revenue, and policy details on the major issues where all three were in disagreement. Table 9.4 (p. 184) identifies the final decisions. In some cases, more than one rule applied. For example, the president threatened to veto the reconciliation spending bill unless the GOP agreed to drop the minimum-wage and workfare provisions in the unified plan. Those were apparently matters of principle, though they also violated the budget agreement and were opposed in the original Senate bill. Many final decisions were decided on the basis of the rule of two-thirds and a host of policy decisions, including several tax provisions and the children's health initiative, resulted from tradeoffs.

The final tax changes were brought about by a number of compromises. Republicans agreed to a White House demand to allow some taxpayers who receive

Table 9.4

*Final Provisions on Major Items of the Reconciliation Spending and
Tax Bills by Three Broad Decision Rules*

A. Provisions dropped or restored by informal veto due to violation of principle or terms of the budget agreement

Medicaid	Restored Medicaid benefits to legal immigrants and disabled children no longer eligible for SSI (part of the budget agreement removed from House bill).[a]
Welfare	(1) Dropped House provisions to restrict workfare participants' eligibility for federal labor and minimum-wage laws (Clinton veto threat and not included in the budget agreement).[a]
	(2) Dropped House provision to restore SSI benefits to legal immigrants who were disabled or elderly as of 22 August 1996, but not to those who become disabled thereafter.[a]

B. Provisions decided by the rule of two-thirds

Medicare	(1) Dropped Senate provisions to raise the eligibility age and add a $5 copayment for home health services passed in Senate (Clinton and House Republicans opposed).
	(2) Dropped Senate provisions to apply a means test for Part B premium (two proponents—Senate and White House—could not agree on details of implementing the policy).
	(3) Medical Savings Accounts (MSAs) demonstration project a compromise between proponents in House and Senate 390,000 beneficiaries eligible with the House provision c a $6,000 maximum deductible.
Welfare	Extended SSI benefits to disabled legal immigrants who were in the United States before 22 August 1996, regardless of when they became disabled (Clinton and Senate agreed).
Children's health	(1) Increased cigarette tax by 15 cents over 5 years and increased spending for children's health from $16 to $24 billion (Clinton and Senate agreed).
	(2) Hyde amendment prohibiting federal funding of abortions, though states can spend their own money for this purpose (House and Senate agreed).

a. The rule of two-thirds also applied.

Table 9.4 (Continued)

C. Tradeoffs

Medicaid	Spent $1.5 billion on block grant to states to help pay Medicare Part B premium for elderly with incomes between 120 and 175 percent of the poverty line. Up from the House's $700 million, but complied with House rules for eligibility.[a]
Children's health	Allowed states to choose among several benefit packages or develop their own plans. The discretion granted to the states was a tradeoff for House leaders who agreed with the tobacco tax.
Child tax credit	Republicans agreed to make the child credit partially refundable for low-income families with three children in exchange for making the credit available to couples earning up to $110,000 per year and for more oversight of fraud and abuse in the EITC program.
Capital gains	Republicans exchange indexation of capital gains for rate cuts down to 10 percent for individuals in the 15 percent tax bracket and 20 percent for those in higher brackets until 2001. In 2001 rates drop to 8 percent and 18 percent on assets held at least 5 years.
Estate taxes	Tax exemption from estates increased to $1.3 million immediately for family farms (more than the $900,000 the White House wanted) and businesses and to $1 million for all other estates by 2007 (slightly less than the $1.2 million Republicans wanted).
Individual retirement accounts	Basically the Republican bill, though income limits for eligibility for the full tax deduction and tax deferral were to be increased at a slower rate over the years at the urging of the White House.

Table 9.4 (Continued)

Education tax breaks	Clinton received more than he originally requested in education tax breaks ($40 billion over 5 years, up from $35 billion in his budget proposal), in exchange for Republican priorities on estate taxes, IRAs, and the alternative minimum tax. Plan allowed the HOPE tax credit up to $1,500 in the first 2 years and up to $1,000 the next 2 years increasing to as much as $2,000 after 2002. Plan also included a $500 tax-free contribution to an education savings account (less than Clinton's proposal of $1,000), student loan deductions, penalty-free withdrawals from IRAs, and extension of exemption of employer-provided tuition assistance.
Alternative minimum tax	Plan included a cut in the alternative minimum tax for corporations and small businesses totaling $6.8 billion over 5 years. The tax cut was lower than the GOP unified plan, though Clinton opposed any change in the AMT.

the earned income credit and pay no income tax to take the child tax credit.[29] In exchange, the White House agreed to make the credit available to families with incomes up to $110,000 (Clinton's bill phased out the credit at $60,000) and to accept Speaker Gingrich's proposal to reduce fraud and abuse in the Earned Income Tax Credit program. In exchange for the tobacco tax, the expanded child credit, and more total education tax breaks, the White House agreed to increase the net tax cut from $85 billion to $95 billion over five years and from $250 to $275 billion over ten years. As part of a general tradeoff, the president succeeded in getting all of his HOPE tax credit and a larger package of education tax breaks in exchange for giving the Republicans the lion's share of their investment-related tax breaks and a portion of the AMT proposal.

Making Divided Government Work

On 29 July, Republicans gathered on the steps of the Capitol for a triumphant rally. Republican leaders nestled around a cluster of microphones in front of a crowd of Boy Scouts standing shoulder to shoulder on the steps as red, white, and blue balloons floated gracefully in the breeze. Gingrich and Lott sent the message that the president had joined Republicans by agreeing to a balanced budget, less government spending, and tax cuts. Republican leaders agreed that it was a day all Americans could celebrate, as both parties cooperated to make the system work. Domenici said: "This bipartisan effort is what the American people expect of those who claim to be leaders of this country. We are proud to join with the president . . . to join hands and say, 'American people, we heard you.' Now the American people have a victory—not the Democrats and not the Republicans."[30] Moments before, congressional Democrats loaded into buses in front of the Capitol and proceeded to the White House, where President Clinton held a separate ceremony attended by over 100 Democratic Senators and House members. Clinton touted his administration's record on reducing the deficit and highlighted the benefits of a balanced budget and the host of new "investments" in education, children's health, and welfare reform. Still, he praised fellow Republicans for "working with us across the lines of substantial philosophical and practical differences to reach a good faith agreement that is an honorable and principled compromise."[31]

A minimal level of trust is necessary to carry on bipartisan negotiations. Basic governing principles and expectations of rank-and-file partisans will induce negotiators to push as far as they can for as long as they can to achieve their policy goals. Thus partisan positioning took place as leaders of both parties attempted to strengthen their bargaining leverage. At the end, President Clinton had a political and institutional advantage over congressional Republicans, yet he needed their support to achieve his policy goals. This meant maintaining independence from congressional Democrats who wanted to prolong the process and allowing Republicans to claim policy success. Clinton reminded his negotiators, "This isn't '95." He instructed them to "fight as hard as you can. But don't overplay your hand."[32] In response to Democratic criticisms that the president compromised too quickly and squandered his advantage in the negotiations process, Gene Sperling noted: "I think this achieves an enormous accomplishment for Democrats. But we have a divided government now, and the price of those accomplishments was being willing to cooperate and compromise with Republicans on priorities important to them."[33]

Restoring bipartisanship depended also on the will of leaders to find ways to resolve their differences. At the final stage of the process, the stakes can never be higher as leaders seek to strike compromises without abandoning their principles or losing the support of members. Before Clinton officials and Republican leaders could find this balance, Speaker Gingrich literally walked away from the table when he sensed the administration had pushed too far. Reassurances that the White House sought an honorable compromise and the ultimate threat of undermining the remainder of the president's legislative agenda were enough to resume talks. The conference reported two reconciliation bills—one for taxes and another for spending—which passed both chambers with large bipartisan majorities. The deal was finally done.

10

The 1997 Budget Agreement in Realist Perspective

The 1997 budget agreement was a gradual but historic step in budget policy. Since the late 1970s, the political system operated under fiscal constraints, and policymakers sought ways to reduce the deficit and address other tax and spending priorities. The 1997 agreement completed the long-term effort to balance the budget, and although neither party won a total victory, the budget shifted priorities in a Republican direction. President Clinton achieved several domestic policy goals: children's health care, higher education tax breaks, and additional welfare funding. Yet the big ticket items in the budget—the first net tax cut in sixteen years, the largest Medicare savings ever enacted into law, and constraints on domestic discretionary spending below the expected rate of inflation over five years—are Republican priorities. Those changes would not have occurred without the election of Republican majorities to the House and Senate in 1994 and 1996.

This chapter identifies several important lessons about governing and leadership from the politics of the 1997 budget agreement, and it applies a realist expectations view of governing to several criticisms of the budget agreement. A realist would argue that although the 1997 budget agreement was no one's "ideal" solution to the nation's fiscal challenges, it took reasonable steps toward addressing several problems. Still, the budget agreement falls short of addressing the long-term fiscal challenges related to the aging of the baby boom generation, leaving serious policy decisions for policymakers in the future.

Governing and Political Leadership

Variation, flexibility, adaptation, and uncertainty define the realist expectations view of governing. As chapter 2 illustrated, over the years numerous efforts to reduce the deficit passed under a variety of institutional, political, and policy conditions, and most occurred during periods of divided government. The 1997 budget agreement adds more evidence to support the claim that divided government does not inevitably lead to gridlock.[1] This study identifies the short-term political and policy conditions that created a bipartisan budget agreement and demonstrates how leaders managed numerous forces that could have thwarted the agreement. Now that we have accounted for the development of the budget agreement from start to finish, we should review the important lessons about governing and leadership under divided government.

Divided government can produce a variety of strategies, patterns of interaction, and policy outcomes, depending on short-term conditions and how leaders adapt to them. To begin with, the 1997 budget process was a continuation of the budget battles of 1995 and 1996, albeit with different negotiators working on behalf of President Clinton. In 1995 the Republicans pushed the system too far, and party leaders learned to lower their sights in order to advance their policy goals. Moreover, previous experience clarified the priorities of both parties and narrowed some major differences. Although difficult issues remained as the negotiations began in 1997, policy leaders were not starting from scratch, and they were not competing over two different budgets. Of course, familiarity can also breed contempt. The intense budget battles of the 104th Congress and the nasty election campaign in 1996 left the parties suspicious of one another. But after several closed negotiating sessions, Republican policy leaders and White House officials established trustworthy relations. They realized a bipartisan process was the best way to address their common goals of balancing the budget and shoring up Medicare, and to pursue limited versions of their particular policy objectives through bargaining and compromise.

The economy is another key short-term factor that helps explain the bipartisan budget agreement. Strong economic growth coupled with low inflation increased revenues, decreased spending, and reduced the amount of savings needed to balance the budget. Thus balancing the budget required fewer fiscal sacrifices and created opportunities for leaders to satisfy other policy goals: tax cuts for Republicans and education, health, and welfare initiatives for President Clinton. Though an unexpected surge in revenues created uncertainty during the bipartisan negotiations and caused a delay in the process, the strong economy generally made it easier for leaders to accommodate more interests and build support for the budget agreement.

The 1996 election is a third important factor in explaining why leaders were able to develop a bipartisan budget agreement. Despite the divided outcomes of the 1996 elections, Republican congressional leaders and President Clinton agreed on this message: the voters wanted both parties to work together. This recognition of public expectations for a bipartisan process encouraged both sides to address budget problems. It is important to note that the 1996 elections produced a consensus among leaders about public expectations of the "process," not necessarily the "policy."

Realist Expectations

The distinction between a "process" message and a "policy" message goes to the heart of the difference between the realist expectations view and the inevitable gridlock model. Applying the inevitable gridlock model, it would seem odd for an election that delivered a divided government to create the setting for a major budget deal. Since the inevitable gridlock model assumes the two parties do not share common policy objectives, it does not expect bipartisan interaction under divided government. Split-party electoral results presumably indicate that the voters have sent mixed signals. Thus it makes more sense politically for the two parties to contend for popular support than to bargain and compromise.

There are several problems with this logic. First, it falsely assumes the two parties do not share enough in common to address national problems in a bipartisan fashion. Over the years, both parties came to view a balanced budget as a common national goal, and more recently, they agreed that Medicare needed urgent attention. Of course, the parties generally differ over the means for achieving those ends, and those differences sometimes lead to stalemate. But their agreement on the ends gives leaders of both parties a reason to negotiate. Second, the responsible party solution to inevitable gridlock focuses too heavily on the need for a "policy message," one that normally does not materialize from election campaigns. Divided government has been the norm since World War II, a reality that compels leaders to consider ways of dealing with the other party even on issues where they do not share a common interest. Third, perhaps because the parties have gotten so used to divided government and because they recognize the political dangers of assuming responsibility for budget decisions, leaders see certain advantages to governing in divided government where responsibility is diffused rather than given to one party. Thus leaders engage in a bipartisan strategy partly because they want to solve common national problems and partly because they see bipartisanship as a way to advance their policy goals without bearing full responsibility for the results.[2] Finally, the inevitable gridlock model places too much faith in elections as a means of developing a policy consensus and over-coming the obstacles in the political system. Policy decisions are affected by a va-riety of factors, and leaders play key roles in managing the obstacles that stand in the way of consensus.

Bipartisan Policymaking: Rewards and Risks

By elaborating further, the realist expectations view helps explain how the budget process works in divided government. For example, we can explain why leaders pursue a bipartisan strategy in an era of intense partisanship if we think about the dual purpose of bipartisan negotiations. The common interests of the two parties may be enough to draw the leaders into negotiations because, as policymakers, they seek to address national problems. Yet political realities and partisan differ-ences dictate that bipartisanship must also provide an opportunity for both sides to pursue their goals. In realist terms, since the election did not offer a popular mandate for one party to control the process, leaders decided to take a chance and try to advance their policy objectives through bipartisan compromise. After all, if recent history is any guide, the next election is not likely to deliver unified con-trol of Congress and the presidency to one party. Besides, given the recent experi-ences President Clinton and congressional Republicans have had with asserting their responsibility to govern alone (with the Democrats losing a majority in 1994 after two years of unified government, and Republicans barely holding on to con-gressional majorities and failing to defeat President Clinton in 1996 after pursu-ing a confrontational strategy), it makes perfect sense for leaders of opposite parties to consider the advantages of pursuing a bipartisan process.

Of course, there are risks as well as rewards to a bipartisan strategy. The bud-get process is full of uncertainties, especially as the agreement develops beyond the closed doors of the bargaining room. As the congressional budget process de-velops, numerous politicians and groups representing a diverse range of constitu-encies attempt to influence policy decisions. The trust leaders developed with one another does not automatically trickle down to rank-and-file partisans, some of whom believe bipartisanship is a threat rather than an opportunity. Thus leaders spend a good deal of energy trying to reassure colleagues that a bipartisan strategy is a good one. Not all will agree, and the process exposes underlying tensions within the two parties. Realizing the high stakes involved, opponents will try to alter the agreement or undermine it altogether. In some cases, the interests of op-ponents can be accommodated with policy adjustments; in others, intraparty dif-ferences over strategy and priorities cannot be reconciled. For example, liberal

Democrats distrusted President Clinton's efforts to compromise with congressional Republicans from the outset, and many believed they had more to gain from confrontation than cooperation. The White House made some attempts to respond to the concerns of liberal Democrats, but the president was more interested in achieving his policy goals than serving as a foil for the political aspirations of congressional Democrats.

Variations in Policymaking Patterns

This study also identifies the variations in policymaking patterns and the mix of policy ideas that are brought into play as the process unfolds. We think of the 1997 budget deal as bipartisan because it emanated from bipartisan negotiations and because the budget resolution and the final reconciliation bills were passed with the support of majorities from both parties. But between the beginning and the end, we witnessed a combination of bipartisan and partisan strategies, depending on particular institutional and political circumstances related to congressional committees and the styles of individual policy leaders. The various tax and spending decisions are based on competing principles, policy effects, political calculations, and concerns about public opinion. The process provides multiple points of entry for numerous participants to add their special ingredients (e.g., a cigarette tax, a change in the formula for calculating the CPI, or a means test for Medicare) into the mix of policy ideas served up in the legislative process.[3] Of course, some ideas are extracted from the mix too in order to broaden the appeal. Thus at each stage along the way, the budget agreement is altered, shaped, and molded in response to the various forces that converge on the budget process.

Chapters 7 and 8 furnish numerous examples of the variation in policymaking across committees and chambers: Thomas develops a bipartisan Medicare package on the Ways and Means Committee, while Bilirakis fails to unite the two sides on the Commerce Committee. The House ultimately passes a reconciliation spending bill containing scores of conservative policy initiatives and gets almost no support from Democratic members who voted in favor of the budget resolution. The Senate pushes major entitlement reforms that stretched beyond the imagination of budget negotiators, and they pass with the support of large numbers of Democrats. Archer pushes a Republican tax bill that manages to offend members of his own party, whereas Roth bends over backward to incorporate Democratic ideas into his tax proposal. Ultimately, party leaders play key roles in resolving the tensions and contradictory policy outcomes that result from the various patterns of policymaking.

Shifting Strategic Advantages

The strategic advantages of the president and Congress also shift as the process develops and conditions change. They begin as coequal branches in a tug-of-war to define the general terms of the budget agreement. The executive branch has more at stake at this stage because virtually anything can happen when the agreement goes to Congress. Thus the president's negotiators want specific language to bind the majority party in Congress, while congressional negotiators must hold their ground to protect the discretion of legislative committees. Since the agreement is malleable, congressional committees have the discretion to push their policy goals to the point of violating the instructions of the budget resolution. White House officials may or may not be invited to participate in the formulation of a committee's reconciliation legislation, and the president is normally relegated to outsider status. The president can threaten a veto, but that might do more to escalate conflict.

In this instance, the president urged Democrats to let the process move forward to the conference committee where the president would have more leverage. Most liberal House Democrats ignored his plea, believing they would be better off playing defense. At the conference stage, in addition to reconciling differences between the chambers, the congressional majority must reckon with the president's priorities, for he will decide if the legislature's product will be enacted into law. The veto always gives the president an advantage at the end of the process, but the veto only allows the president to say no. If the president wishes to achieve his policy goals, he needs the congressional majority as much as they need him.

Interest Groups and Constituent Concerns

As the budget process grinds along, members of Congress naturally seek to avoid decisions that might offend allies or turn off constituents. They are hard pressed to pass up opportunities to help friendly interest groups or improve their electoral prospects. Thus interest-group demands and constituent concerns place constraints on the degree to which policy leaders can impose "tough choices" on the members. For example, pressure from elderly groups and concerns about reelection help explain the decision process for proposals to adjust the CPI. Even after Budget Committee Republicans expressed their opposition to a budget deal containing an adjustment in the CPI, Chairman Kasich endorsed the initial budget agreement, which contained a small change in the formula for computing the CPI. Yet after the CBO reported additional revenues for the upcoming fiscal year,

Kasich went along with a White House proposal to drop it. He later justified his decision on the grounds that Budget Committee Republicans opposed changing the formula anyway. Efforts to adjust the CPI and other attempts at major entitlement reform were limited by the specter of the "Mediscare" campaign of 1996 as incumbent politicians wondered about stirring up opposition from angry seniors in the next election.

Nevertheless, policy leaders sometimes push ideas that impede the electoral goals of individual members or disappoint the hopes of particular groups. Deficit-reduction plans can hardly avoid disappointing some groups, and several powerful interests did not get their way in 1997. The hospital and home health industries absorbed the costs of the Medicare reforms, and tobacco companies paid the price for the expanded children's health initiative. Many senators voted against the expressed wishes of the AARP, one of the most powerful and organized lobby groups in Washington, by passing Medicare reforms that imposed direct costs on beneficiaries. In the area of tax policy, Chairman Archer used various tactics to fend off a range of Republican-leaning groups thirsting for privileged tax breaks. Most came away disappointed. In the area of transportation policy, members had to forego direct benefits to constituents in order to advance a budget that sought to advance the national interest. Many members of the House resisted the temptation of pork-barrel politics by voting against Shuster-Oberstar.

Theories of policymaking that view interest groups as all-powerful entities and individual members as cowardly slaves to pork-barrel benefits cannot explain why some groups lose and a majority of representatives reject a budget resolution that holds out the promise of a federal project. The realist expectations perspective offers two plausible explanations. First, party leaders play key roles in managing the tensions between groups and policy leaders and mitigating the effects of tough votes on the electoral prospects of individual members. Second, budget decisions are based on a variety of factors: principles, political considerations, policy analysis, and responsiveness to public opinion. Party leaders sometimes can overrule the bold designs of policy leaders, as when Speaker Gingrich forced Chairman Archer to redistribute the benefits of tax cuts to small businesses, or when he pulled the plug on Archer's proposal to scratch the ethanol subsidy. The Speaker had leverage over the Ways and Means chairman because, without such changes, the entire tax bill might have failed.

In some instances, though, leaders cannot devise a solution, and the narrow interests of particular groups or the local concerns of individual members are pitted against the collective good of a balanced budget. Then leaders make appeals to the "big picture." Since individual decisions are based on many criteria, they make the case for the budget agreement on various grounds. They try to persuade members that voting for the collective good is a smart political decision, or they appeal to the members' principles, sense of good policy, or duty to the country. Moreover, the multistage budget process, incremental policy change, and realist expectations supply their own logic. Leaders try to prepare members in advance that the conditions require a compromise that is less than ideal and that everyone must be willing to accept half a loaf or gain nothing at all. Leaders might also encourage dissatisfied groups and disgruntled members to try to change policy at a later stage in the process.

In sum, the budget process is likely to produce winners and losers, and occasionally the process forces individual members to make a tough choice. Of course, members of Congress are not irrational actors who want to vote against a bill that might bring a transportation project to their district or vote for an amendment opposed by a well-organized group. But, like it or not, members have to decide between a narrow benefit (a road or a bridge) and a collective good (a balanced budget, tax cuts, and extending the life of the Medicare Trust Fund).

Leadership Is the Key

Leadership is a critical element in explaining how the budget process works. It is virtually impossible to explain bipartisan cooperation, managing internal partisan tensions, overriding narrow group interests, or persuading individual members to choose a collective good over a particular benefit without accounting for the role of leaders. Even when conditions are right for a bipartisan budget deal, the process cannot produce a successful outcome without leadership. Party leaders must protect their parties' principles in bipartisan negotiations, frame the policy choices in favorable terms, convince members to vote for those choices, and look out for the political interests of individual members. Since these roles are discussed elsewhere in the book, this section focuses mainly on the interactive effects of individual skills and the institutional, political, and policy conditions that affect leadership strategies and styles.

Political scientists have long recognized that leadership strategies and styles are constrained by institutional, political, and policy conditions.[4] Party leaders must be responsive to the wishes and policy preferences of the members who elect them, or they may be removed from office.[5] This study includes numerous instances in which leaders intervened, sometimes perhaps even against their personal wishes, to accommodate the preferences of members. Budget Committee Chairman Kasich often reminded House Republicans that he was their "agent" in negotiating with the White House, for he knew the fate of the agreement was ultimately in the hands of members who would vote either for or against it. Speaker

Gingrich pulled the plug on the CPI, and later he and Majority Leader Armey vetoed the Senate Medicare proposals in response to concerns raised by Republican members. Majority Leader Lott grudgingly gave in to bipartisan forces to pass a cigarette tax in order to fund additional health coverage for children and accommodate particular tax initiatives by members of the Senate Finance Committee. Examples abound of how the institutional, political, and policy environment dictated the actions and decisions of party leaders.

Yet while the broader conditions set the parameters within which leaders operate, the conditions inherent to the budget process do not always offer a clear course of action. The political strategies and tax and spending decisions that might result from the variations in institutional, political, and policy conditions are endless. If party leaders decide to enter into bipartisan negotiations, leadership involves identifying, promoting, and defending priorities and knowing when to compromise without abandoning basic principles. Building support in Congress requires leaders to convince colleagues that a bipartisan budget agreement is worthy of their support and to block attempts to throw the budget process off track. With so many individuals seeking to influence budget policy and so many forces threatening to disrupt the process—disputes between the parties, divisions within the parties, interest-group demands, concerns about reelection, and arguments over priorities—leaders constantly labor over strategies, tradeoffs, and choices in an unpredictable environment. Should we cooperate and bargain? If so, when and how? On which issues should we compromise, and when should we hold firm?

In responding to these questions, leaders are guided by prevailing conditions, but conditions alone do not dictate how they will act and what effect they will have on the process. Leaders have discretion to choose strategies and make decisions based on both the conditions under which they are operating and their personal preferences and individual skills. The contrast between Archer and Roth in chapter 8 illustrates that policy outcomes and the budget process are affected by the ways in which leaders interpret and respond to prevailing conditions. Intelligence, persistence, tenacity, integrity, salesmanship, and bargaining skills are among the important attributes effective leaders must have to make the process work. In terms of coalition building, for example, it is hard to measure the total effect of Chairman Kasich's persistent efforts to sell the budget agreement to his colleagues and defeat the Shuster-Oberstar substitute to the bipartisan budget resolution. Yet it is also hard to imagine the budget resolution passing without those efforts.

All leaders operate in an uncertain environment in which conditions are constantly changing. Thus leaders must alter strategies and adjust their policy objectives in response to reactions by rank-and-file members, new information about policy outcomes, their counterparts' strategy, and the degree of leverage they have at particular stages of the process. Given all these factors, it is not surprising to find that leadership strategies are a combination of circumstances and personal factors.

In sum, governing, policy, and leadership conditions are critical components of explaining how the budget process works. The political system permits a wide range of governing arrangements and policy choices, and politicians base their decisions on a variety of goals, making it difficult to predict policy outcomes. Leaders play key roles in interpreting the prevailing circumstances, deciding which policy changes should be pursued and determining which strategies offer the best chance of advancing their parties' policy goals and political interests.

Evaluating the Budget Agreement

Evaluating the merits of budget policy is inherently a normative exercise. When realists, policy analysts, and ideologues apply different values to the same budget, they reach different conclusions. In 1997 conservatives were disappointed with the lack of spending cuts and tax cuts, while liberals argued that the tax cuts and spending cuts were too big. Policy analysts concentrated on the long-term effects of policy changes in the budget agreement. Judging by any of these norms, the 1997 budget agreement was variously described as a "nonevent," an "illusion," a "violation of principle," an "act of fear," a "dead fish," a "missed opportunity," or just plain "awful."[6] Conceding the obvious facts that the 1997 budget agreement was limited in scope, did not solve the long-term problems with Social Security and Medicare, and added more complexity to the tax code, a realist would disagree with most of these judgments.[7]

A realist assumes that policy outcomes are likely to be a mixture of principled demands, popular choices, political calculations, and rational policy decisions. Thus a bipartisan budget agreement cannot possibly meet the ideals of a staunch liberal or conservative, or the strictly rational expectations of a policy analyst. It can only do better or worse by those standards without being unresponsive to public opinion or naive to political goals. In 1997 the institutional, political, and policy conditions did not permit leaders to attain the lofty long-term goals of budget reformers or the grand ambitions of ideological foot soldiers, worthy as they may be. Perhaps one day the conditions will suit the policy outcomes desired by one or more of the critics of the budget agreement. In the meantime, we should recognize the accomplishments and limitations of a budget that passed the ultimate test: winning the support of majorities in the House and Senate and the signature of the president.

Views from the Right and Left

James Glassman, one of the most vociferous conservative opponents of the budget agreement, complained that Republicans had to abandon basic principles to reach a budget agreement with President Clinton.[8] Glassman concluded that the budget deal was "bad for everyone" because it increased overall spending even beyond the amount Clinton proposed in February, added $32 billion more for Clinton's new program initiatives, and contained "minuscule tax cuts." Though Glassman conceded that the budget agreement moved government policy slightly in a Republican direction, the compromise fell short of the Republicans' goals after the 1994 congressional elections. Despite the tax cuts and Medicare savings, Glassman said, "This is hardly the promised land." Politicians should "kill the budget deal. Let the Democratic president and the Republican Congress contend in the clear light of day. Let them each decide what's right and fight on principle."[9]

Of course, principles are an important part of the budget process, and the positions taken by legislators of both parties were not void of principle. But governing requires compromise and the modification of principles in order to achieve tangible policies. As they seek to advance principles, policymakers must deal with the realities of the governing circumstances and policy constraints. In a separation-of-powers system with divided government, it does little good to fight one's ideological opponent to a bitter end.[10] Politicians seek to advance principles *as far as possible* and compromise when necessary to make *progress* toward ultimate policy goals. Moreover, parties are not simply agents of ideological principles, they are institutions that seek to gain power in order to advance those principles. Thus party leaders need to recognize and respond to the public's will and judgment. Republicans attempted dramatic reforms in 1995, and those reforms were rejected. Party leaders must also tolerate and manage the internal divisions among elected officials. Even when a party is unified internally, it must operate in a separation-of-powers system that checks its capacity to enact major reforms.[11]

Budget Committee Chairman Kasich's response to Glassman reflected a realist perspective of governing.[12] Kasich pointed out that Glassman's critique of the budget agreement overlooked certain basic facts. First, according to the CBO, the budget agreement spends $115 billion less over five years than the budget President Clinton presented in February. Second, the $70-billion-dollar increase in total spending from 1997 to 1998 is largely due to entitlement spending, especially Social Security. Kasich indicated, as he had all along, that the budget agreement was only a step in the right direction and that Congress and the president needed to do more in the future to trim entitlement spending. Third, the tax cuts are hardly "minuscule" when one considers the effects on individual taxpayers. Kasich noted: "When I tell parents of two children in Ohio that their taxes are going to be cut by $1,000 through our family tax credit, they are grateful, not critical." In terms of compromising with President Clinton, Kasich wondered why Glassman and others would take the view that "if you cannot accomplish everything you wish to, then you should not try to accomplish anything." Moreover, "Mr. Glassman and other Beltway critics refuse to listen to what most Americans are telling us. A little more than six months ago, the American people elected both a Republican Congress and a Democratic president. They told us to work it out together." Reflecting on Glassman's alternative strategy, Kasich concluded: "Of course, Republicans in Congress could have gone it alone, seen our plans vetoed and not accomplished anything. No tax cuts. No solvency for Medicare over the next 10 years. No entitlement reform. No restraint in Washington spending. No balanced budget."

While some conservatives complained about "minuscule" tax cuts, increased domestic spending, and insufficient funds for defense, liberals argued that President Clinton caved in to Republicans by capitulating to their demands for tax cuts and defense spending, and he failed to keep his promise to restore welfare benefits.[13] Though they may be justified in grumbling about the overall shift in priorities to the right, liberals understated the president's initiatives to increase spending for social programs. Without compromising, no progress would have been made on children's health, aid to legal immigrants, and welfare policy. Under the governing conditions, President Clinton pursued a sensible strategy. He gave ground to Republicans in terms of defining the general direction of budget agreement in exchange for several specific policy changes that a Republican Congress would not have passed on its own. Of course, Clinton's initiatives had to be paid for with spending reductions in other parts of the budget, or the tobacco tax in the case of the health initiative, but that is part of the process of allocating resources to specific spending priorities. In response to disappointed liberals, White House negotiators OMB Director Franklin Raines and National Economic Council Director Gene Sperling asked: "Do the critics believe that holding out for the purest position and certain gridlock is preferable to an agreement that puts the deficit on a path to zero while investing more in education, the environment, and children's health?"[14]

Policy Analysts

Policy analysts from Washington think tanks and government watchdog groups critiqued the budget agreement using rational criteria to evaluate the potential long-term effects of policy changes on the government's fiscal situation and the nation's economy.[15] Policy analysts play an important role in reminding politicians of future demographic, social, and economic trends, and they act as the consciences of politicians tempted to place short-term demands ahead of long-term fiscal considerations. Organizations such as the Concord Coalition and the Committee for a Responsible Federal Budget constantly prod elected officials to "do more" to curb entitlement spending. For example, Warren Rudman, the co-chair of the Concord Coalition, remarked: "Our real budget challenge is not about 2002, but 2022 and 2032. The budget agreement will buy some time, but Congress and the President must not squander this opportunity by declaring victory over the short-term deficit and ignoring the fiscal tidal wave heading toward us when the baby boomers start to retire."[16] While their critical analyses provide valuable information to policymakers and their watchdog role contributes to the process by pushing politicians to think beyond the next election, policy analysts might ignore the realistic constraints on governing and sell short the progress of gradual policy changes.[17] Still, their criticisms need to be taken into account, for they point to the limitations of the 1997 budget agreement.

Robert D. Reischauer, former CBO director, used several rational criteria to evaluate the budget agreement.[18] Reischauer was interested in whether any sacrifices were made, whether the budget was credible, whether it dealt with long-term problems, and whether it made the tax code simpler, fairer, and more conducive to economic growth. In a nutshell, Reischauer concluded that few sacrifices were made in terms of spending restraint, there were no major entitlement reforms, the savings in Medicare were "unavoidable," and the tax cuts were inequitable, complicated, and insignificant to economic growth. Reischauer stated correctly that the budget agreement does not address the long-term solvency of Medicare (beyond ten years), the tax cuts are mainly a hodge-podge of political tradeoffs, and the president and Congress may be more prone to violate the spending caps on discretionary spending as they operate under budget surpluses. Yet while Reischauer's conclusions are compelling when judged by the criteria he chooses, those criteria do not account for the opportunities and constraints of the governing situation.

For example, Reischauer called the Medicare reforms "substantial" but "unavoidable," and his analysis emphasized the shortcomings of the reforms, rather than the accomplishments. He concluded that policymakers lacked the political will to do something significant and that the "failure to reform the entitlements represented a missed opportunity."[19] A realist would make at least three points in response to Reischauer's judgments. First, while the $115 billion package of Medicare savings over five years did not solve the long-term problems with Medicare financing, it is by far the largest in history and therefore must be deemed "historic" by any prior standards. In comparison, the 1990 and 1993 budget deals contained Medicare savings of $44 and $56 billion respectively. Second, enacting reforms that keep the Medicare Trust Fund solvent for ten years is a significant accomplishment for a political system that is not set up to plan for a half-century. Ten years may be long enough for a clearer consensus on long-term reforms. Of course, a long-term solution may never transpire, in which case politicians will have to continue to make adjustments to keep a popular entitlement program afloat, maybe for ten years at a time.

A third key point is that the timing was not right for a major overhaul of Medicare, and attempts to develop major reforms could very well have resulted in stalemate. Ideally, leaders from both parties would have come together and designed Medicare reforms that guaranteed benefits to every senior citizen until the year 2050. But after the intense political fights over Medicare in 1995 and 1996, nobody knew whether or how leaders of opposing parties would deal with Medicare. Negotiations in the 104th Congress reduced the differences between Clinton and Republican leaders, but they still needed to close a $50 billion gap in total savings, and they disagreed on the policy changes to do it. One could argue reasonably that the 1997 budget agreement exceeded expectations by containing a package with twice the savings than the system had ever produced before, and those changes were not simply unavoidable. Of course, the Senate wanted more significant Medicare reforms, but policy differences and political considerations prevented the House and the president from going along. To push the system further might have resulted in stalemate, as it did in the 104th Congress. Thus the policy changes in Medicare depended as much on the willingness and ability of leaders to reach a feasible compromise as they did on "unavoidable" forces pushing the process to an inevitable end.

In the area of tax policy, Reischauer points out that the budget agreement makes major tax reform less feasible by creating new commitments and complicates the tax code by introducing new investment options, each with a new set of standards, tax rates, eligibility rules, and the like.[20] Ultimately, Reischauer concludes: "In the end, the nation's long-run economic interests would have been better served by building slightly larger surpluses rather than by enacting . . . 'junk tax cuts.'"[21]

Simplicity, equity, and stimulating economic growth are traditional values economists use to evaluate tax policy. Everyone agrees the Taxpayer Relief Act made the tax code more complicated, and most will conclude the overall effects on economic growth are limited by the size of the tax cuts in relation to the economy. On the other hand, the issue of tax fairness is controversial enough to be debated by reasonable people who disagree about how the tax cuts are distributed across income levels.[22] Moreover, while politicians from both parties have introduced plans to simplify the tax code, they are a long way from a consensus about how to do it. While congressional Republicans agree that the tax code should be dismantled, for example, they continue to debate whether it should be replaced by a consumption tax or a flat income tax.

In 1997, since President Clinton opposed major tax reform, the debate was not about how to simplify the tax code. The central questions concerning taxes were whether to provide tax relief and, if so, to whom. If tax relief is not a legitimate policy goal, then tinkering with the tax code makes no sense. But if a reasonable case can be made for tax relief, then policymakers were not about to wait for Steve Forbes to be elected king, abolish the IRS, and "drive a stake through the tax code."[23] Aside from the 1986 Tax Act, changing tax policy has traditionally meant increasing complexity through incremental policy changes that respond to particular interests or broad societal needs. The political scientist John Witte, author of a definitive work on the history of tax politics, observes: "In a sense [the tax code] is an incrementalist paradise, most changes in tax bills consist of simple adjustments to existing policy provisions."[24] Once President Clinton and Republicans agreed to cut taxes, the policy choices would almost certainly be biased toward maximizing political interests, attempting to address social needs, and attaining microeconomic objectives.

Though politicians suggested that tax cuts would stimulate economic growth, most rationalized the tax cuts in terms of helping families raise their children, assisting individuals to pay for college, or providing incentives for personal savings and investment. Policy analysts who seek to maximize efficiency and simplicity in the tax code criticize the microeconomic and social benefits of the tax bill. For them, tax breaks for families with children, incentives for individuals to save and invest, relief to a family-owned business when the principal owner dies, and assistance to middle-class college-bound students with tuition costs may be noble ends in themselves. Indeed, all can be rationalized in terms of meeting societal needs. Yet the policy analyst is bound to ask whether the same social goals can be attained more efficiently through other means. Moreover, once specific tax breaks are added to the tax code, they are very difficult to take away, and traditionally they can become very costly. Thus, according to Witte, "decisions that appear to be rational and proper in each individual case are in the aggregate and over time a disaster."[25]

Time will tell whether the tax policy changes contained within the Taxpayer Relief Act of 1997 will turn out disastrous. For now, the myriad new benefits and complex formulas that contradicted the basic principle of tax simplification were the price to pay for tax relief. The tension between the values of simplification and relief are embodied in the policy goals of House Ways and Means Chairman Bill Archer, the principal author of the House tax bill. Archer ideally prefers to replace the current income tax with a national sales tax.[26] That goal is further away today than it was before the 1997 Taxpayer Relief Act became law. But when confronted with the choice between a theoretical ideal and a real possibility of providing tax relief, Archer and many others placed the latter value over the former. An aide to Chairman Archer described the realist dilemma of tax reform: "Chairman Archer wants a consumption tax, but he recognizes reality. As long as you have a Democratic President in the White House, there's no guarantee of an overhaul of the tax system. So, for now he is more interested in making first downs than touchdowns, which means cutting taxes under the current system we've got and rewriting the tax code later."[27]

Facing the Fiscal Challenges Ahead

Despite the important policy changes contained in the budget agreement, policy analysts raise legitimate concerns about the budget's limitations when matched against the fiscal challenges of the twenty-first century. Key budget policy leaders also recognize that more needs to be done. In a series of speeches, Kasich recognized that the budget agreement was a gradual but important step and that more challenges remained. Here is an illustration of the perspective shared by Kasich and Domenici:

> While our balanced budget plan does not pretend to solve all our problems, it does provide us time to develop additional steps that will be needed down the road. There is no question that more must be done to secure the long-term future of Medicare and Social Security as the baby boom generation retires over the next 20 years.[28]

We should be encouraged by the fact that policy leaders were willing to push ambitious reforms in 1997, even though governing constraints limited their extent. Yet we cannot ignore the demographic changes that will place a massive burden on taxpayers and policymakers beginning in the year 2010. Consider the facts regarding eligibility for Medicare. Today about 38 million people are enrolled in Medicare (13.7 percent of the population); by 2010 it will be 47 million (15.2 percent of the population), and by 2030 it will be over 75 million (22 percent of the population). In 1965 when Medicare began, the average life expectancy was seventy; by 1990 it rose to seventy-five, and by 2010 it is projected to be seventy-eight. Medicare spending will continue to grow. In 1996 Medicare spending totaled $191 billion; by 2002 CBO projects Medicare spending will grow to $314 billion, and by 2007 it is expected to reach $464 billion. Once the baby boomers become eligible for Medicare, increased program costs will rise, from 2.7 percent of GDP in 1996 to 4.4 percent by 2010 and 7.4 percent by 2030.[29]

The aging baby boomers also present problems for Social Security. Though the Social Security Trust Fund is currently running surpluses of as much as $65 billion and the Treasury's assets of $550 billion will continue to grow, using modest projections, annual Social Security spending will exceed annual revenues by 2013. If present policies continue, by 2025 Social Security will run an annual deficit of over $300 billion as it draws on the remaining principal left in the Trust Fund. By 2031, the annual deficit will equal $766 billion and the Trust Fund will be insolvent. Debt to the Trust Fund is expected to reach $2.1 trillion by 2040 and $5.1 trillion by 2050 if current policies remain in effect. Moreover, the current Social Security system contains serious generational inequities. For example, an individual worker who retired in 1980 will get back $39,000 more than he and his employer paid into the Trust Fund plus interest. Whereas a single individual with an average income who retires in 2010 will get back $36,000 less than he or she contributed under present policy.[30]

No wonder President Clinton drew thunderous applause from members of Congress in his 1998 State of the Union address when he contended that any future budget surpluses should be used to save Social Security. Clinton invited the AARP and the Concord Coalition to present a year-long series of forums to educate Americans about Social Security in 1998 so that Congress could consider serious reform proposals in 1999. Some observers believe a gradual consensus is emerging that at least some of the Trust Fund surpluses should be invested in stocks, either by the individual taxpayer or directly from the Trust Fund. But allocating more funds to equities, instead of devoting all surplus revenues to government bonds and securities, as we do under current law, will not by itself solve the long-term funding problems facing Social Security. Additional steps will have to be taken, which means either additional tax increases or benefit reductions. The choices will not be easy.

The good news is that, assuming reasonably stable economic conditions, budget analysts predict a decade of annual surpluses adding up to $1.6 trillion.[31] Yet we should not assume that surpluses will produce the antidote to the fundamental conflicts over values and priorities that defined the deficit era. Even before the surpluses arrived, policy analysts, political commentators, and elected officials were fighting over ways to utilize the extra funds. Should we pay off the national debt? Cut taxes? Invest more in human development and physical infrastructure? Save Social Security and Medicare? Restore our national defense capabilities?

The budget battle between Clinton and congressional Republicans in 1998 offered a glimpse into the future of surplus politics. House Republicans passed an $80 billion package of tax cuts with the stipulation that the remaining surplus funds over the next decade would go to toward shoring up the Social Security Trust Fund. The Senate never even voted on the bill, and President Clinton promised to veto any tax cuts passed by Congress anyway. Meanwhile, the president held out for concessions in the appropriations process as the fiscal year came to a close and members eagerly sought an exit from Washington so they could campaign for the November 1998 elections. Before leaving town, Republicans succumbed to the president's wish to spend $20 billion out of the projected $80 billion surplus for FY 1999, exceeding the discretionary spending caps for the first time since they were enacted in 1990. Optimists suggested that the lapse in fiscal discipline could have been worse: they could have spent the entire surplus.

If the past is any guide, attempts to predict what *will* happen next are premature at best, though the policy debate over what *should* happen sounds familiar. Policy analysts, elected officials, and organized interests will debate budget decisions in terms of the fundamental values, national priorities, and practical implications of policy changes. At the same time, they will calculate the effect of prospective policy changes on their political goals. The surpluses will never be large enough to serve everyone's needs, and even if consensus emerges about the long-term problems that deserve the most attention, we should not be surprised if the system does not solve them quickly or completely. The process that never ends will continue on an uncertain course as leaders attempt to balance principles and political goals under varying institutional, political, and policy conditions. The 1997 budget agreement is a done deal, but it is not the last deal to be done.

Notes

Chapter 1: The Puzzle of Budget Politics

1. Quoted in "Statements by Clinton and Congressional Leaders on the Agreement," *New York Times*, 2 May 1997, A13.

2. Woodrow Wilson, *Congressional Government: A Study in American Politics* (Boston: Houghton Mifflin, 1885).

3. The responsible party doctrine traces its roots to American Political Science Association Committee on Political Parties, *Toward a More Responsible Two-Party System* (New York: Rinehart, 1950). For a more recent defense of the thesis, see James L. Sundquist, *Constitutional Reform and Effective Government* (Washington, D.C.: Brookings Institution, 1992).

4. For a review of this argument, see Morris P. Fiorina, *Divided Government* (New York: Macmillan, 1992), chap. 6.

5. See, for example, Mathew D. McCubbins, "Government By Lay-Away: Federal Spending and Deficits under Divided Party Control," in *The Politics of Divided Government*, ed. Gary W. Cox and Samuel Kernell (Boulder, Colo.: Westview, 1991), 113–53.

6. George Hager and Eric Pianin, *Mirage* (New York: Random House, 1997), 12.

7. Ibid., 9. It is worth noting that *Mirage* won the praise of more than one Washington political columnist. See, for example, David S. Broder, "What the Nation Cares About," *Washington Post*, 16 April 1997, A17; and Morton M. Kondracke, "Chronic Partisanship Makes a Budget Deal a Recurring Mirage," *Roll Call*, 14 April 1997, 10. Hager and Pianin's thesis about budget politics dovetails with other studies about how partisan politics undermine the capacity of policymakers to address the nation's toughest problems. E.J. Dionne Jr. argues that Americans despise politics because politicians are busy playing partisan games and arguing about "false choices" instead of addressing the problems faced by ordinary Americans. E.J. Dionne Jr., *Why Americans Hate Politics* (New York: Simon and Schuster, 1991). Political scientists Benjamin Ginsberg and Martin Shefter argue that institutional struggles between the president and Congress replaced elections as the main source of competition between political parties. Thus the political system is deadlocked, unable to respond effectively to national problems, including the deficit. Benjamin Ginsberg and Martin Shefter, *Politics by Other Means* (New York: Basic Books, 1990).

8. See, for example, Anthony King, *Running Scared* (New York: Free Press, 1997), chap. 6.

9. Peter G. Peterson, *Facing Up: How to Rescue the Economy from Crushing Debt and Restore the American Dream* (New York: Simon and Schuster, 1993).

10. Studies that track public opinion on various entitlement programs over time show mixed results. The most costly programs with the largest "middle class" recipient populations (Social Security, Medicare, and Medicaid) have been consistently supported by large majorities of the American public. See, for example, Benjamin I. Page and Robert Y. Shapiro, *The Rational Public* (Chicago: University of Chicago Press, 1992), 118–21, 129.

11. In general, see Jonathan Rauch, *Demosclerosis: The Silent Killer of American Government* (New York: Random House, 1994). With respect to tax and spending policy in particular, see Steven R. Eastaugh, *Facing Tough Choices: Balancing Fiscal and Social Deficits* (Westport, Conn.: Praeger, 1994), chap. 2.

12. The largest group and the one with the biggest stake in the entitlement system is the American Association of Retired Persons (AARP) with over 33 million members and an annual budget of over $300 million. See Peterson, *Facing Up*, 82.

13. For more on this point, see Robert J. Samuelson, *The Good Life and Its Discontents* (New York: Random House, 1995), 171.

14. Jessica Korn, *The Power of Separation: American Constitutionalism and the Myth of the Legislative Veto* (Princeton: Princeton University Press, 1996), 12. For more on this point, see James W. Ceaser, "In Defense of Separation of Powers," in *Separation of Powers: Does it Still Work?*, ed. Robert A. Goldwin and Art Kaufman (Washington, D.C.: American Enterprise Institute, 1986), 168–93.

15. Charles O. Jones, *The Presidency in a Separated System* (Washington, D.C.: Brookings Institution, 1992), 17.

16. David R. Mayhew, *Divided We Govern* (New Haven: Yale University Press, 1991), chap. 7.

17. For a more complete account of this perspective, see Joseph White and Aaron Wildavsky, *The Deficit and the Public Interest* (Berkeley: University of California Press, 1989).

18. I develop this point in chapter 2. For case studies that explore some of the major successes and failures, see Timothy J. Penny and Steven E. Schier, *Payment Due: A Nation in Debt, a Generation in Trouble* (Boulder, Colo.: Westview, 1996), chaps. 4 and 5; Hager and Pianin, *Mirage*; and White and Wildavsky, *Deficit and the Public Interest*.

19. I use "bipartisan" to describe policymaking processes that involve representatives of both parties. Charles O. Jones develops a more refined conceptual framework that includes four different patterns of presidential-congressional interaction: partisan, copartisan, crosspartisan, and bipartisan. Jones, *Separated Presidency*, 19–23.

20. E.J. Dionne Jr., "A Political Classic," *Washington Post*, 1 August 1997, A21.

Chapter 2: Budget Choices and Deficit Politics: 1980–96

1. Quoted in George Hager and Eric Pianin, *Mirage* (New York: Random House, 1997), 201–2.

2. Aaron Wildavsky, *The New Politics of the Budgetary Process*, 2d ed. (New York: HarperCollins, 1992), 480.

3. Several scholars have developed this argument. See Wildavsky, *New Politics of the Budgetary Process*; Joseph White and Aaron Wildavsky, *The Deficit and the Public Interest* (Berkeley: University of California Press, 1989); Dennis S. Ippolito, *Uncertain Legacies: Federal Budget Policy from Roosevelt through Reagan* (Charlottesville: University Press of Virginia, 1990); and R. Douglas Arnold, *The Logic of Congressional Action* (New Haven: Yale University Press, 1990), chap. 5.

4. For a more comprehensive description and analysis of the federal budget, see, for example, Stanley E. Collender, *The Guide to the Federal Budget: Fiscal 1997* (Lanham, Md., and London: Rowman and Littlefield, 1996).

5. The Constitution does not explicitly grant the president authority to submit a budget to Congress. The Budget and Accounting Act of 1921 gave the president that authority and created a Bureau of the Budget, later renamed the Office of Management and Budget, to assist the president in developing and implementing a budget.

6. For a more comprehensive description of the federal budget process, see Allen Schick, *The Federal Budget: Politics, Policy, and Process* (Washington, D.C.: Brookings Institution, 1995).

7. Hager and Pianin, *Mirage*, 45.

8. The number of important budget concepts are virtually endless. For a more comprehensive glossary of concepts, see Gary R. Evans, *Red Ink* (San Diego: Academic Press, 1997).

9. Not all user fees generate revenues, and many are counted as "offsetting receipts" to cover specific purposes. Unlike taxes, user fees are "voluntary, businesslike" transactions used to offset costs for government services, and they do not go to general fund revenues.

10. For a more comprehensive description of the differences between deficits and the debt, see Evans, *Red Ink*, chap. 1.

11. For a more precise description of entitlement programs, see Congressional Budget Office, *Reducing Entitlement Spending* (Washington, D.C.: Government Printing Office, 1995), x–xi.

12. General Accounting Office, *Federal Fiscal Trends: Fiscal Years 1971–1995*, GAO/AIMD-97-3 (Washington, D.C.: Government Printing Office, 1996), 4.

13. James D. Savage, *Balanced Budgets and American Politics* (Ithaca, N.Y.: Cornell University Press, 1988).

14. Wildavsky, *New Politics of the Budget Process*, 470.

15. For a summary of the main reasons for the deficit problem, see Robert D. Reischauer, "The Budget: Crucible for the Policy Agenda," in *Setting National Priorities*, ed. Reischauer (Washington, D.C.: Brookings Institution, 1997). See also Ippolito, *Uncertain Legacies*, chap. 1; and Allen Schick, *The Capacity to Budget* (Washington, D.C.: Urban Institute Press, 1990), chaps. 2 and 3.

16. See R. Kent Weaver, "Controlling Entitlements," in *The New Directions in American Politics*, ed. John E. Chubb and Paul E. Peterson (Washington, D.C.: Brookings Institution, 1985).

17. John H. Makin and Norman J. Ornstein, *Debt and Taxes* (New York: Times Books, 1994), 155.

18. Numerous programs were indexed for inflation during the 1960s and 1970s, including civil service pensions, military pensions, coal miners' disability, railroad retirement, food stamps, Medicaid, and Supplemental Security Income. See R. Kent Weaver, *Automatic Government: The Politics of Indexation* (Washington, D.C.: Brookings Institution, 1988).

19. Timothy J. Penny and Steven E. Schier, *Payment Due: A Nation in Debt, A Generation in Trouble* (Boulder, Colo.: Westview, 1996), 31.

20. David M. Cutler, "Restructuring Medicare for the Future," in *Setting National Priorities*, ed. Robert D. Reischauer (Washington, D.C.: Brookings Institution, 1997). See also Wildavsky, *New Politics of the Budgetary Process*, chap. 8.

21. Budget of the United States Government, Fiscal Year 1999, *Historical Tables* (Washington, D.C.: Government Printing Office, 1998), 24.

22. For a good discussion of how deficits affected the budget process, see Schick, *Capacity to Budget*, chap. 6.

23. Schick, *Federal Budget*, 86. This is probably a safe estimate of the cumulative aggregate "effects" of legislation that aimed to reduce the deficit, though it is very difficult to calculate the precise effects of such changes.

24. For more on entitlement spending, see Weaver, "Controlling Entitlements," in *New Directions in American Politics*, ed. Chubb and Peterson. Despite the conventional wisdom that entitlements are untouchable, Weaver shows that some entitlements grow more than others. From 1965 to 1974, entitlement spending increased at an inflation-adjusted annual rate of 10 percent, but after a period of consolidation and retrenchment, from 1975 to 1985 entitlement spending growth slowed to 4 percent. For more on this point, see Wildavsky, *New Politics of the Budgetary Process*, 309.

25. Marilyn Moon and Janemarie Mulvey, *Entitlements and the Elderly: Protecting Promises, Recognizing Realities* (Washington, D.C.: Urban Institute, 1996), 3.

26. Congressional Budget Office, *Universal Health Insurance Coverage Using Medicare's Payment Rates* (Washington, D.C.: Government Printing Office, December 1991). Allen Schick counted more than 200 changes in Medicare during the Reagan years, most of which affected payments to hospitals and physicians. Schick argues that those changes created instability in the program, and not all of them saved money. Schick, *Capacity to Budget*, 190–92.

27. For a comprehensive analysis of the politics of Social Security reform, see Paul Light, *Still Artful Work: The Continuing Politics of Social Security Reform* (New York: McGraw-Hill, 1995). Light argues that, in a crisis atmosphere, leaders from both parties negotiated in secret, compromised their highest priorities, set a deadline for completing the legislative process, operated under the premise of shared sacrifice, and created political cover so that no single individual or party could be punished for making unpopular policy changes.

28. Wildavsky, *New Politics of the Budgetary Process*, 287.

29. For an account of budget savings from tax revenue increases in 1980, 1982, 1984, 1985, and 1987, see Schick, *Capacity to Budget*, 136. Political scientist Dennis Ippolito estimates the tax changes of 1982 through 1984 offset revenue losses from the 1981 tax cuts by about one-third. Ippolito, *Uncertain Legacies*, 67–75.

30. Interest groups paid a price for tax policy changes of the 1980s and 1990s. With respect to business interests and the TEFRA, see White and Wildavsky, *Deficit and the Public Interest*, 249–58. Elderly lobbies were also unable to block initiatives that increased the tax liability of senior citizens. See Moon and Mulvey, *Entitlements and the Elderly*, 27–28.

31. I am not suggesting that tax increases alone caused Bush to lose in 1992 and Democrats to lose their congressional majorities in 1994. Yet contrary to popular opinion, politicians have not always ducked the so-called tough choices required to reduce the deficit. See Robert D. Reischauer, "Light at the End of the Tunnel or Another Illusion? The 1997 Budget Deal," *National Tax Journal* (March 1998): 143–67.

32. Reischauer discusses the various ways in which analysts measure spending growth and prefers to use a "real," or inflation-adjusted, measure. Real spending, as distinguished from "nominal" spending, takes into account the costs of goods and services rather than simply the total amount of money spent in a given year. Robert D. Reischauer, "The Unfulfillable Promise: Cutting Nondefense Discretionary Spending," in *Setting National Priorities*, ed. Reischauer, 130.

33. For a summary of why GRH failed to balance the budget, see Schick, *Capacity to Budget*, 204–6. For the redeeming qualities of the GRH law, see Lance T. LeLoup, Barbara Luck Graham, and Stacy Barwick, "Deficit Politics and Constitutional Government: The Impact of Gramm-Rudman-Hollings," *Public Budgeting and Finance*, 7 (Spring 1987): 100–101.

34. The GRH deficit target for 1990 was $74 billion, but in March the CBO estimated that the effects of the savings-and-loan bailout and a lingering recession would raise the deficit to $161 billion. In order to avoid as much as $80 billion in automatic spending cuts under the GRH and reduce pressures on the stock market, President Bush sought to initiate negotiations with Democratic leaders in Congress.

35. See Elizabeth Drew, *On the Edge: The Clinton Presidency* (New York: Simon and Schuster, 1994), chap. 4.

36. Hager and Pianin, *Mirage*, 211–12.

37. For more details of changes Congress made in Clinton's original package, see David W. Brady and Craig Volden, *Revolving Gridlock* (Boulder, Colo.: Westview, 1998), 110–11. For other details on political and legislative developments in the budget process in 1993, see Drew, *On the Edge*, chaps. 11, 16, 20.

38. For more on the 1985 budget resolution, see White and Wildavsky, *Deficit and the Public Interest*, 432–38; and Richard F. Fenno Jr., *The Emergence of a Senate Leader: Pete Domenici and the Reagan Budget* (Washington, D.C.: CQ Press, 1991), 211–20.

39. For more background on this case, see Penny and Schier, *Payment Due*, 74–89.

40. The following account of events in the 1995 budget cycle relies mainly on Hager and Pianin, *Mirage*, chaps. 1–2, 8–9; and Elizabeth Drew, *Showdown* (New York: Simon and Schuster, 1996), chaps. 8, 16, 18, 23–24.

41. Boehner and Gingrich quoted in Hager and Pianin, *Mirage*, 243–44.

42. Quoted in ibid., 259.

43. For a review of the negotiations, see ibid., 271–79.

44. See Schick, *Capacity to Budget*, chaps. 4–6; and Wildavsky, *New Politics of the Budgetary Process*, chaps. 5–6.

Chapter 3: Aligning the Stars . . . Governing, Policy, and Leadership

1. Quoted in Peter Baker, "Clinton Calls Budget His Top Priority," *Washington Post*, 11 November 1996, A18.

2. See Lawrence C. Dodd and Bruce I. Oppenheimer, "Revolution in the House: Testing the Limits of Party Government," in *Congress Reconsidered*, 6th ed., ed. Lawrence C. Dodd and Bruce I. Oppenheimer (Washington, D.C.: CQ Press, 1997), 49.

3. See David Rogers, "Spending Pact Marks Major Retreat by GOP Leaders," *Wall Street Journal*, 30 September 1996, A20.

4. Thomas B. Edsall and Mario A. Brossard, "Clashing Coalitions Produce Split in Government Power," *Washington Post*, 7 November 1996, A1. Rhodes Cook also found that "nearly three out of four congressional districts were carried by a presidential candidate of the same party." Rhodes Cook, "Actual District Votes Belie Ideal of Bipartisanship," *Congressional Quarterly Weekly Report*, 12 April 1997, 859.

5. See David W. Rohde, *Parties and Leaders in the Postreform House* (Chicago: University of Chicago Press, 1991).

6. Ruth Marcos, "Taking 'Voter Guides' to the TV Audience," *Washington Post*, 17 October 1996, A16.

7. Lawrence C. Dodd and Bruce I. Oppenheimer, "Congress and the Emerging Order: Conditional Party Government or Constructive Partisanship?" in *Congress Reconsidered*, ed. Dodd and Oppenheimer, 395.

8. George Hager, "A Bipartisan Budget? No Duress, No Deal," *Congressional Quarterly Weekly Report*, 23 November, 1996, 3322. See also Richard E. Cohen, "Don't Place Your Bet on Bipartisanship," *National Journal*, 1 February 1997, 233.

9. Personal interview with a Republican staff person, anonymity guaranteed. (Some members and staff allowed me to cite their names, others preferred to remain anonymous.) Other points in this paragraph about the attitudes and perspectives of Republican members are based on personal observations of caucus meetings with Republicans on the House Budget Committee and personal interviews with members and staff personnel.

10. William Hoagland, staff director of the Senate Budget Committee, interview by author.

11. See George Hager and Andrew Taylor, "GOP Looks for New Strategies as Talks Stall Yet Again," *Congressional Quarterly Weekly Report*, 20 January 1996, 150.

12. Based on personal observations of Republican House Budget Committee caucus meetings and illustrated in the following chapter.

13. See Robert D. Reischauer, "Light at the End of the Tunnel or Another Illusion? The 1997 Budget Deal," *National Tax Journal* 51 (1998): 145–46.

14. See Dodd and Oppenheimer, "Congress and the Emerging Order," 390–413.

15. Jackie Koszczuk and Congressional Quarterly Staff, "Members Move to Claim Center as Voters Demand Moderation," *Congressional Quarterly Weekly Report*, 9 November 1996, 3199.

16. Personal communication with Congressman Robert L. Ehrlich (R-Md.).

17. Clinton quoted in Roger K. Lowe and Jonathan Riskind, "Parties See New Voter Mandate," *Columbus Dispatch*, 7 November 1996, A1.

18. Gingrich quoted in Kevin Merida, "Gingrich Pledges to Find 'Common Ground' with Clinton," *Washington Post*, 7 November 1995, A35.

19. Lott quoted in Dan Balz, "Republicans Sound Conciliatory Tone; Hill GOP would defer to the Reelected President but Warns of Conflict," *Washington Post*, 7 November 1996, 1.

20. Personal interview with Republican staff person, anonymity guaranteed.

21. Personal interview with Congressman John Kasich (R-Ohio).

22. The role of policy leaders in the budget process takes on another dimension after Congress passes a budget resolution and committee chairs are given the responsibility of drafting specific legislation to meet the goals and priorities of the resolution. Committee chairs are policy leaders too, but they are not direct participants in the process of negotiating the budget agreement. Thus they are even more apt to diverge from the preferences of party leaders.

23. For a good discussion of conditions under which politicians will prefer disagreement over compromise, see John B. Gilmour, *Strategic Disagreement: Stalemate in American Politics* (Pittsburgh: University of Pittsburgh Press, 1995).

24. Personal interview with member of Congress, anonymity guaranteed.

25. Personal interview with Republican staff person, anonymity guaranteed.

26. Personal interview with Congressman David Hobson (R-Ohio).

27. Quoted in Peter Baker, "Clinton Calls Budget His Top Priority," *Washington Post*, 11 November 1996, A1.

28. Quoted in John F. Harris, "A Break with the Past, in More Ways Than One," *Washington Post*, 4 May 1997, A18.

29. Personal interview with Congressman Ben Cardin (D-Md.).

30. The White House knew that many congressional Democrats preferred partisan conflict to bipartisan cooperation. See, for example, Morton M. Kondrake, "Credit for Budget Deal Should Go to Clinton's Man on the Hill Hilley," *Roll Call*, 5 May 1997, 6.

31. Personal interview with Democratic member of Congress, anonymity guaranteed.

32. See, for example, Morton M. Kondrake, "Clinton Faces War with Gephardt over Budget Pact," *Roll Call*, 1 May 1997, 8.

33. See Dodd and Oppenheimer, "Revolution in the House," 48–49.

34. For Gingrich's views on compromising in the budget process in the fall of 1995, see his response to former CBO director Robert Reischauer's prediction that the GOP would compromise with the White House to avert a "train wreck" at the end of the fiscal year. Newt Gingrich, "Cooperation Yes—Compromise, No," *Washington Post*, 25 September 1995, C7. Gingrich rebuked Reischauer's suggestion that a compromise was in the cards: "Unfortunately, [Reischauer] completely misses what is at the heart of the Republican revolution—a commitment to actually changing the system that has been making the nation sicker and sicker financially."

35. Quoted in Dale Russakoff, "On the Stump, Gingrich Adjusts to Reduced Stature," *Washington Post*, 24 October 1996, A1.

36. Personal interview with Republican staff person, anonymity guaranteed.

37. Quoted in Harris, "A Break with the Past," A18.

38. Personal interview with Republican staff person, anonymity guaranteed.

39. Quoted in John F. Harris, "As Clinton's Deal-Maker, Bowles Means Business," *Washington Post*, 12 May 1997, A9.

40. All quotations in this paragraph are from Harris, "As Clinton's Deal-Maker, Bowles Means Business," A9.

41. Personal interview with Congressman David Hobson (R-Ohio).

42. Personal interview with Congressman John Kasich (R-Ohio).

43. Personal interview with Republican member of Congress, anonymity guaranteed.

44. Quoted in Laurie Kellman, "Speaker Exults Over Success on Budget Pact," *Washington Times*, 3 May 1997, A4.

45. William Hoagland, staff director of the Senate Budget Committee, interview by author.

46. See, for example, Kondrake, "Credit for Budget Deal Should Go to Clinton's Man on the Hill Hilley," 6.

47. Quoted in Eric Pianin, "Kasich's Ambitions May Be 'Wild Card' in Budget Talks with the White House," *Washington Post*, 24 March 1997, A4.

48. Quoted in Pianin, "Kasich's Ambitions," A4.

49. Richard F. Fenno Jr., *The Emergence of a Senate Leader: Pete Domenici and the Reagan Budget* (Washington, D.C.: CQ Press, 1991), 96.

50. Fenno, *The Emergence of a Senate Leader*, 72.

51. Quoted in Jerry Gray, "For Senate's Budget Expert, a Long Climb Gets Tougher," *New York Times*, 13 May 1995, 1.

52. See George Hager and Eric Pianin, *Mirage* (New York: Random House, 1997), 61.

Chapter 4: Tug-of-War

1. William J. Clinton, "Address Before a Joint Session of Congress on the State of the Union," *Weekly Compilation of Presidential Papers* 33, no. 6 (4 February 1997): 136.

2. Statement by House Budget Committee Chair John Kasich during Republican Budget Committee caucus meeting, 13 February 1997.

3. Quoted in Alissa J. Rubin, "House Man of the Hour Archer Says He's Ready to Deal," *Congressional Quarterly Weekly Report*, 22 February 1997, 481.

4. Bill Archer, "Let's Make a Deal, Mr. President," *Washington Post*, 26 January 1997, C01.

5. Quoted in Helen Dewar, "Despite Some Tensions, Hill Leaders Confident of Budget Agreement," *Washington Post*, 10 January 1997, A4.

6. Personal interview with William Hoagland, staff director of the Senate Budget Committee.

7. The account of this meeting is based on personal observation.

8. Both quotations in this paragraph are from a personal interview with John Kasich.

9. Personal interview with Rick May, staff director of the House Budget Committee.

10. Quoted in "Clinton Unveils $1.7 billion Proposal; Tax Cut 'Trigger' Included," *National Journal's CongressDaily*, 6 February 1997, 1.

11. Domenici and Kasich quoted in "GOP Leaders: Proposal Falls $50B Short of 2002 Balance," *National Journal's CongressDaily*, 6 February 1997, 2.

12. Personal interview with William Hoagland, staff director of the Senate Budget Committee.

13. The account of this meeting is based on personal observation.

14. Personal interview with John Kasich.

15. The following assessment of economic projections is from George Hager, "War Over Predictions Goes On Despite History of Bad Calls," *Congressional Quarterly Weekly Report*, 29 March 1997, 735–36.

16. Income shares are calculated from the size of corporate profits and employee wages, the inflation rate is based on the Consumer Price Index (CPI), and interest rates are the expected yield on ten-year Treasury notes.

17. Penner quoted in Hager, "War Over Predictions Goes On," 735–36.

18. Quoted in David Baumann and Mary Ann Akers, "Kasich Wants New Clinton Budget in Redux of 104th," *National Journal's CongressDaily/AM*, 4 March 1997, 1.

19. Quoted in "Raines Challenges GOP to Produce Alternative Budget," *National Journal's CongressDaily*, 4 March 1997, 2.

20. Daschle quoted in Jerry Gray, "Frustration on All Sides at the Budget Struggle," *New York Times*, 6 March 1997, A1.

21. Quoted in George Hager, "GOP Demands New Clinton Budget as CPI 'Magic Bullet' Misfires," *Congressional Quarterly Weekly Report*, 15 March 1997, 620.

22. The account of this meeting is based on personal observation.

23. Personal interview with John Kasich.

24. Although the determination of the CPI is an inexact science, several studies have found that the CPI overstates inflation. In 1995 the Congressional Budget Office (CBO) reported the annual inflation overstatement of the CPI ranged between .2 and .8 percent. Federal Reserve Chairman Alan Greenspan cited an overstatement range of .5 to 1.5 percent.

25. Lott and Domenici quoted in Hager, "GOP Demands New Clinton Budget," 619–20.

26. Quoted in Patrice Hill, "Gingrich Advises Balancing Budget Before Cutting Taxes," *Washington Times*, 18 March 1997, A3.

27. Polls showed Americans favored balancing the budget over tax cuts. See Charles E. Cook, "Gingrich Goes Out on a Limb by Putting Off Tax Cuts in Budget," *Roll Call*, 20 March 1997.

28. Quoted in Sandy Hume, "GOP Rank-and-File Protests Proposal to Remove Tax Cut from Budget Bill," *The Hill*, 19 March 1997, 1.

29. The account of this meeting is based on personal observation.

30. Personal interviews with William Hoagland and John Kasich.

Chapter 5: Bipartisan Deal Making under Divided Government

1. "Gingrich Seeks Elimination of Capital Gains, Estate Taxes," *National Journal's CongressDaily*, 9 April 1997, 1.

2. William Hoagland, staff director of the Senate Budget Committee, interview by author.

3. Quoted in David Baumann, "GOP Negotiators Insist on Larger Discretionary Cuts," *National Journal's CongressDaily*, 9 April 1997, 7.

4. Quoted in David Baumann, "Budget Negotiators Vow to Crank Up Efforts Next Week," *National Journal's CongressDaily/A.M.*, 19 April 1997, 5.

5. Quoted in "Both Sides Issuing Ultimatums over Budget Negotiations," *National Journal's CongressDaily*, 21 April 1997, 1.

6. Quoted in "Daschle Says Rebellious Dems Soothed on Negotiations," *National Journal's CongressDaily*, 18 April 1997, 1. For more on Congressman Frank's argument on the defense issue, see Barney Frank, "Cut Defense, Too," *Washington Post*, 2 May 1997, A19.

7. Quoted in Jerry Gray, "Conservative Senators Pressure G.O.P. Leaders in Budget Talks," *New York Times*, 23 April 1997, A19. For a description of Gramm's budget priorities, see Phil Gramm, "Budget Discretion," *Wall Street Journal*, 18 April 1997, A18.

8. Quoted in "Nickles Warns Budget Talk Delay Jeopardizes Agreement," *National Journal's CongressDaily*, 22 April 1997, 1–2. The other eight senators included John Aschcroft (R-Miss.), Larry E. Craig (R-Idaho), Lauch Faircloth (R-N.C.), Jesse Helms (R-N.C.), James M. Inhofe (R-Okla.), Rick Santorum (R-Pa.), Richard C. Shelby (R-Ala.), and Robert C. Smith (R-N.H.).

9. Quoted in "Nickles Warns Budget Talk Delay Jeopardizes Agreement," 1.

10. Quoted in George Hager, "Time Pressure Prods Both Sides, but Party Wings Yield Little," *Congressional Quarterly Weekly Report*, 26 April 1997, 949.

11. Quoted in Hager, "Time Pressure Prods Both Sides," 947.

12. The account of this meeting is based on personal observation.

13. Quoted in Eric Pianin and Clay Chandler, "White House Weighs GOP Budget Plan," *Washington Post*, 26 April 1997, A4.

14. Personal interview with Congressman John Kasich.

15. Quoted in Eric Pianin, "Budget Dialogue Narrows Divide over Tough Issues," *Washington Post*, 27 April 1997, A10.

16. Quoted in Greg Hitt, "Lott Says Reduction in Inflation Index Is Dead Issue in Balanced-Budget Talks," *Wall Street Journal*, 29 April 1997, A20.

17. Quoted in "Deal Is 'Close, But Not Done' as Archer Issues Warning," *National Journal's CongressDaily*, 1 May 1997, 1.

18. The account of this meeting is based on personal observation.

19. Based on interviews with members and staff present at the meeting on 1 May. See also Adam Clymer, "Democrats in Congress Fume over Clinton Budget Process," *New York Times*, 2 May 1997, A1, A21.

20. Personal interview with a Democratic member of Congress, anonymity guaranteed.

21. Personal interview with a Democratic member of Congress, anonymity guaranteed.

22. Quoted in "GOP Says a Budget-Balancing Deal with Clinton Is at Hand," *CQ Monitor*, 2 May 1997, 3.

23. Quoted in David Baumann and Lisa Caruso, "Divided Democrats Pose Highest Hurdle for Budget Deal," *National Journal's CongressDaily*, 1 May 1997, 1.

24. Quoted in Eric Pianin, "Tax-Cut Details Delay Pact on Balanced Budget," *Washington Post*, 2 May 1997, A1.

25. Quoted in George Hager, Alissa J. Rubin, and Andrea Foster, "Negotiators Say They're Close to a Budget Agreement," *CQ Monitor*, 1 May 1995, 6.

26. Quoted in Pianin, "Tax-Cut Details Delay Pact on Balanced Budget," A1.

27. Quoted in Baumann and Caruso, "Divided Democrats Pose Highest Hurdle for Budget Deal," 4.

28. All passages in the paragraph are from Eric Pianin and John F. Harris, "President, GOP Agree on Balanced Budget Plan: Deal Includes $85 Billion in Tax Cuts, Funds for Clinton Domestic Priorities," *Washington Post*, 3 May 1997, A1 and A14.

29. Personal interview with Republican staff person, anonymity guaranteed.

30. Personal interview with William Hoagland, staff director of the Senate Budget Committee.

31. Jackie Calmes, "In the Unusual Logic of Budget Negotiations, a Windfall Is Something That Can Kill a Deal," *Wall Street Journal*, 5 May 1997, A20.

32. The account of the Thursday evening Democrat caucus meeting is based on interviews with participants. See also Clay Chandler, "Hitting the Jackpot on Capitol Hill," *Washington Post*, 3 May 1997, A14.

33. Quoted in Chandler, "Hitting the Jackpot on Capitol Hill," A14.

34. Personal interview with William Hoagland, staff director of the Senate Budget Committee.

35. Domenici and Gephardt quoted in "Gephardt Charges GOP Trying to Stampede Budget Deal," *National Journal's CongressDaily*, 8 May 1997, 1.

36. Personal interview with Congressman Ben Cardin (D-Md.).

37. Quoted in Patrice Hill, "Details Bedevil Balanced Budget," *Washington Times*, 2 May 1997, A13.

38. Quoted in Jerry Gray, "In Budget Battle, Advantage Goes to G.O.P. Chairman," *New York Times*, 4 May 1997, 30.

39. Quoted in Sandy Hume, "GOP Chairman Blasts Leaders on Budget Deal," *The Hill*, 7 May 1997, 1.

40. Quoted in Patrice Hill, "Parties Continue to Squabble Despite Agreement on Budget," *Washington Times*, 9 May 1997, A5.

41. Quoted in "Lott Hits White House 'False Claims' about Budget Deal . . . but Says Negotiators Have 'Understanding' on Taxes," *National Journal's CongressDaily*, 9 May 1997, 1–2.

42. The account of this meeting is based on personal observation.

Chapter 6: "Don't Let the Perfect Be the Enemy of the Good"

1. *Congressional Record*, 105th Congress, 1st sess., vol. 143, no. 67, 20 May 1997, H.2965.

2. Arnold argues that leaders play a crucial role in building coalitions for macroeconomic policy goals in spite of the tendency members have to focus on particular constituent needs. R. Douglas Arnold, *The Logic of Congressional Action* (New Haven: Yale University Press, 1990), chap. 5.

3. The account of the markup session is based on personal observations.

4. "Concurrent Resolution on the Budget—Fiscal Year 1998," *Report of the Committee on the Budget*, House of Representatives, 105th Congress, 1st sess., 18 May 1997, 74.

5. The account of the markup session is based on personal observations.

6. Quoted in David Baumann and Lisa Caruso, "Budget Deal Clears Two More Hurdles," *National Journal's CongressDaily*, 20 May 1997, 1.

7. For the theoretical basis for most of the scholarship on how electoral motives affect "distributive policy," see David Mayhew, *Congress: The Electoral Connection* (New Haven: Yale University Press, 1974). For a good review of the literature on the relationship between pork barrel and congressional elections, see Robert M. Stein and Kenneth N. Bickers, *Perpetuating the Pork Barrel: Policy Subsystems and American Democracy* (New York: Cambridge University Press, 1995), chap. 7.

8. See, for example, David Rogers, "Mississippi's Senators Continue a Tradition: Getting Federal Money," *Wall Street Journal*, 6 March 1998, A1, A8.

9. Quoted from a memorandum, "Bipartisan Amendment to the Budget Resolution by the Leadership of the Transportation and Infrastructure Committee," *House Committee on Transportation and Infrastructure*, 19 May 1997.

10. Personal interview with Congressman John Kasich.

11. David Hosansky, "ISTEA Reauthorization Stalls Over Highway Funding," *Congressional Quarterly Weekly Report*, 10 May 1997, 1066.

12. Jennifer Bradley, "Members Make Their Play for Road Dollars," *Roll Call*, 17 March 1997, 10.

13. Personal interview with Republican staff person, anonymity guaranteed.

14. In Congressman Robert L. Ehrlich's (R-Md.) office, we received letters or faxes requesting support for Shuster-Oberstar from the following associations, alliances, and unions representing over 150 organizations: American Public Transit Association, American Portland

Cement Alliance, Marylanders for Efficient & State Highways, Transportation Construction Coalition, Alliance for Truth in Transportation Budgeting, Keep American Moving, Building and Construction Trades Department, the Canadian Transit Company, Baltimore Department of Public Works, Design Professionals Coalition, American Society of Civil Engineers, International Brotherhood of Teamsters, National Association of Manufacturers, National Governors' Association, and Small Business Legislative Council.

15. The account of this meeting is based on personal observations.

16. "Where from Here on the Budget?" *Washington Times*, 20 May 1998, A20.

17. Not only did most Republicans on the Budget Committee shy away from changing the CPI, but on 7 May the House adopted a resolution stating that it was the sense of the House that any changes in the CPI be made only by the Bureau of Labor Statistics. The resolution passed 399–16, and Republicans supported it by a vote of 212–7.

18. Only five members of the House voted against every budget resolution: David Weldon (R-Fla.), Henry Hyde (R-Ill.), Philip Crane (R-Ill.), Dennis Kucinich (D-Ohio), and Mark Sanford (R-S.C.).

19. *Congressional Record*, 105th Congress, 1st sess., vol. 143, no. 67, 20 May 1997, H.2963.

20. Quoted in Eric Pianin and John E. Yang, "Gephardt Denounced Balanced Budget Plan," *Washington Post*, 21 May 1997, A4.

21. Letter from Franklin D. Raines, director of OMB, 20 May 1997.

22. The following account of the Republican conference meeting and leadership strategy is based on interviews with participants, though a few news articles are also cited.

23. Interview with Republican staff person, anonymity guaranteed.

24. "Shuster Mulls ISTEA Options After Amendment Defeated," *National Journal's Congress-Daily*, 21 May 1997, 1.

25. See "House GOP Leaders Wield Rule Book to Defeat Shuster," *National Journal's Congress-Daily*, 22 May 1997, 7. I confirmed this in interviews with several participants.

26. *Congressional Record*, 105th Congress, 1st. sess., vol. 143, no. 67, 20 May 1997, H.2991–2992.

27. Ibid.

28. *Congressional Record*, 105th Congress, 1st. sess., vol. 143, no. 67, 20 May 1997, H.3005.

29. *Congressional Record*, 105th Congress, 1st. sess., vol. 143, no. 67, 20 May 1997, H.3062.

30. Personal interviews with Republican members, anonymity guaranteed.

31. Political scientist Richard Fenno was the first to identify and analyze the effects of "multiple goals" (reelection, gaining prestige or influence in the institution, and good public policy) on the behavior of members and committees. Congressional scholars have debated the role of various individual goals ever since. See Richard F. Fenno Jr., *Congressmen in Committees* (Boston: Little, Brown, 1973).

32. Quoted in David Hosansky and Alissa J. Rubin, "Shuster's Steamroller Stopped—for Now," *Congressional Quarterly Weekly Report*, 24 May 1997, 1183.

33. Arnold, *The Logic of Congressional Action*, 7.

34. Personal interview with Republican staff person, anonymity guaranteed.

35. I know of one case in which party leaders reminded John Ensign (R-Nev.) about the help he was given on a previous issue. Ensign was on the floor, but he hesitated long enough not to vote. After the result was announced, he reported to the chair that he intended to vote yes in favor of Shuster-Oberstar. *Congressional Record*, 105th Congress, 1st sess., vol. 143, no. 67, 20 May 1997, H.3065.

36. *Congressional Record*, 105th Congress, 1st sess., vol. 143, no. 67, 20 May 1997, S.4723.

37. *Congressional Record*, 105th Congress, 1st sess., vol. 143, no. 67, 20 May 1997, S.4729.

38. ". . . As Hatch, Kennedy Predict Close Vote on Amendment," *National Journal's Congress-Daily*, 20 May 1997, 1–2.

39. Passages from Hatch's speech are from the *Congressional Record*, 105th Congress, 1st sess., vol. 143, no. 68, 21 May 1997, S.4783.

40. *Congressional Record*, 105th Congress, 1st sess., vol. 143, no. 68, 21 May 1997, S.4784.

41. *Congressional Record*, 105th Congress, 1st sess., vol. 143, no. 68, 21 May 1997, S.4789.

42. *Congressional Record*, 105th Congress, 1st sess., vol. 143, no. 68, 21 May 1997, S.4803.

43. *Congressional Record*, 105th Congress, 1st sess., vol. 143, no. 68, 21 May 1997, S.4809.

44. *Congressional Record*, 105th Congress, 1st sess., vol. 143, no. 68, 21 May 1997, S.4810.

45. For an overview of Clinton's efforts to defeat the amendment, see Adam Clymer, "Clinton Helps Kill Proposal to Raise Tax on Cigarettes," *New York Times*, 22 May 1997, A1.

46. *Congressional Record*, 105th Congress, 1st sess., vol. 143, no. 68, 21 May 1997, S.4828.

47. Personal interview with member of Congress, anonymity guaranteed.

Chapter 7: Reconciliation Medley

1. Personal interview with Congressman Clay Shaw (R-Fla.), chair of the Ways and Means Subcommittee on Human Resources.

2. Personal interview with Congressman Tom Bliley (R-Va.), chair of the House Commerce Committee.

3. For a discussion of how reconciliation procedures affect budget policy, see John B. Gilmour, *Reconcilable Differences?* (Berkeley: University of California Press, 1990).

4. For more background on postcommittee adjustments and omnibus reconciliation bills, see Barbara Sinclair, *Unorthodox Lawmaking* (Washington, D.C.: CQ Press, 1997), chaps. 2, 5.

5. Quoted in Christopher Georges, "GOP Plans to Target Workfare Pay," *Wall Street Journal*, 22 May 1997, A6.

6. Quoted in ibid., A3.

7. Quoted in Robert Pear, "G.O.P. in House Moves to Bar Minimum Wage for Workfare," *New York Times*, 12 June 1997, B16.

8. "Supplemental Security Income: Recent Growth in the Rolls Raises Fundamental Program Concerns," General Accounting Office, January 1995.

9. Under the welfare reform legislation, noncitizens currently receiving SSI were scheduled to lose benefits in August 1997 unless they became citizens, worked in the United States for at least ten years, or were military personnel.

10. Personal interview with Congressman Shaw.

11. Concurrent Resolution on the Budget–Fiscal Year 1998. Report of the Committee on the Budget, House of Representatives, 105th Congress, 1st sess., 18 May 1997, 144.

12. The subcommittee passed an amendment by Jim McCrery that denied SSI to any legal immigrant whose sponsor earned at least $40,000 a year.

13. Personal interview with Congressman Shaw.

14. Levin quoted in Cheryl Wetzstein, "GOP Proposes Welfare Changes; Gore Sees Need for Safety Net," *Washington Times*, 5 June 1997, A9.

15. Quoted in "Gore Calls GOP Immigrant Welfare Plan 'Un-American,'" *National Journal's CongressDaily*, 20 June 1997, 6.

16. Clay Shaw, "Cut the Rhetoric on Noncitizens," Dear Colleague letter, 26 June 1997.

17. Raines and Shaw quoted in "Panel Passes Welfare Provisions on Party Line Vote," *National Journal's CongressDaily*, 6 June 1997, 5.

18. "Bipartisan Medicare Preventive Benefits Bill Introduced," Press Release from Congressman Ben Cardin, 7 January 1997.

19. Personal interview with Congressman Ben Cardin (D-Md.).

20. Quoted in Bud Newman and Julie Rovner, "House Panel to Act on Medicare Bill," *National Journal's CongressDaily*, 4 June 1997, 1.

21. Quoted in Newman and Rovner, "House Panel to Act on Medicare Bill," 8.

22. See Samuel Goldreich, "GOP Rolls Medicare Plan for Balanced-Budget Deal," *Washington Times*, 4 June 1997, A1, A8.

23. There were three important policy differences between the two committees' Medicare bills. First, Bilirakis's bill contained a "carve out" provision for graduate medical education. The carve out essentially meant that funds for graduate medical training and charity care (about $11 billion) would go directly to the institutions rather than through HMOs. The Ways and Means bill did not contain the carve out provision. Second, the Ways and Means Committee calculated Medicare payments on the basis of a formula that uses 50 percent local and 50 percent national costs, which tends to favor rural areas, whereas Commerce used a 70/30 blend. Third, Ways and Means phases in the transfer of spending for home health care from Part A to Part B, and Commerce did it immediately.

24. Not all Democrats agreed with the consumer protections, however. During the markup session, Peter Deutsch (D-Fla.), a strong advocate of managed care, gave a blistering critique of the amendments.

25. See "Minority Views on Title IV–Medicare," in *Balanced Budget Act of 1997, Report of the Committee on the Budget*, House of Representatives, 105th Congress, 1st sess., Report 105–149, 24 June 1997, 1650–51.

26. Opponents of the bill included the most liberal Democrats (Pallone, Eshoo, and Engel) and the most conservative Republicans (Stearns, Crapo, Cox, and Largent) on the Commerce Committee.

27. The inability of the Commerce Committee to come up with enough savings for spectrum auctions is another complicated and interesting story that deserves more attention than I can give in this chapter. Under the budget agreement, the Commerce Committees were instructed to raise $26.3 billion from spectrum auctions to broadcasters. The CBO estimated that policy proposals by the House Commerce and Senate Commerce, Science, and Transportation Committees fell short of reaching the level of savings specified by the budget agreement. For more details, see Juliana Gruenwald, "Auction of Broadcast Spectrum Gets Senate Panel Approval," *Congressional Quarterly Weekly Report*, 21 June 1997, 1439.

28. The Budget Committee does not "mark up" the reconciliation bill. It can adopt motions with a majority vote of committee members to instruct the chairman to request policy changes to the Rules Committee. The motions gave Budget Committee Democrats one final chance to go on record to protest various parts of the reconciliation bill. For motions made by Budget Committee members, see *Balanced Budget Act of 1997, Report of the Committee on the Budget*, House of Representatives, 105th Congress, 1st sess., Report 105–149, 24 June 1997, 1620–25.

29. By then, most of the problems were worked out, but a few remained. In some cases, the differences were not resolved at all, and policymakers agreed informally to deal with remaining problems in the conference with the Senate. For example, when the reconciliation bill went to the House floor, the Ways and Means and Commerce Committees continued to differ on the "carve out" provision for teaching hospitals from managed-care fees. They also differed in terms of the fee structure for reimbursing hospitals in rural areas; the Ways and Means bill would distribute more fees to hospitals in rural areas.

30. Waxman and Stark quoted in "House OKs Reconciliation Rule; Senate Voting Continues," *National Journal's CongressDaily*, 25 June 1997, 3.

31. *Congressional Record*, 105th Congress, 1st sess., 25 June 1997, H.4555.

32. Quotations from Spratt's floor speech are from ibid.

33. Ibid.

34. Most of the following account of how budget enforcement legislation developed is from an interview with Tim Bromelkaamp, legislative assistant to Congressman David Minge (D-Minn.).

35. The amendment raised the annual deductible from $100 to $540 for individuals with incomes of $50,000 and married couples with $75,000. The deductible increased upward along a sliding income scale, topping off at $2,160 for individuals with incomes of $100,000 and couples with $125,000.

36. Quoted in Robert Pear, "Senate Finance Panel Adjusts a 'Means Test' for Medicare," *New York Times*, 24 June 1997, A13.

37. Roth's original bill called for a maximum deductible of $6,000. Rockefeller's amendment lowered the maximum deductible to between $1,500 and $2,500. Maximum out-of-pocket expenses were capped at $3,000.

38. Roth quoted in Mary Agnes Carey, "Medicare Overhaul Heads for Senate Floor Battle," *Congressional Quarterly Weekly Report,* 21 June 1997, 1447.

39. See Christopher Georges and Laurie McGinley, "Senate GOP Plan to Overhaul Medicare Will Seek to Raise Eligibility Age to 67," *Wall Street Journal*, 11 June 1997, A4.

40. Quoted in Samuel Goldreich, "Both Houses OK Medicare Bills, but the Differences are Dramatic," *Washington Times*, 26 June 1997, A18.

41. "Means Testing Is Not an Answer to The Medicare Problem," Seniors Coalition, Press Release, 18 June 1997.

42. Raines quoted in "OMB Letter Warns Senate GOP over Medicaid Provisions," *National Journal's CongressDaily*, 17 June 1997, 1.

43. Gramm quoted in Robert Pear, "Capitol in Discord over Plan to Aid Uninsured Youths," *New York Times*, 17 June 1997, A1.

44. The decision to use a means test was based on practical policy effects. Applying a means test to the deductible would be inequitable, difficult to administer, and ineffective for wealthier seniors who most likely have Medigap health plans to pay for most deductible costs. See Robert D. Reischauer, "Midnight Follies," *Washington Post*, 22 June 1997, C7.

45. *Congressional Record*, 105th Congress, 1st sess., 23 June 1997, S.6079.

46. Ibid.

47. See Kerrey's speech, *Congressional Record*, 105th Congress, 1st sess., 24 June 1997, S.6122.

48. See Daschle's speech, *Congressional Record*, 105th Congress, 1st sess., 24 June 1997, S.6129.

Chapter 8: The Politics of Tax Policy

1. *Congressional Record*, 105th Congress, 1st sess., 26 June 1997, H.4810.

2. *Congressional Record*, 105th Congress, 1st sess., 25 June 1997, S.6332.

3. Those factors are key elements of Fenno's classic work on committee politics. Richard F. Fenno Jr., *Congressmen in Committees* (Boston: Little, Brown, 1973).

4. The budget agreement also included several proposals made in the Clinton administration's FY 1998 budget: welfare-to-work tax credit, capital gains tax relief for home sales, brownfields legislation, and incentives to spur growth in the District of Columbia.

5. For more discussion of differences among key Republican groups, see Ben Wildavsky and Kirk Victor, "Fighting Over Taxes," *National Journal*, 21 June 1997, 1283.

6. "Gramm Predicts 'Destructive' GOP Battle over Tax Cuts," *National Journal's Congress-Daily*, 5 May 1997, 1.

7. The agreement assumed about $32 billion would come from the airline-ticket tax, but Archer estimated he could find only another $7 to $8 billion in loophole closings.

8. See especially Fenno, *Congressmen in Committees.* With respect to the Ways and Means Committee, see Randall Strahan, *New Ways and Means: Reform and Change in a Congressional Committee* (Chapel Hill: University of North Carolina Press, 1990), chap. 5.

9. After the Democratic reform era of the 1970s, the goals of Ways and Means shifted from influence and prestige to a combination policy interests plus influence and prestige. Some members linked policy interests with constituent interests as an important goal, but none considered constituent interests or reelection the primary goal. See Strahan, *New Ways and Means*, 75–78.

10. Except for a short time in the mid-1970s, it was rare for members from marginal districts to be appointed to the committee. Strahan, *New Ways and Means*, 68–69.

11. See Jim Vande Hei, "Republicans Fill 'Big Three' with Vulnerable Members," *Roll Call*, 1 December 1997, 1; and Gregg Hitt, "Tale of Two House Republicans Show Rewards and Risks of Seat on Ways and Means Committee," *Wall Street Journal*, 1 October 1997, A24.

12. See Richard E. Cohen, "Grumbling Over Lott's Power Plays," *National Journal*, 19 July 1997, 1475.

13. Some congressional scholars argue that personal qualities of individual leaders are irrelevant to explaining how they will lead; others argue that personal qualities are critical to understanding leadership style. I favor the latter view. See Daniel J. Palazzolo, *The Speaker and the Budget: Leadership in the Post-Reform House of Representatives* (Pittsburgh: University of Pittsburgh Press, 1992). See also Strahan, *New Ways and Means*, chap. 5.

14. See Jackie Koszczuk, "Unheralded Roth Is Front and Center," *Congressional Quarterly Weekly Report*, 9 September 1995, 2701.

15. See Erika Niedowski, "Senator William Roth; Packwood's Successor as Finance Chairman is Low-Key Consensus Builder," *The Hill*, 17 January 1996, 34.

16. See Bud Newman, "Tax Package Looms as Archer's Test," *National Journal's CongressDaily*, 19 May 1997, 1, 3–4; and Richard W. Stevenson, "Texan Faces Big Challenge in Shaping Tax Policy," *New York Times*, 30 May 1997, A24.

17. In comparison with previous Ways and Means Committee chairs, Archer liked to compare himself with Wilbur Mills, the long-time Democratic chair who served from the late 1950s to 1975, rather than to Dan Rostenkowski, who served in the 1980s and early 1990s. Clay Chandler and Eric Pianin, "Bill Archer's Tough Target: Turning Budget Deal into Tax Bill to Test Chairman's Ways and Means," *Washington Post*, 23 May 1997, G01.

18. Ibid.

19. Quoted in Clay Chandler and Eric Pianin, "Hill Republicans Offer Plan to Cut Taxes," *Washington Post,* 10 June 1997, A4.

20. The AMT passed as part of the Tax Reform Act of 1986 had good intentions—to make sure wealthy individuals and corporations could not avoid paying taxes. But the AMT produced unintended consequences, especially for capital-intensive businesses, and it was widely recognized by Democrats and Republicans as a punitive tax on investment. Under the AMT, investment in business machinery and equipment is treated as income rather than expense, and the estimated cost of investing in business machinery and equipment is increased by 10 percent for companies paying the AMT. Many businesses lack the means or the incentive to invest in machinery and equipment that will depreciate over time. When manufacturing companies fail to invest, they fail to build profits and pass on their profits to workers in the form of higher wages, and they fail to create high-paying jobs. The most important component of the Ways and Means bill regarding the AMT is that it repeals the AMT depreciation adjustment. Still, phasing out the AMT eased the tax burden of corporations, making it a big target for Democrats opposed to the tax proposal in general.

21. Quoted in Nancy E. Roman, "GOP's Tax-Cutting Plan Favors Relief for Families," *Washington Times*, 10 June 1997, A10.

22. "Dear Republican Colleague" letter from Bill Archer, chairman of the House Committee on Ways and Means, 9 June 1997.

23. Personal interview with Democratic member of the House Committee on Ways and Means, anonymity guaranteed.

24. Personal interview with Congressman Clay Shaw (R-Fla.), member of the House Committee on Ways and Means.

25. Quoted in Chandler and Pianin, "Hill Republicans Offer Plan to Cut Taxes," A04.

26. Ibid.

27. Quoted in Alissa J. Rubin, "Archer-Backed Tax-Cut Package Finds Critics in All Corners," *Congressional Quarterly Weekly Report*, 14 June 1997, 1359.

28. Quoted in Laurie Kellman, "Archer Manages to Avoid Instant Condemnation for Tax Bill," *Washington Times*, 10 June 1997, 19.

29. Quoted in "NFIB Calls Death Tax Provision in House Tax Package 'Unacceptable,'" *U.S. Newswire*, 9 June 1997. The NFIB represents 600,000 business owners and gave 93 percent of its $1.1 million in PAC and soft-money contributions to Republicans in 1996.

30. See Bud Newman and Lisa Caruso, "GOP, Democrats Still Scrambling Before Tax Markup," *National Journal's CongressDaily*, 11 June 1997, 8.

31. Bloomfield quoted in Lisa Caruso, Matthew Morrissey, and Daryl Richard, "GOP, Business Give Mixed Reviews to Archer Tax Plan," *National Journal's CongressDaily*, 10 June 1997, 8.

32. See Greg Hitt, "GOP Targets Estate Taxes, Capital Gains," *Wall Street Journal*, 10 June 1997, A1, A3.

33. Under the depreciation recapture provisions in the bill, any long-term gain from the sale of commercial real estate that had taken depreciation deductions in prior taxable years would be taxed at a maximum rate of 26 percent instead of the new rate of 20 percent.

34. The issue of airline-ticket taxes has traditionally split the seven big airlines and discount competitors. Though the new tax shifted some of the burden to regional discount carriers (because they have lower fares and more takeoffs and landings), both sides opposed the new tax. For airline industry reaction, see Peter Kaplan, "Airlines Opposed Tax-Cut Proposal," *Washington Times*, 10 June 1997, A9.

35. Quoted in "Daschle Demands Tax Cut Stay in Budget Resolution," *National Journal's CongressDaily*, 4 June 1997, 2.

36. Quoted in Phillip Brasher, "Archer Targets Indian Revenue Again," *Associated Press Newswire*, 9 June 1997.

37. Gregg Hitt, "GOP Drops Plan to Scrap Corporate Tax," *Wall Street Journal*, 12 June 1997, A2. For a description of the leadership meeting, see Clay Chandler, "Democrats Show Unity on Tax Plan," *Washington Post*, 12 June 1997, A11.

38. Under the original bill, the estate tax exemption was scheduled to increase from $600,000 to $1 million over seventeen years, while the substitute raised the exemption to $1 million over ten years. The estimated cost of changing the schedule was about $10 billion over ten years.

39. Chandler, "Democrats Show Unity on Tax Plan," A11.

40. Quoted in Hitt, "GOP Drops Plan to Scrap Corporate Tax," A2.

41. Quoted in "New Archer Proposal Alters AMT, Estate and Ticket Taxes," *National Journal's CongressDaily*, 11 June 1997, 1.

42. Quoted in Hitt, "GOP Drops Plan to Scrap Corporate Tax," A2.

43. Jackie Calmes, "How Cash, Caucuses Combined to Protect a Fuel on the Hill," *Wall Street Journal*, 18 August 1997, A1.

44. Ibid.

45. Interestingly, six of the eight Republicans who voted against the chairmen were from marginal districts and the other two, Jim Ramstad (R-Minn.) and Dave Camp (R-Mich.), represented constituencies with direct interests in agriculture or corn processing.

46. Archer quoted in Jill Zuckman, "Indian Tax Faces Opposition on Panel; Some Try to Kill Bid, Face Leader's Threat," *Boston Globe*, 12 June 1997, A10.

47. Quoted in Hitt, "GOP Drops Plan to Scrap Corporate Tax," A2.

48. Quoted in Clay Chandler, "Roth Tax Plan Sets Up New Battle with Clinton," *Washington Post*, 18 June 1997, C11.

49. Ibid.

50. Quoted in Clay Chandler, "Key Senate Democrats Backing Roth Tax Bill," *Washington Post*, 17 June 1997, A4.

51. *Congressional Record*, 25 June 1997, S.6335.

52. Quoted in Clay Chandler, "Some Telling William Overtures; House, Senate Panel Chiefs Use Contrasting Styles to Advance Their Tax Proposals," *Washington Post*, 22 June 1997, A18.

53. See Helen Dewar, "Tax Bills Open Way for Policy Initiatives: Sen. Hatch, Among Others, 'Seized the Moment' for a Bipartisan Appeal," *Washington Post*, 30 June 1997, A04.

54. For example, the committee passed amendments by Gramm to transfer 4.3 cents of gas tax to the Highway Trust Fund, by Connie Mack (R-Fla.) to give a $5,000 income tax credit for first-time buyers of a principal residence in Washington, D.C., and by Richard Bryan (R-Nev.) to allow IRAs to be invested in gold bullion. See Richard W. Stevenson, "Compromise Included in Senate Panel's Tax Bill," *New York Times*, 21 June 1997, 11.

55. Quoted in Eric Pianin, "Senate Passes $77 Billion in Tax Relief," *Washington Post*, 28 June 1997, A01.

56. The Senate passed one significant amendment sponsored by Paul Coverdell (R-Ga.) to allow individuals to use the child tax credit and savings accrued through IRAs to pay for elementary and secondary school tuition. The amendment was passed 59–41, mainly along party lines.

57. Quoted in Pianin, "Senate Passes $77 Billion in Tax Relief," A01.

58. One advertisement sponsored by the National Association of Realtors targeting Archer and DeLay, both of Houston, Texas, announced: "Houston, We Have a Problem. Congress is considering changing the rules on investment real estate." The association ran a radio advertisement played in marginal districts represented by Hayworth, Nussle, and Hulshof, saying that the Ways and Means Committee had "broken a promise" made in 1963 about how investment real estate was to be taxed.

59. The following description of the problems facing the party leadership is based partly on interviews with various Republican members and key staff personnel, anonymity guaranteed. Also see Jackie Koszczuk, "Gingrich under Fire as Discord Simmers from Rank to Top," *Congressional Quarterly Weekly Report*, 21 June 1997, 1415–18.

60. The antishutdown provision was designed to give the Republican Congress leverage at the end of the legislative session. In 1995 President Clinton vetoed Republican appropriations bills, leading to a government shutdown that the public blamed on Republicans. The census sampling issue was based as much on political concerns about redistricting as it was on statistical accuracy. Sampling tends to increase the minority count in the population and the number of potential Democratic voters. Republican National Committee Chairman Jim Nicholson estimated that Republicans could lose as many as 25 seats if sampling procedures are used in the 2000 census. See Juliana Gruenwald, "Statistics Stir the Passion of Parties' Boosters," *Congressional Quarterly Weekly Report*, 21 June 1997, 1436.

61. Quoted in "President Details Rejection of Supplemental Bill," *Congressional Quarterly Weekly Report*, 14 June 1997, 1393.
62. A Gallup poll for CNN and *USA Today* showed that 55 percent of respondents blamed Republicans and only 25 percent blamed Clinton for delaying disaster aid. Andrew Taylor, "Clinton Signs 'Clean' Disaster Aid After Flailing GOP Yields to Veto," *Congressional Quarterly Weekly Report*, 14 June 1997, 1362.
63. For more on Daschle's tactics, see Nancy E. Roman, "Daschle Earns GOP Plaudits for 'Shrewd' Senate Tactics," *Washington Times*, 13 June 1997, A1, A14.
64. Shays quoted in Koszczuk, "Gingrich under Fire as Discord Simmers from Rank to Top," 1416.
65. Comments by Republican members based on my personal observations.
66. Quoted in Calmes, "How Cash, Caucuses Combined to Protect a Fuel on the Hill," A1.
67. Personal interview with Republican member of the House Committee on Ways and Means, anonymity guaranteed.
68. Their concerns were certainly legitimate. A *Wall Street Journal*/NBC poll showed that 60 percent of the public supported the Democratic package of tax cuts and only 31 percent favored the Republican version. See *"Wall Street Journal*/NBC: Most Agree with Dems on Tax Cuts," *Hotline*, 26 June 1997. See also Al Hunt, "This Republican Tax-Cut Dog Won't Hunt," *Wall Street Journal*, 26 June 1997, 19.
69. Clay Chandler, "Clinton Says GOP's Child Tax Credit Plan Would Hurt Two-Income Families," *Washington Post*, 13 June 1997, A4.
70. Rangel quoted in "Archer Offers Child Tax Credit Compromise to Clinton," *National Journal's CongressDaily*, 19 June 1997, 3.
71. Gephardt quoted in Clay Chandler and Eric Pianin, "Hill Democrats, GOP Duel Statistically Over Tax Plans," *Washington Post*, 20 June 1997, A04.
72. Gingrich quoted in John E. Yang, "Gingrich Says Tax Cut Drive Just Starting; GOP Bill Called 'Moral Imperative,'" *Washington Post*, 22 June 1997, A18.
73. The Republican Conference faxed daily talking points from 20 June until 26 June, the day the House passed the bill.
74. The following account of the whip meeting is based on my personal observations.
75. The letter, signed by several powerful Republican business allies, including the Mortgage Bankers Association of America, the National Association of Home Builders, and the National Reality Committee, was designed to counteract the letter-writing campaign organized by the National Association of Realtors.
76. All of the heavyweight groups representing small businesses, families, and investment companies endorsed the tax bill, including U.S. Chamber of Commerce, Family Research Council, and the NFIB.
77. Ever since Secretary Rubin released a Treasury Department analysis of how the tax cuts would be distributed across income levels, the parties sparred over the definition of income. The Treasury data on the effects of tax cuts showed a disproportionate share of the cuts went to upper-income Americans. But the Joint Economic Committee found that the Treasury inflates income levels by counting items most people would not consider part of their income and do not include on their income tax return. In calculating an individual's income the Treasury includes the rental value of a taxpayer's home even if it is not rented, fringe benefits, inside buildup of IRAs and pensions, life and health insurance, and most nontaxable transfer payments.
78. *Congressional Record*, 105th Congress, 1st sess., 26 June 1997, H.4809.
79. *Congressional Record*, 105th Congress, 1st sess., 26 June 1997, H.4668.
80. Ibid.

Chapter 9: Conference Politics: Staking Out Positions and Restoring Bipartisanship

1. For a detailed description of the evolution, functions, and influence of conference committees, see Lawrence D. Longley and Walter J. Oleszek, *Bicameral Politics: Conference Committees in Congress* (New Haven: Yale University Press, 1989).

2. Stephen D. Van Beek, *Post-Passage Politics: Bicameral Resolution in Congress* (Pittsburgh: University of Pittsburgh Press, 1995), chap. 1.

3. Richard Morin, "New Friends Help Boost Clinton to Record Approval," *Washington Post*, 14 July 1997.

4. Gerald F. Seib and Gregg Hitt, "Public Supports Budget Deal, Despite Doubts," *Wall Street Journal*, 26 June 1997, A20. A poll conducted for the Republican National Committee yielded a 60 percent approval rating for Clinton and found that almost half of Americans thought Republican tax cuts were for the "rich." Moreover, the public ranked the education tax cuts as the most important tax proposal. The Tarrance Group, Public Opinion Strategies, and Voter Consumer Research, "Key Findings from a Nationwide Survey of Voter Attitudes," 24 June 1997.

5. For a good review of events involving the attempted ouster of Speaker Gingrich, see Ceci Connolly, David S. Broder, and Dan Balz, "Shifting Winds of House Rebellion," *Washington Post*, 28 July 1997, A01.

6. For a good description of the underlying tensions within the Republican Party, see Dan Balz and Ceci Connolly, "House Leadership Battle Mirrors Deeper Conflict; Lack of Unifying Themes, Chiefs Frustrate GOP," *Washington Post*, 20 July 1997, A01.

7. House Budget Committee aide and Kasich quoted in John E. Yang, "Paxon Quits House GOP Leadership," *Washington Post*, 18 July 1997, A01.

8. Sperling quoted in Alan Fram, "Clinton, Democrats Differ on Budget," *Associated Press*, 7 July 1997.

9. Gephardt and Bowles quoted in Alan Fram, "Clinton's Medicare Views Detailed," *Associated Press*, 11 July 1997. For Gephardt's critique of Medicare reforms passed in the Senate, see Edward M. Kennedy and Richard A. Gephardt, "Messing with Medicare," *Washington Post*, 26 June 1997, A19.

10. Lott quoted in Andrew Taylor and Mary Agnes Carey, "Hopeful Negotiation Schedule Threatened by Tax Battles," *Congressional Quarterly Weekly Report*, 12 July 1997, 1612.

11. Clay Chandler, "A Costly Medicare Question: Who Collects Premium Hike?" *Washington Post*, 23 July 1997, A04.

12. Personal interview with William Hoagland, staff director of the Senate Budget Committee.

13. Daschle quoted in Robert Pear, "G.O.P. Feud in House Stalls Budget Talks," *New York Times*, 22 July 1997, A1.

14. Archer quoted in John F. Harris and Eric Pianin, "Clinton Offers, Seeks Concessions on Tax Cuts," *Washington Post*, 1 July 1997, A01.

15. Rangel quoted in Eric Pianin and Ann Devroy, "President, Congress Close in on Tax Deal; House Democrats Wary of Clinton's Concessions," *Washington Post*, 3 July 1997, A01.

16. Both Kasich and Armey assured Republicans at House party whip meetings during July that negotiators assured them Clinton wanted to sign a tax bill.

17. Clinton quoted in Harris and Pianin, "Clinton Offers, Seeks Concessions on Tax Cuts," 1 July 1997, A01.

18. See, for example, Jeff Plungis, "Tax Cut Plans Spawn a Battle of Competing Statistics," *CQ Monitor*, 7 July 1997, 11.

19. For a good overview of those differences, see Clay Chandler, "Tax Cut Debate Centers on Fairness," *Washington Post*, 21 July 1997, A1. See also Donald Lambro, "GOP Accuses Rubin of Misusing Data," *Washington Times*, 8 July 1997, A4.

20. Sperling and Clinton quoted in Eric Pianin, "Democrats Give Republican Budget-Tax Plan a Cool Reception," *Washington Post*, 24 July 1997, A12.

21. Daschle quoted in "Lott, Daschle Give Conflicting Views on Tax Bill Progress," *National Journal's CongressDaily*, 21 July 1997, 1.

22. Daschle Quoted in Alan Fram, "White House Has Upper Hand in Budget," *Associated Press*, 25 July 1997.

23. Raines quoted in Pianin and Chandler, "Newfound Trust Held Budget Deal Together: Talks Nearly 'Blew Up' at the Last Minute," *Washington Post*, 5 August 1997, A01.

24. Domenici and Kasich quoted in Eric Pianin, "Clinton Signals Readiness to Wait for Deal He Likes," *Washington Post*, 25 July 1997, A04.

25. Pianin and Chandler, "Newfound Trust Held Budget Deal Together," A01.

26. The account described in this paragraph, including quotations, is from ibid.

27. Quotations by Bliley and Kasich from personal interviews.

28. Quoted in David Hosansky, "Scouting Out the Final Deal," *Congressional Quarterly Weekly Report*, 2 August 1997, 1832.

29. The amount of the refundable child credit is based on a complicated formula. In simple terms, the child credit may be refundable for families with three or more children when the amount of the employee's portion of the payroll tax exceeds the earned income tax credit. The child credit may be used to offset the balance of the employee's portion of the payroll tax remaining after the earned income credit.

30. Quoted in "GOP Leaders Extol Tax Cuts, Other Budget Deal Features," *Congressional Quarterly Weekly Report*, 2 August 1998, 1889.

31. Quoted in Alissa J. Rubin, "Desire to Spread the Benefits Leads to More Complexity," *Congressional Quarterly Weekly Report*, 2 August 1997, 1837.

32. Clinton quoted in Pianin and Chandler, "Newfound Trust Held Budget Deal Together," A01.

33. Sperling quoted in Alan Fram, "Clinton, Democrats Differ on Budget," *Associated Press*, 7 July 1997.

Chapter 10: The 1997 Budget Agreement in Realist Perspective

1. See also Charles O. Jones, *The Presidency in a Separated System* (Washington, D.C.: Brookings Institution, 1992); and David R. Mayhew, *Divided We Govern* (New Haven: Yale University Press, 1991).

2. "Diffusion of responsibility," as Jones describes it, means that both parties share credit and accept blame, resulting in policy changes that might not be possible when a single party controls both branches. Jones, *Presidency in a Separated System*, 18.

3. Political scientist John W. Kingdon refers to this mix of policy ideas as the "policy primeaval soup." John W. Kingdon, *Agendas, Alternatives, and Public Policies* (New York: HarperCollins, 1995), chap. 6.

4. See, for example, Joseph Cooper and David W. Brady, "Institutional Context and Leadership Style: The House from Cannon to Rayburn," *American Political Science Review* 75 (1981): 411–25; and Barbara Sinclair, *Majority Leadership in the U.S. House* (Baltimore: Johns Hopkins University Press, 1983).

5. Charles O. Jones, "Joseph G. Cannon and Howard W. Smith: An Essay on the Limits of Leadership in the House of Representatives," *Journal of Politics* 30 (1968): 617–46.

6. References to those kinds of criticisms can be found in the following assessments of the budget agreement: Jonathan Rauch, "The Easy Way Out," *National Journal*, 10 May 1997, 928-30; E.J. Dionne Jr., "A Political Classic," *Washington Post*, 1 August 1997, A21; Phil Gramm, "Deceptive Budget Deal," *Washington Post*, 9 May 1997, A25; and Mary McGrory, "Shades of Awful," *Washington Post*, 11 May 1997, C01.

7. For a defense of the budget agreement from a "realist" perspective, see Norman J. Ornstein, "A Bad Rap on the Budget Deal?" *Washington Post*, 4 June 1997, A23.

8. James K. Glassman, "Bad for Everyone," *Washington Post*, 20 May, A19. For other criticisms by conservatives, see, for example, George F. Will, "The Republicans' Mayday," *Washington Post*, 15 May 1997, A23; and "No Deal," *Weekly Standard*, 12 May 1997, 9–16. Some conservative writers accepted the realities of the governing situation. See Tod Lindberg, "The Art of the Balanced Budget Deal," *Washington Times*, 7 May 1997, A15; Tod Lindberg, "The Real, the Ideal, the Budget," *Washington Times*, 21 May 1997, A15; and Merrill Matthews Jr., "One Small Step for the Budget?" *Washington Times*, 5 June 1997, A21.

9. James K. Glassman, "The Budget Deal: Kill It," *Washington Post*, 6 May 1997, A19.

10. For more on this point, see Norman J. Ornstein's response to Glassman in "Budget Deal Makers Deserve Kudos, Not Scorn, from Kibitzers," *Roll Call*, 26 May 1997.

11. As political scientist Richard Fenno argues, the Republican Party failed to attain its policy and political goals in 1995 and 1996 because of a lack of governing experience in a separation-of-powers system. Indeed, Glassman was calling for Republicans to make some of the same mistakes they made in the previous Congress: failing to set priorities, recognize accomplishments, accept tradeoffs, or calculate feasible outcomes. See Richard F. Fenno, *Learning to Govern* (Washington, D.C.: Brookings Institution, 1997).

12. The following paragraph is based on Kasich's rebuttal to Glassman. See John R. Kasich, "The Budget Deal," *Washington Post*, 1 June 1997, C08. See also "The Best Budget Pact We Can Get," *Wall Street Journal*, 2 June 1997, A18.

13. See McGrory, "Shades of Awful"; Dionne, "A Political Classic"; and E.J. Dionne, "Status Quo Budget," *Washington Post*, 9 May 1997, A25.

14. Gene Sperling and Franklin D. Raines, "Bogus Facts about the Budget," *Washington Post*, 9 June 1997, A19.

15. I leave out of this classification such liberal organizations as the Center on Budget and Policy Priorities or Citizens for Tax Justice, or such conservative organizations as the Heritage Foundation or the CATO Institute. They engage in policy analysis, but their values are decidedly ideological.

16. Quoted in "Concord Urges Congress and the President to Quickly Take Up Long Term Issues," Press Release, 29 July 1997.

17. Of course policy analysts are not all alike, and some are more sensitive to political realities than others. For example, Concord Coalition's Executive Director Martha Phillips took a more realistic view: "This is not the budget Concord would have written. In fact it is clearly no one's first choice, but that's what happens in the real world of legislative compromise." Quoted in "Concord Urges Congress and the President to Quickly Take Up Long Term Issues."

18. The following description of Reischauer's analysis is from Robert D. Reischauer, "Light at the End of the Tunnel or Another Illusion? The 1997 Budget Deal," *National Tax Journal* (March 1998), 143–65.

19. Ibid., 161.

20. For brief descriptions of the variety of tax breaks and their complications, see Alissa J. Rubin, "Desire to Spread the Benefits Leads to More Complexity," *Congressional Quarterly Weekly Report*, 2 August 1997, 1837–42.

21. Reischauer, "Light at the End of the Tunnel or Another Illusion?" 163. For similar criticisms, see William G. Gale, "The Budget Deal: An Opportunity Lost," *Washington Post*,

1 August 1997, A21; and Robert J. Samuelson, "The Demolition of Tax Reform," *Washington Post*, 21 May 1997, A23.

22. This became very clear in the debate over the Treasury Department's income distribution analysis. See chapters 8 and 9.

23. The main justification for Forbes's argument can be found in several publications. See, for example, "Tear Down This Tax Code," *Wall Street Journal*, 15 July 1997, A15.

24. John Witte, *The Politics and Development of the Federal Income Tax* (Madison: University of Wisconsin Press, 1985), 246. According to Witte, the history of tax policy has been a steady march toward complexity. For a summary of other historical patterns, see pp. 248–68. Witte's book was published just prior to the passage of the Tax Reform Act of 1986, a major reform of the tax code, which reduced marginal tax rates, eliminated many tax preferences enjoyed by corporations, and made the tax code more progressive. For an overview of the major tax policy changes in the 1986 Tax Reform Act, see Henry J. Aaron, "The Impossible Dream Comes True: The New Tax Reform Act," *Brookings Review*, Winter 1987, 3–10. For more on the politics of the 1986 Tax Reform Act, see Jeffrey H. Birnbaum and Alan S. Murray, *Showdown at Gucci Gulch* (New York: Random House, 1987).

25. Witte, *Politics and Development of the Federal Income Tax*, 381.

26. See Greg Hitt, "Texans Plan Texas-Size Drive for Big U.S. Sales Tax," *Wall Street Journal*, 11 February 1997, A1. Hitt notes the differences within the Republican Party reflected in the opposing positions taken by Archer, a proponent of the sales tax, and House Majority Leader Richard Armey, who favors a flat income tax.

27. Quoted in Morton M. Kondrake, "Budget Plan May End GOP Dreams of Big Tax Reform," *Roll Call*, 9 June 1997, 10.

28. Pete V. Domenici and John R. Kasich, "The Budget Deal: Good for Families," *Washington Post*, 20 May 1997, A19.

29. The facts presented in this paragraph can be found in several publications. I refer to "Raising the Eligibility Age for Medicare," *Concord Coalition*, 2 July 1997.

30. Peter G. Peterson, *Will America Grow Up Before It Grows Old?* (New York: Random House, 1996), 42. See chapter 3 of Peterson's book for a summary of the current problems of the Social Security system.

31. Congressional Budget Office, *The Economic and Budget Outlook: An Update* (Washington, D.C.: Government Printing Office), August 1998.

Glossary of Terms

Appropriations act. A statute, under the jurisdiction of the House and Senate Appropriations Committees, that generally provides authority for federal agencies to incur obligations and to make payments out of the Treasury for specified purposes. Currently, there are thirteen regular appropriations acts for each fiscal year. From time to time, Congress also enacts supplemental appropriations acts. *See also Continuing resolution; Supplemental appropriation.*

Budget baseline. Projected federal spending, revenue, and deficit levels based on the assumption that current policies will continue unchanged for the upcoming fiscal year. In determining the budget baseline under Gramm-Rudman-Hollings, the directors of OMB and CBO estimate revenue levels and spending levels for entitlement programs based on continuation of current laws. For estimating discretionary spending amounts (both defense and nondefense), the directors assume an adjustment for inflation (GNP deflator) added to the previous year's discretionary spending levels.

Budget deficit. The amount by which the government's total outlays exceed its total revenues for a given fiscal year. *See also Outlays; Revenues.*

Budget resolution. A concurrent resolution passed by both chambers of Congress setting forth, reaffirming, or revising the congressional budget for the U.S. government for a fiscal year. Concurrent resolutions do not require a presidential signature because they are not laws but are a legislative device for Congress to regulate itself as it works on spending and revenue bills.

Budget surplus. The amount by which the government's revenues exceed its outlays for a given fiscal year. *See also Outlays; Revenues.*

Continuing resolution. Appropriations legislation enacted by Congress to provide temporary budget authority for federal agencies to keep them in operation when their regular appropriations bill has not been enacted by the start of the fiscal year. A continuing resolution is a joint resolution, which has the same legal status as a bill. A continuing resolution is a form of appropriations act and should not be confused with the budget resolution.

Deficit. *See Budget deficit.*

Discretionary spending. A category of spending (budget authority and outlays) subject to the annual appropriations process. *See Appropriations act.*

Entitlement. Programs governed by legislation in a way that legally obligates the federal government to make specific payments to qualified recipients. Payments to persons under Social Security, Medicare, and veterans' pensions programs are considered entitlements. *See Mandatory spending.*

Federal debt. All Treasury and agency debt issues outstanding. Current law places a limit or ceiling on the amount of debt. Debt subject to limit has two components: debt held by the government and debt held by the public.

> *Debt held by the government.* The holdings of debt by federal trust funds and other special government funds. For example, when a trust fund is in surplus, as is true with Social Security, the law requires that this surplus be invested in government securities.

> *Debt held by the public.* The holdings of debt by individuals, institutions, other buyers outside the federal government, and the Federal Reserve. The change in debt held by the public in any given year closely tracks the unified budget deficit for that year.

Fiscal policy. Federal government policies with respect to taxes, spending, and debt management intended to promote the nation's macroeconomic goals, particularly with respect to employment, gross national product, price level stability, and equilibrium in balance of payments. The budget process is a major vehicle for determining and implementing federal fiscal policy.

Fiscal year. A twelve-month accounting period. The fiscal year for the federal government begins 1 October and ends 30 September. The fiscal year is designated by the calendar year in which it ends; for example, fiscal year 1997 is the year beginning 1 October 1996 and ending 30 September 1997.

Mandatory spending. Outlays for programs whose level is governed by formulas or criteria set forth in authorizing legislation rather than by appropriations. Examples of mandatory spending include Social Security, Medicare, veterans' pensions, rehabilitation services, members' pay, judges' pay, and the payment of interest on the public debt. Many of these programs are considered *entitlements*.

Net deficit reduction. Savings below the defined budget baseline achieved for the upcoming fiscal year because of laws enacted or final regulations promulgated since 1 January. CBO and OMB independently estimate these savings in their initial and final sequester reports.

Outlays. Disbursements by the Treasury in the form of checks or cash. Outlays flow in part from budget authority granted in prior years and in part from budget authority provided for the year in which the disbursements occur.

Pay-as-you-go (PAYGO). Arises in two separate contexts: a point of order in the Senate and a sequester order from OMB.

> *Pay-as-you-go and sequestration under the BEA.* The Budget Enforcement Act requires OMB also to enforce a pay-as-you-go requirement, which has an effect similar to the Senate's point of order. Congress is required to "pay for" any changes to programs that result in an increase in direct spending, or in this case risk a sequester. If OMB estimates that the sum of all direct spending and revenue legislation enacted since 1990 will result in a net increase in the deficit for the fiscal year, then the president is required to issue a sequester order reducing all nonexempt direct-spending accounts by a uniform percentage in order to eliminate the net deficit increase. Most direct spending is either exempt from a sequester order or operates under special rules that minimize the reduction that can be made in direct spending. Social Security is exempt from a pay-as-you-go sequester, and Medicare cannot be reduced by more than 4 percent.

President's budget. The document sent to Congress by the president in January or February of each year, requesting new budget authority for federal programs and estimating federal revenues and outlays for the upcoming fiscal year.

Revenues. Collections from the public arising from the government's power to tax. Revenues include individual and corporate income taxes, social insurance taxes (such as Social Security payroll taxes), excise taxes, estate and gift taxes, and customs duties.

Reconciliation process. A process by which Congress includes in a budget resolution "reconciliation instructions" to specific committees, directing them to report legislation that changes *existing* laws, usually for the purpose of decreasing spending or increasing revenues by a specified amount by a certain date. The legislation may also contain an increase in the debt limit.

Supplemental appropriation. An act appropriating funds in addition to those in the thirteen regular annual appropriations acts. Supplemental appropriations provide additional budget authority beyond the original estimates for programs or activities (including new programs authorized after the date of the original appropriations act) in cases where the need for funds is too urgent to be postponed until enactment of the next regular appropriations bill. *See also Appropriations act.*

Tax expenditures. Revenue losses attributable to a special exclusion, exemption, or deduction from gross income or to a special credit, preferential rate of tax, or deferral of tax liability.

Unified budget. A comprehensive display of the federal budget, including all revenues and spending for all regular federal programs and trust funds. The 1967 President's Commission on the Budget recommended the unified budget, and it has been the basis for budgeting since 1968, when it replaced a system involving an administrative budget, a consolidated cash budget, and a national income accounts budget.

Source: Excerpted from "The Congressional Budget Process: An Explanation," Committee on the Budget of the United States Senate, 104th Congress, 2nd sess., S. Print 104–70, December 1996, 51–57.

Index